WISDOM OF THE MYTHTELLERS

Wisdom

of the

Mythtellers

Sean Kane

broadview press

Portions or all of the following tales are reproduced in this book by permission. *The Wonguri-Mandjigai Song Cycle of the Moon Bone,* translated by
Ronald M. Berndt, © 1948 by Ronald M. Berndt. Published in *Oceania*
19:1 (1948). *Nanlgdldastlas / One They Gave Away* by Qquuna Qii-
ghawaay Skaai (John Sky), translated by Robert Bringhurst, ©1992 by
Robert Bringhurst. *Sttluujagadang / Sapsucker* by John Sky, translated by
Robert Bringhurst, ©1994 by Robert Bringhurst. *Xhuuya Qagaangas /
Raven Travelling* by John Sky and Job Moody of the Sttawaas Xhaayda-
gaay, translated by Robert Bringhurst, ©1994 by Robert Bringhurst.
"The Earth-Shapers" by Ella Young, from *Celtic Wonder Tales* by Ella
Young, published by Maunsel, 1910, reissued by Floris Books, ©1910,
and renewed 1985 by the Estate of Ella Young / Save the Redwoods
League, San Francisco. From *The Odyssey* by Homer, translated by
Robert Fitzgerald, ©1961, 1963 by Robert Fitzgerald and renewed 1989
by Benedict R.C. Fitzgerald. Published by Vintage Books, a Division of
Random House Incorporated.

Canadian Cataloguing in Publication Data
Kane, Sean,
Wisdom of the mythtellers
Includes bibliographical references.
ISBN 1-55111-041-5
1. Mythology — Comparative studies.   2. Nature — Religious
aspects.   I. Title.
BL435.K35 1994   291.1'3   C94-931608-3

Broadview Press
Post Office Box 1243, Peterborough, Ontario, Canada K9J 7H5

in the United States of America:
3576 California Road, Orchard Park, NY 14127

in the United Kingdom:
B.R.A.D. Book Representation and Distribution Ltd.
244A London Road, Hadleigh, Essex SS7 2DE

Broadview Press gratefully acknowledges the support of the Canada
Council, the Ontario Arts Council, the Ontario Publishing Centre,
and the Ministry of Canadian Heritage.

PRINTED IN CANADA
5 4 3 2   95 96

FOR OWEN KANE

CONTENTS

PROLOGUE

FROM: THE SONG OF THE MOON-BONE

Sung by the Sandfly clan of the Wonguri People of Arnhem Land

bili gorunala durdula nalindi wirmu
wiribuklili kopeinaranara kalukarpumiri banbanala
bala'durulama djareindja dirlpunara lanara dumerunumi
boiwerauwal manguldji biliwili manbulbul gurulnora biniwara
nalindi durdula banbanala wirmu kopeinaranara
kurulnandji kurulnanadjinadji bogulnu wirmu
bala'gumorwilpulun likandja lupteruna marnalili
likandja barawaitnura likandja'wilpulun gunumulnura
walmindji kalawala kurulnanadjinadji wirmu
    banbanala nalindi kopeinaranara
kapu'nama bogulnu kapu'nama goruna gurumbalnbalnor
bala'durulama gorulma wirmu gumorwilpulun
gorulma dudulama runijiri gorulma malkanarawala
    dodowala dagitshbomawala wulananawala
    nakunakuwala manaritshkala
linanura wirmu gorunala djeidjulkamauwala
    warawarawala kapulukanawala
bili nara kalukarpumiri durdula kalawala walmindji
    banbanala kopeinaranara
likan'walpulun durdula durulama gorulma milingimbi
bala gorulma barku namoijani wirwara karupu kamindja
nalindi durdula kalawala kurulnanadjinadji
    banbanala wirmu durulunana
djareiwonara nalindi durdula likan'wilpulun
wirmu bala kalukarpumiri
djareindja gorulnala dipunura lanara
durulama durinar'mardji wirmu gurumbalbalju kapulili
luptunar'mardji kapuli bogulnoiju durijuna lupkai
durduleiju bilina lupteruna nalindi
   ...

FROM: THE SONG OF THE MOON-BONE

Translated by Ronald M. Berndt (1948)

Now the New Moon is hanging, having cast away his bone:
Gradually he grows larger, taking on new bone and flesh.
Over there, far away, he has shed his bone: he shines
      on the Place of the Lotus Root, the Place of the Dugong,
On the Place of the Evening Star, of the Dugong's Tail,
      of the Moonlight Clay-pan ...
His old bone gone, now the New Moon grows larger;
Gradually growing, his new bone growing as well.
Over there, the horns of the old receding Moon bent down,
      sank into the Place of the Dugong:
His horns were pointing towards the Place of the Dugong.
Now the New Moon swells to fullness, his bone grown larger.
He looks on the water, hanging above it, at the Place of the Lotus.
There he comes into sight, hanging above the sea,
      growing larger and older ...
There far away he has come back, hanging over the clans
      near Milingimbi ...
Hanging there in the sky, above those clans ...
« Now I'm becoming a big moon, slowly regaining my roundness ... »
In the far distance the horns of the Moon bend down, above Milingimbi,
Hanging a long way off, above Milingimbi Creek ...
Slowly the Moon-Bone is growing, hanging there far away.
The bone is shining, the horns of the Moon bend down.
First the sickle Moon on the old Moon's shadow; slowly he grows,
And shining he hangs there at the Place of the Evening Star ...
Then far away he goes sinking down, to lose his bone in the sea;
Diving towards the water, he sinks down out of sight.
The old Moon dies to grow new again, to rise up out of the sea.

Up and up soars the Evening Star, hanging there in the sky.
Men watch it, at the Place of the Dugong, the Place of the Clouds,
    the Place of the Evening Star.
Far off, at the Place of Mist, the Place of Lilies,
    the Place of the Dugong.
The lotus, Evening Star, hangs there on its long stalk
    held by the Spirits.
It shines on that Place of the Shade, on the Dugong Place,
    and on to the Moonlight Clay-pans ...
The Evening Star shines, back towards Milingimbi,
    over the Wulamba People ...
Hanging there in the distance, toward the Place of the Dugong.
The Place of the Eggs, of Tree-Limbs-Rubbing-Together,
    Place of the Moonlight Clay-pan ...
Shining on its short stalk, the Evening Star; always there
    at the clay-pan, at the Place of the Dugong ...
There, far off, the long string hangs at the Place of the Evening Star,
    the Place of Lilies
Away there at Milingimbi ... at the Place of the Full Moon,
Hanging above the head of that Wonguri headman:
The Evening Star goes down across the camp,
    among the white gum trees ...
Far away in those places near Milingimbi ...
Goes down among the Ngurulwulu People,
    toward the camp and the gum trees
At the Place of the Crocodiles, Place of the Evening Star,
    away toward Milingimbi ...
Evening Star going down, lotus flower on its stalk ...
Going down among all the western clans ...

It brushes the heads of the uncircumcised people ...
Sinking down in the sky, the Evening Star, the lotus ...
Shining on to the foreheads of all those headmen ...
On to the heads of all those Sandfly people ...
It sinks into the place of the white gum trees at Milingimbi.

PROLOGUE

As civilization feels its way forward to practices of living with the earth on the earth's terms, we are discovering the respect for nature demonstrated by archaic humanity. We are now realizing that early humanity negotiated a dialogue with nature that has gone on variously for the better part of 100,000 years. It is still going on today – in places where a jungle or tundra or rainforest shelters one of the few remaining archaic peoples; and it is continuing, though in different forms, in places where shattered aboriginal communities revive their ancestral traditions. By all accounts, this dialogue was – and still is – an affectionate counterpoint to the earth's voices, with no ambition to direct them or force them to give up their meanings. To this dialogue I give the name _mythtelling_, with the hope of understanding it as much as possible in the way it has understood itself.

This is a tall hope. To start with, we have no records of myths told in the primeval past. No source can tell us directly what mythtelling meant to those who practised it and heard it. We do have records of myths told in cultures of great antiquity that still existed in very recent times – but these cultures are not the same as they were eons ago. We have literary recreations of myth written by famous poets like Ovid and by anonymous poets like the Irish monastic scribes. Yet however fine these versions are, they are literature, not mythtelling (I will distinguish between these media later). Finally, we have scores of books in the Mythology and Religion sections of book stores – but the student of myth needs to steer a careful course through these publications. Much revivalist mythology is really psychology, cutting across cultural difference with the mistaken assumption that there is a universal world of myth which is true to all peoples past and present because it is true to eternal powers in the human psyche.

This mix of anthropology, literature and psychology – in combination with the huge information gap about actual mythtelling – raises a greater question than it can answer. How do the mythtellers dwell on this earth? In answering this question we can only reconstruct mythtelling intuitively, basing our intuitions on certain common patterns recognizable in a few selected mythtelling traditions. That is what I have done in this book – though I am aware that I am an individual shaped by modernity, an outsider to myth. There is always the danger of coloring mythtelling with our own inclinations about the way we want to hear the stories now. Mindful of a temptation to primitivism, this is the tall hope I have in writing this book – to recreate imaginatively something of the dialogue with nature of the mythtellers. I invite the reader to join me in the adventure.

Adventures involve the crossing of boundaries – in this case, the boundaries that separate us from the mythtellers, and that separate the mythtellers from each other. Boundaries are the crossing-points into autonomous cultural worlds, so we have to be careful. The term *prehistory* is the first boundary. The term refers to everything in the life of a civilization before literacy arises – before the society consciously becomes the source of records about itself. Before that, all is prehistory, stretching back 750,000 years or so to the time hominids migrated (it is believed, from Africa) across the joined continental masses into what became Europe and Asia. Whether or not the societies of these ape-like people were held together by myths, we do not know. I have said the better part of 100,000 years of mythtelling because this is the span of time at the beginning of which the human brain became as large as it is today, and it is the span of time within which emergent *homo sapiens* became capable of culture. Since about a hundred millennia ago, the ancestors of the human species evolved a new organ, called culture: it allowed patterns of behavior to be transmitted variably in stories and other communications, instead of fixed in molecules in the genetic code.

This vast expanse of prehistoric time is divided by archaeologists into ages, according to the varying relationships to the environment implied by the particular kinds of tool used by early humanity. They are the Paleolithic, the Mesolithic, and the Neolithic – that is, Early, Middle and Late Stone Age. It is from these different kinds of earth-relatedness that we will take our stories, with the understanding that cultures are not stages on the line of time. Cultures flower at their own rates within their own boundaries of land, resources, and belief. Some archaic cultures still flower in the present.

The form of mythtelling in the Paleolithic will be represented by examples from the Native Australian peoples. Using chipped stone tools, hunting and collecting their food, and making camps as they travelled, instead of living in houses, they carried a 40,000-year hunter-gatherer culture virtually intact almost into the twentieth century. Paleolithic experience in European antiquity was one of hunting nomadically the great mammals of the receding Ice Age: the mammoth, the cave bear, the wooly-haired rhinoceros, and other extinct species. There were megafauna in Australia too, all of them marsupial. The great animals died out – but the basic style of Paleolithic existence remained, held in stories that evolved over millennia of living with the land.

In Europe, this kind of hunter-gatherer existence did not come to an end – rather, it changed in important details, such as the use of polished stone tools instead of chipped stone tools, when the peoples of north and north-central Europe shifted from hunting the great creatures of the steppes and tundra to exploit instead the variety of smaller forest-dwellers, like the deer and wild boar, and when they began to fish for food, using hooks and other composite tools. The use of these more complicated tools for catching food defines the

Mesolithic – though, again, chronology is not the issue; cultural context is. There are Mesolithic societies even in the near present which subsisted in this way almost exclusively by hunting and fishing and gathering. One example is the Haida civilization of the Pacific Northwest, and it is the example I will refer to for mythtelling in the Mesolithic. Resident for some thirty centuries in the Queen Charlotte Islands of British Columbia – in Haida Gwaii, the Islands of the People – this was a culture of settled villages, high technology, fine art, some polished stone and virtually no agriculture. Dogs were domesticated by the Haida – the only domesticated animal in Mesolithic contexts. A settled village existence typified these Middle Stone-age people who depended on the scheduling of food resources within a defined territory. They did not have to chase the food; the food came to them in the form of salmon and halibut and the various animals attracted to the fish run. I will refer a great deal to the Haida in this book because we have in Skaai of the Qquuna Qiighawaai, whose work was transcribed in the year 1900, a genuine Stone-age storyteller, present through Robert Bringhurst's translation.

The last period of the Stone Age is the Neolithic, which in Europe began to shape itself through the transitional Mesolithic about 10,000 years ago, when the ice caps melted and the oceans rose to their present level. As the marker of a boundary we must cross in order to distinguish a further type of mythtelling, the term Neolithic implies a radically altered relationship to the earth achieved through agriculture. The domestication of plants and animals began around 7000 BC in the Middle East (about 5000 BC in Mesoamerica). This change in livelihood shows in the use of polished, not chipped, stone tools – blades with a sheen on their edges and other ground stone artifacts such as hand-mills for grinding corn. And also knives, axes, adzes, hoes and sickles. These are the tools of planters and herders, not hunters and foragers, the equipment of a people rooted in village life and agriculturalism. From learning to grind and polish tools, it was a short step in European Neolithic experience to begin smelting metal and work it into tools that outperformed their stone equivalents. The domestication of minerals (if we can call it that) began about 3500 BC, so that contained in the most technologically developed phase of Stone-age existence is the beginning of the age of metals.

Copper and tin are rare, and consequently bronze is an expensive commodity. Its possession is largely restricted to a warrior nobility, which is why the Bronze Age is associated with highly 'structured societies dominated by a heroic warrior caste. However, the use of bronze weapons is not enough to account for these complex expansionary civilizations. Bronze merely puts a finer point on a set of impulses hidden in the Neolithic, when there was suddenly a radically altered relationship between humans and plants and animals. For this reason, I will take examples of mythtelling from the Celtic and Greek civilizations, when what has been called the Neolithic Revolution achieves its confirmation.

The Neolithic technique of domestication marks a transformation of most of the life on this planet from a nomadic to an agrarian existence, from a forager to a producer economy. I need to overstate the total effect of this transformation because, thanks to the literature of Europe since its beginnings in Greek experience, most popular notions of myth are agriculturalist ones. Coming at us from the Neolithic slope of a great divide, these notions speak too readily to our own experience as the inheritors of the agricultural revolution. Our present civilization, with its fields full of rice and wheat and corn and livestock, is based on the Neolithic technique of actually managing food into being. Without leaving that world of managed natural resources, it is practically impossible to feel our way to the spirituality of human beings who lived without agriculture. <u>These were people who greeted all forms of life on earth as intelligent kin and, as far as we can tell, saw themselves as just another species sharing a habitat.</u> The hunter-gatherers of the Paleolithic and Mesolithic participated in a vast ecology in which the bodies occupied by essentially spiritual beings – the body-masks – were borrowed for food. The plants and animals would give of themselves for food, so long as certain rules were followed and an attitude of respect for the providers was maintained. <u>Many of the stories warn that it is disrespectful to the spirit-keepers of the animals to try to hoard food or manipulate it into being.</u> With the crossing into the Neolithic, however, the barriers go up between human effort and providential nature. To build a fence around a field or pasture, to tether an animal, to harbor seeds and plant them at just the right time – these activities put humanity into a state of contest with nature. That contest is called work – it takes work to keep a garden going. It is work to keep it free of the weeds and rodents and pests whose populations explode in the open track of the plow. The Book of Genesis, written by agriculturalists out of older myths about a snake-being who teaches nature's secrets, remembers this transition from a time when humans knew the speech of the animals to a time of domestication when humans feared them:

> *And the Lord God said unto the serpent, Because thou hast done this, thou art cursed above all cattle and above every beast of the field; upon thy belly shalt thou go, and dust shalt thou eat all the days of thy life.*
>
> *And I will put enmity between thee and the woman, and between thy seed and her seed; it shall bruise thy head, and thou shalt bruise his heel.*
>
> *Unto the woman he said, I will greatly multiply thy sorrow and thy conception; in sorrow thou shalt bring forth children;*

and thy desire shall be to thy husband, and he shall rule over
thee.

(Genesis 3:14-16)

The domestication of a variety of creatures from the horse to the honey-bee – indeed, as Genesis suggests, the domestication of woman – involves unceasing toil shaped by a sense of the finality of natural death: "In the sweat of thy face shalt thou eat bread, till thou return unto the ground" (3:19).

The Book of Genesis declares a new attitude to nature, while silencing an old one. The focus of this attitude of resource-management is the custom of hoarding. With the hoarding of resources that previously had been left to the animal spirits to look after, there sounds in myth the note of fear that is heard in Genesis. This is a different kind of fear from the fear of hunter-gatherers about, say, breaking a taboo. Taboo wariness often turns out to serve a practical purpose. For example, among the Gunwinggu people of Australia's West Arnhem Land there is a complexity of prohibitions concerning the Rainbow Snake. This great sky serpent is known throughout most of Aboriginal Australia as the spirit of rain and water. Her tongues light up the sky of Arnhem Land at the beginning of the monsoon season:

> *The tongues of the Lightning Snakes flicker and twist*
> *one to the other ...*
> *Flashing among the cabbage palm foliage ...*
> *Lightning flashing through clouds, flickering tongue*
> *of the Snake ...*
>
> *Always there, at the wide expanse of water, at the place*
> *of the sacred tree ...*
> *Flashing above the people of the western clans ...*

According to the Gunwinggu, in her female form the Rainbow Serpent swallows her victims in a sudden flood – that is to say, she drowns them. She is the reference point for warnings and taboos about certain stretches of a river, or certain deep pools with steep sides, or certain low-lying coastal plains. These are places subject to sudden flooding during the northwest monsoon. In one story, the sizzling of a small animal over a fire brings the punitive face of the Rainbow Snake because the cooking is being done on sand or on a flat rock near the water's edge, not on high ground where cooking is supposed to happen. This wariness about natural catastrophe in a landscape of spirits who otherwise provide for the Gunwinggu is radically different from the fear of the world-ending Death, Pestilence, Disease and Famine (Revelation 6:2-8) created by intensive agriculture. Writing of "the terror that nature would not furnish enough," Calvin Luther Martin shows how this fear on the part of the hoarder of resources is projected onto the novel sky-gods of the post-Neolithic – gods of the sun like Apollo, gods of rain and storm like Zeus, gods of time and periodic order like Kronos. The schedules of plant life are felt to depend on these and other deities, who need to be appeased by an agricultural people. So begins organized religion. Calendars are drawn up to mark the seasons for planting and harvesting; the stars are consulted; priest classes are formed to safeguard the esoteric knowledge of the heavens; and mythtelling becomes an instrument for keeping the expanding populations of the Neolithic in line. Where ten thousand years ago there were probably not more than 10 million people on the earth – all of them hunters and foragers – with the food-surplus inventions of the Neolithic the lid comes off population controls. No longer constrained by the checks and balances of survival in nature, populations are now controlled by social class. A class system arises out of the necessities of agriculture. For agriculture to work, you need to have a concept of property. For a concept of property to work, you need to have a state. For a state to work, you need to have armies to defend it. Consequently, developed agricultural societies evolve a new mythology featuring three classes of deities – deities who stand respectively for the functions of priest, farmer, and warrior. Odin, Frey, and Thor are the Norse versions. Such a myth of the divine prototypes of the three classes is part of the panoply of kingship and hereditary prestige by which the burgeoning populations created by agricultural wealth are controlled.

All of this has consequences for the mythtelling traditions carried across the great divide between the Paleolithic and the Neolithic. As we know from so many ruined indigenous communities, the consequences for human behavior are often tragic when this transition is abrupt. Uncle Bul, an Aborigine elder from Nowra, New South Wales, told the author Robert Lawlor about the effect of a new style of dependence on the psyche of the Native Australian hunter-gatherer: "Some of the young Aboriginal men today talk and act very smart, they no longer have the vision, 'cause they have the same fear inside as white fellas. That's because they can't go off in the bush and feed themselves like I do. I know where all the roots and berries and fruits are. Anyone who does not know how to find food and feed himself is always frightened inside like a little child who has lost his mother and with that fear the vision of the spirit world departs."

I have over-elaborated the transition between hunter-gatherer and agriculturalist experience for the sake of making their representative mythtelling traditions brighter by the contrast. Myths which evolve in sympathy with nature are different from myths which compete with it. Of course, there are whole kinds of Neolithic mythtelling that escape generalization about the agricultural revolution and its aftermath. Just to take some instances, that mythtelling goes on in the

Amazon basin, in Africa, in Polynesia, in New Zealand among the Maori. In North America, it is found among the Zuni, the Hopi, the Iroquois. It went on in late Stone Age Europe. So we cannot be too categorical.

Indeed, we cannot be too categorical even about the selected mythtelling traditions demarcated in this prologue. While the Australian Aboriginal cultures were isolated in the Paleolithic by the rising oceans that created the great continents 10,000 years ago, and while the Mesolithic cultures of the Haida and their neighbors were intact until the coming of the white man's plagues, the cultures of the Celts do not show a matching coherence. Celtic culture incorporates differing archaeological strata, into which certain of the myths reach with their long memory. The Stone Age is a period which Irish and Welsh mythtelling never entirely escapes. The Celts had metal from about 2000 BC on – but this does not mean they stopped using stone, nor stopped relating to the landscape in the way of Stone-age peoples. The sense of power, strangeness and wonder given by Irish mythtellers to Goibnu, the metal-working god, is Stone Age in mentality. So too is a shamanistic tradition that jumps out suddenly from the Welsh myths. The early Irish poets, who were priestly visionaries as well as experts on the laws of kingship, wore cloaks of bird-feathers, like shamans of the Paleolithic. Irish mythology is animistic beyond summary, matriarchal, and involved with the processes of the earth. It expresses agriculturalism on the small scale – cattle raids rather than clashes between cities. There is much Stone-age behavior beneath the shine of Celtic bronze. Similarly, the culture of the Hellenic settlers of Greece is a scratch away from an earlier indigenous stratum of village agriculture that was rich in local fertility cults.

Paleolithic, Mesolithic, Neolithic, Bronze. These terms do not presume to be categorical. They serve to affirm the distinctiveness of the mythtelling traditions they frame, reminding us that human dialogues with the earth and sky vary with the relationship humanity has with its environment.

— To these general categories of experience in nature I add a fifth term. That term is Modernity. The context of, not a dialogue, so much as a monologue in search of an answer, it is nevertheless a part of the subject of mythtelling. Modernity must also have a place in this book because it is the context from which we survey and use antiquity. We cannot ignore our own context in relation to past peoples — nor the fact that myth continues to have meaning to people who live, removed from nature, in cities. Modern revivalist mythtelling is represented by one of its best examples — a reconstruction of the myth of the Celtic goddess Brigit, written in 1910 by Ella Young during a period of nationalism and feminism in literary Ireland, and retold here by Alice Kane, one of the leading figures in the revival of storytelling that is happening in many places.

Alice Kane is my Aunt Alice — she brought me up on stories and turned me into a listener. Formed in her childhood by the songs and sayings of her native Ireland, she is one of a company of master-storytellers who have carried the oral tradition into the late twentieth century. It is in her voice — I cannot say precisely how it is in her voice — the music of humanity at peace with time, and with the earth, and with mortality. In places where this book breathes more deeply as it tells a story, or when it makes a point in the half-said way of the storyteller, that is where the spirit of a distinguished teacher and teller of myth is present.

The other teacher, present everywhere in this book, is the poet Robert Bringhurst. He has made himself the denizen of several oral cultures, having taken the trouble to study the languages of each. Like the oral sages whose thinking he reconstructs in his poetry, Bringhurst speaks in the silence "at the thought's edge" where "The gods come, unseen, to drink." This makes him a teacher of personal and very private meaning, and I doubt if what I have learned from him resembles his thinking, if he ever took the trouble to write it all out. This book is richer for Bringhurst's translations of two myths by the great oral poet, Skaai of the Qquuna Qiighawaai.

Among the things I learned from my teachers is that it is cleaner to step into one or two mythtelling traditions, and feel one's way around their spiritual powers, than to make generalizations among many. With each of the myths reproduced at the beginnings of chapters in this book, the opening phrases are given in the original language (the exception is the modern myth written by Ella Young). This propriety reminds us that myths belong to the peoples who once told them. If the mythtellers still speak to us in our time, they do so in voices that are theirs, not ours. And reproducing a part of a myth in its own tongue reminds us that the indigenous voice of myth is oral poetry, which is a form of song.

The singing of Homer is suggested in Robert Fitzgerald's translation of *The Odyssey*, excerpted as an introduction to the chapter on oral tradition. Skaai's music, used as overtures to the first two chapters of the book, has a counterpart in Bringhurst's poetry. Ronald Berndt provides a lyrical translation of the Moon song of the Wonguri people. Alice Kane's storytelling voice could be set down in a musical score. However, with the longer narrative introductions to the other chapters, I have had a problem finding versions that re-enact the sung quality of myth. Here I have had to offer my own work.

I have further acknowledgments to make. I place them at the end of the volume so as not to obscure the debt I owe to Alice Kane and Robert Bringhurst. This book is theirs, and is written as a homage to them.

CHAPTER ONE / PATTERN

[STTLUUJAGADANG]

Skaai of the Qquuna Qiighawaai (John Sky). Skidegate, October 1900

Anang qqayghudiyis hau, qqan aa, qqayghudaayang wansuuga.
Lagut la qaaganggwangas, sttluujagadang aa.
L ttaaghun dlsguxhan laagha gawus.

Gyanhau unsiiya gu qaayt yuuwan qqalgaugyagangas.
Giiyagang la kkutdlskidas.
Gyan la kkuudadighan di xhan giina l suuwudas,
« Dang tsin'ga quunigaay gwahlang dang qaattsixhalga.»
Gyan gii la qiixhagasi.
Gam giina gut qqaahlghaghangas.

Gyan ising gangang giina l suuwudaghaay dluu
qaaydaay naxhul xhiilaayasi gii la qiixattsiyaay dluu
tajxwaa nang ghaadaghaghaagha sqqin gangang ghiida qqaawas.
Gyan l qattsaayas.

Nang qqayas anggha ghuuda skajiwaay ghii daayaangisi.
Gut ghiista la la dangttsisatliihliyaay dluu
ghin l xiyaay ttaghun la ttawustaasi.
Waaaaa.
Gyan l kkiida ising waghei la giijas
gyan la la tlghuuhlghadlstlas.
Sagwi la la sghiithltapxiyaangdas.
Gyan han la la suuwudas,
« Hay ttakkin'gha hittaghan naqaayt [dii ghiiga daa hl gaaguyinggan].
Hauhau giina gagi diiga daa iijiniittsi.»

28

SAPSUCKER

Translated from the Haida by Robert Bringhurst (1994)

Grass surrounded something round, they say.
He travelled around in it, Sapsucker did.
All his feathers were missing.

Now then, up the hill stood a big spruce with its skin missing.
He whacked it with his beak.
And as he drummed his beak against it, something said,
«Your father's father asks you in.»
He looked for what had spoken.
Nothing stood out.

When it said the same thing to him again,
he looked inside the hollow of the tree.
Someone shrunken and sunken, white as a gull, sat at the back.
And he stepped in.

The old one reached into his little box.
He took out four more boxes, one within another,
and in the last box were wing feathers.
Ooooooooooh my!
He gave him tailfeathers too,
and shaped him with his hands.
He painted the upper part of him red.
And he said to him,
«Now, my grandson, a moment ago [I called you into my] treehouse.
This is why you have been with me.»

Gyan l qasuwalasi, gyan l xidas.
Gyan tlgu l waagansas gangang qaaydaay gii agang la ttahlghaasgitsi
gyan la kkuudadiigangasi.
Hau tlan l ghiida.

Then he went out, and then he flew.
And he clutched the tree and drummed his beak against it
just the way he did before.
So it ends.

Definitions

It is difficult nowadays to talk intelligently about myth, and to speak about it at all is to mark our distance from some hundred thousand years of life on this planet when most of human knowledge was conveyed by oral memory. Now, even our definition of myth is a poor remembrance. The word comes to us from a Greek word meaning "story." Since the ancient Greek stories were stories about the gods, the term recalls those statuesque personages whose functions are as obscure as the domestic squabbles they seem perpetually locked in.

Myths – stories about the gods. That is the truncated definition which has been kept alive through the ages by literature. Those of us brought up on the old storybooks will connect the term with a particular mythology. We may think of the Greek gods – Zeus, Aphroditê, Kronos, and Hermes who became winged Mercury. Today they lend their names and aura to makes of cars. Others of us may prefer to imagine the older matriarchal goddesses who were themselves eclipsed by these deities – the snake goddesses of Crete, the harvest goddess Demeter, Gaia, whose name has been regiven to the planet Earth. Whatever we make of these figures today, we are at least prepared for a greater than human world, and, insufficient as that definition of myth is, "stories about the gods" is at least a starting-point for an exploration of mythtime.

But who, or what, are the gods? Are they like those statues of a Greek temple gazing eyelessly into the distance? "Apollo, son of Zeus, appeared on the Kyllenian mountain, his broad shoulders clad in purple cloud." That is how the singer of a Homeric hymn sees a god. The figure is idealized, humanized, immortal – someone to be supplicated. He is the sun burning through early morning cloud-cover and mountain mist, but even more than that he is a recognizably human effigy answering to a human psychology. The sun god, the god of the silver bow, is a deity of a warrior agricultural civilization prominent in the eastern Mediterranean for some eleven centuries. Yet for all his distance from us in time, Apollo's effect is like that of one of those faceless figures in a modern magazine advertisement for the good life, or like those hulking video superheroes who offer the ten-year-old images of power and sexuality. They are all gods, to be sure – but they are not the gods of Stone-age peoples. For those peoples, who gave us myth, we need a different conception altogether.

A starting-point for that conception is the activity I call mythtelling. The word calls attention to the oral nature of myth. It means the passing on of stories from generation to generation – forms that exist only in the tenuous moment of their actual performance, and forms that take their inspiration, not from texts, temples or other monuments at the center of human effort, but from the life of nature surrounding it. Because a people coevolve with their habitat, because they walk the paths their ancestors walked, mythtelling assumes that the stories already exist in nature, waiting to be overheard by humans who will listen for them. Such stories have a semi-wild existence; they are just barely domesticated and so are free to enact the patterns of the natural world. Thus the ovoid formlines of Haida art and narrative reiterate the shapes of life in the rainforest and ocean of the Pacific Northwest, as the voices that sound in the mythtelling echo the songs of intelligent natural beings.

This, then, is prehistory's definition of myth. The definition directs us towards an emotional and philosophical language of coevolution with nature, a language that allows all life, not just human life, to participate in the ecology of the earth. This is a different definition of myth from the one that history gives us, in everything from the storybook deities of developed hierarchical civilization to the superheroes of the present day. History has been brutal to nature and therefore brutal to myth, which it has defined by the Latin equivalent of the Greek word as *fabula*, a persistent lie. Myth is felt by history to be untrue because it articulates a reality that exists outside the more provable worlds that men and women construct for themselves. However much those constructions of civilized effort honor a supernatural world, they also serve an assumption of human power. That assumption of human power we loosely call anthropocentrism. As far as mythtelling is concerned, the term implies a shift from the authority of the plants and animals, each the spirit-children of supernatural progenitors, to the authority of man, considered to dwell godlike at the center of the world he constructs for himself. Once this anthropocentrism settles in the outlook of a people who have learned to domesticate animals, the animals stop talking in myth.

The powers

Myths in their original form – it was a form very much like improvised music – opened their tellers to the proper subject of myth. The proper subject of myth is the ideas and emotions of the Earth. The ideas and emotions of the Earth: you see, I have not used the term "gods." That is because the mythtellers do not speak of "the gods," at least, they do not speak of them in any way that makes that term useful. The Australian mythtellers joined their songs with vast, intangible vibrating fields of energy in which they could narrate the form – or one of the changing forms – of a particular supernatural being who could appear variously as human, plant, star, mountain, or animal. The Haida mythtellers used a word, *sghaana*, that best translates as "power," in the sense of a greater than human power. According to an element that can be suffixed to the Haida agglutinative verb, such powers can be named as being about to become or capable of becoming something or someone else. It is like being able to name energy in a state of transition. And everything in the Haida mythworld is in a state of transition because spiritual powers are living beings and so are subject to mortality: they grow old, they die, they are reborn in another form. In Native Australian thinking, the changing forms of the great characters of myth are the source of a vital, life-giving power (called *dal* in northeastern Arnhem Land, *maia* in the Kimberleys). Bronze-age Celtic civilization was agricultural, and it evolved a loose pantheon of deities related to the goddess Dana, who is associated with the water of life (she gives her name to European rivers from the Danube to the Don). But in ancient Irish mythtelling, where a Stone-age sensibility lies beneath an agriculturalist frame of mind like volcanic rock beneath peat, one encounters all the intelligent energies of animism – that is, of a nature seen as having mentality (*animus*). Neither generically benevolent nor malevolent, these spirits are at best ambiguous. For example, in one eighth-century text, where they are first mentioned, a swarm of "small bodies" (*lúchoirp* or *luchorpáin*) comes out of the sea. Water spirits, they grant the hero the power to travel underwater, like a shaman, and the power is his until he breaks a taboo they have warned against. (It would do nothing for a definition of mythtelling to point out that the word *luchorpáin*, having undergone transposition of the consonant sounds of *c* and *p*, survives as the modern word "leprechaun.") In the unpredictable world of swirling energies that the mythtellers inhabit, there is no place set for "the gods" in the sense in which we inherit the term from literature.

It seems, rather, as if the mythtellers sing of whole sets of ecological relationships which can, or might, reveal their facets as this and as that god. The mythtellers speak of the powers *in relation to* each other, and with an eye to the whole ecology, not separable functions of it. They know that each being has a partner, and each works off the other to its own gain, and in the end forms a pattern. The Red-headed or Pacific forms of the Yellow-bellied Sapsucker (*Sphyrapicus varius*) could not fail to catch the eye of a Haida poet like John Sky. But what catches his eye too is an old spruce tree. The old tree shares a condition with the embryonic or proto-form of the Sapsucker: its skin is missing. This is a situation for sympathy, for compassion on the part of the very old for the very young. Something needs to be passed on from the end of one cycle to the beginning of another. And so the Old Man who is White as a Gull – he is a force of potency who appears in Haida narrative in the most unpredictable things and places – the Old Man White-as-a-Gull reaches into his boxes of dream memory to give the bird its eye-catching identity. Sapsucker goes out from the Old Man,

> *and then he flew.*
> *And he clutched the tree and drummed his beak against it*
> *just the way he did before.*
> *So it ends.*

The story, that is. The process goes on and on, and each time a Red-headed Sapsucker drills its parallel rows of identical holes in a spruce tree, then comes back to feed on the insects drawn to the sap on that tree, the bird takes with that food the spiritual energy of the Old Man who is his kin. "Your father's father asks you in." And the Old Man is reborn in the beauty of the Sapsucker for, according to the logic of Haida kinship, the grandfather is reincarnated in the grandson. Life is served.

The myth, therefore, is not about the Sapsucker in the sense of "How the Sapsucker got its Red Head." And it is not about the Old Man who is everywhere and nowhere. It is about the *relationship* between the two of them. If I were pressed to name the center of the sacred in this story-poem, I would say it is both these beings and the pattern that is between them. Especially, it is the pattern that is between them – for the knowledge of pattern is the beginning of every practical wisdom.

Practical wisdom ▬

Where is the north when you're lost in the forest at night and the sky is overcast? Our ancestors would have known. The smell on the north sides of trees is different. That is because in the northern hemisphere certain mosses grow on the north side of trees, on the damp side, away from the light. You could smell your way north. But you're hungry – you need nourishment as well. What do the elders say? In the Pacific Northwest, the elders know that certain barks from the "sunrise" side of trees, boiled with liquorice fern, sweetened with trailing wild raspberry, will make a good tonic. That kind of knowledge is all very practical – practical enough for today's pharmaceutical companies to send researchers after the stories of native elders in order to find the bases of possible drugs. An Amazon tree provides quinine, an antimalarial drug. Another tree produces curare, used to treat multiple sclerosis and Parkinson's disease. The alkaloids of the Madagaskar Periwinkle (*Catharanthus roseus*) are used in the chemotherapy for Hodgkin's disease and several forms of childhood leukemia. Steroids are derived from the Mexican yam. The popular drug Echinacea, extracted from the Narrow-leaved Purple Coneflower (*Echinacea angustifolia*), was used by the Plains Native Peoples to treat toothache, sore throat and rattlesnake bite. An environmentalist, walking through the rainforest of Sarawak, in northern Borneo, heard Dawatt Lupung, a native guide, explain the vast pharmacopoeia which is the forest. For diarrhea, you chew the stem of this plant. To repel bees, you burn this leaf. To reduce fever, you place the inner bark of this tree on your forehead. You can fold this broad leaf into a drinking cup. This rough leaf polishes blowpipes. This makes loincloths. Dawatt is elucidating the properties of the forest at great length, while listening to the various cicadas giving a running weather report. No wonder the natives say losing an elder is like losing an entire library. We imagine European witches making their potions of such unappetizing things as "eye of newt" – but the Matses people on what is now the border of Brazil and Peru scrape the mucus from the skin of *Phyllomedusa bicolor*, a leaf-nesting tree frog, and rub it into open burn wounds on their skin before they go hunting. The result is a sharpened mental state, a euphoric strength that feels god-like. Could this frog-sweat be used by modern doctors to treat depression and senile dementia? The Gunwinggu people told Catherine and Ronald Berndt about how they distinguish in the behavior of birds and animals the seasonal variations, particularly the all-important monsoon rains: "The *galawan* goanna, people say, stands up on its hind feet during the rain because he likes to feel it, but the *bugbug* 'rain pheasant' does more than enjoy it – 'his cry brings more rain.' When the cicada 'talks' a little, new root foods are just starting to grow, but when she talks loudly and strongly they are ready to be dug." To the east, in Arnhem Bay, the Wonguri-Sandfly clan meets at a sacred lagoon where the cycles of the edible lily and lotus roots are involved in the cycles of the moon and evening star. In its full rendition, the "Song of the Moon-Bone" tells of the other creatures who feed there on the water plants, and of the relationships among them: the diving duck, the water rat – also, the white cockatoos, prawns, catfish, frogs, and leeches that are there in the place where the moon left his reflection. Each has its own voice to add to the song about the fertility of the lagoon.

In traditional cultures much of this practical knowledge is conveyed by mythtelling. It is conveyed by stories. In the eastern boreal forest, for example, it is generally not a good idea to eat any berry that is white. This is something I was told as a child. If you're hungry, don't eat the white berries. But I never knew the story of Nanabozo who made that mistake one day, and had to climb a tree to escape from his mounting pile of diarrhea. Nanabozo is the trickster god of the Algonkians. His name is heard in the Algonkian greeting *"Bozo!"* It is a kind of "God bless you!" (The French settlers in Canada were pleased to think the Indians were saying *Bonjour.*) Nanabozo teaches by negative example. He teaches by telling you what *not* to do. "Nobody eats me! Nobody eats me!" the berry tree screamed at Nanabozo one day. Perverse as always, Nanabozo ate the berries on the white berry tree. Even the birds knew better than he did. Soon enough, he was squatting on the lower limb of a tree. But the stuff came higher – it just kept coming and coming. He moved higher, then higher, until he was sitting on the very top of the tree trying to escape the mountain of diarrhea that was rising up to meet him. No, it is not a good idea to eat *white* berries.

Patterns which think and speak   —

Myths are repositories of practical wisdom. The practical wisdom is what we might now call scientific knowledge, yet it is a mistake to think that the wisdom of the mythtellers is some impure or inaccurate form of science. It is just as useful to consider the scientific a piecemeal form of mythological knowing. Our oral ancestors knew something that the scientific mind doesn't know – or didn't know until after the Second World War when science discovered there was such a thing as information, or the principle of order that creates order. They knew that we live in a world of mysterious relationship.

The whole world seems alive with relationships we cannot see, except as they make their presence felt in other relationships which we *can* see. That is how we get to know a landscape, by intuiting the relationships in it – like that between the Red-headed Sapsucker and a dying spruce tree. There are patterns everywhere, dancing especially around those places that we might think of now as ecologically interesting or complex.) And ecological complexities behave as if they have intelligences or minds guiding them, responsible for them, protecting them. We cannot see these minds, but we can feel them, and we can discover their effects in the things they impinge on. As far as any precise understanding of these beings goes, they are a mystery, or something kept hidden. Indeed, if it is not the case that they go about their affairs oblivious to humans, uninterested in us, these beings much prefer to be kept hidden. It is sometimes better not to know the precise why of the natural powers; the meaning is lost in the secondary mechanics of controlling it. <u>Often it is better that something remain a mystery.</u>

It is a mystery to me, for example, why the tallbush cranberry outside my kitchen window throws out an abundance of berries before an especially long and cold winter. Alive to the rhythms of wind and weather, the tree knows something I don't. The birds seem to know it too. But to me it is a mystery. Both the cranberry bush and the birds seem able to respond to an event *before* it happens, and in a way that suggests events in nature are part of a vast and intricate network that eludes simpleminded explanation. Here, the shape of the coming winter is somehow implied in the behavior of the tree during the preceding summer. If the effect comes before the cause across time, it is because in anything in nature the larger

There is a mystery in knowing, a wonder in discovery

whole dwells as a component of the organization of the discrete particulars. From the shape of clouds, one can guess at the approaching weather pattern. From the design of a particular leaf, one can tell the specific tree it fell from. Nature is full of these patterns (information theorists call them "redundancies") which invite practical divination. These overlapping patterns are the sites for myths and proverbs. Everyone knows the saying:

Red skies at night,
Sailors' delight.
Red skies in the morning,
Sailors take warning.

It can be explained by the fact that weather usually comes from the west. A saying about the moon, which Alice Kane is fond of quoting, also catches a pattern in the spin of things:

O, Lady Moon – your horns point to the East:
Shine, be increased.
O, Lady Moon – your horns point to the West:
Wane, be at rest.

But a saying about the ash and the oak tree is more mysterious:

If the ash is out before the oak,
Then we're going to have a soak.
But if the oak's before the ash,
Then we'll only get a splash.

Some complex wisdom about changing patterns of relationship is caught in that saying of a people – the Celtic people –

whose mythology was based on reverence for trees. Today, some of us still remember:

> *An apple a day*
> *Keeps the doctor away.*

The northern European people, not knowing anything about Vitamin C, told myths about the health-giving properties of the apple. In Norse mythtelling, apples were sacred to Iduna, the goddess of youth and beauty. When the gods fed on her apples, they did not know old age.

> *Health to thee, good apple tree!*
> *Well to bear pockets full, hats full,*
> *Pecks full, bushels full and bags full.*

Perhaps there is a scientific explanation for every mythic site on which there grows the ruins of a superstition. However, the intricacy of pattern can be lost when one begins to analyse it scientifically. Then it is buried under a different intricacy. These complex notional wholes have much to teach us if we don't take them apart to see how they work.

A Dene and Inuit myth about the caribou is a case in point. This myth seemed like superstitious knowledge to wildlife biologists sent to study what appeared to be a dramatic decline in the numbers of the Kaminuriak herd in the early seventies. The biologists attributed the decline to overhunting. But the Dene people knew better. Their myth tells of a great hole in the ground into which the caribou periodically disappear. The hole is covered by a caribou skin and two rabbits guard it. When the time is right, the two rabbits will pull the skin away and the caribou will return from their spirit world. The biologists were not convinced – they had their own set of measurements obtained by aerial survey and statistical model-

I don't agree

ing. Northern ecosystems, however, function over extensive periods of time and they are notoriously unpredictable. The trouble with science in this context is that it takes a mere analytical slice in the time of the whole picture. Native experience, accumulated over ages and organized mythically into informal and flexible systems with natural variation accepted, is better able to account for northern unpredictability. It was a surprise to biologists in 1982 when the rabbits pulled the caribou skin aside and the Kaminuriak herd exploded from a supposed precipitous decline to an estimated 200,000 animals. It turned out that the basic assumptions about caribou biology were wrong. It had been thought that three herds of caribou – the Beverly, the Kaminuriak and the Bluenose herds – were distinct breeding populations. The myth led the biologists to see that they were not discrete herds and that there was migration between them. (To date, the cycling patterns of caribou are still not scientifically modelled.)

The original mythtelling in which relationships in nature were encoded has dwindled down to the kind of superstition that now fills the pages of *The Farmer's Almanac*. Myth has been reduced to anecdote in our time. There is a mysterious relationship between an early end to winter and the thinness of onion skins the preceding fall. There is a relationship, just out of reach of our knowing, between the thick dark band in the middle of the woolly worm and the onset of a severe winter. People of northern European extraction, when they butcher a pig, will look at the spleen. The pig's spleen is referred to as "the winter" in Russian and German folklore. "What's the winter look like?" The shape of the organ tells the farmer when the heavy part of winter is going to come. The clue is in the location of a visible "bulge" in the spleen, which in a pig is about five centimeters long. When the spleen is wide at the base where it attaches to the liver, and then narrows unusually, that means the winter is going to be cold and severe to start with, and then, because the spleen suddenly narrows, milder later on. There is a relationship, not so mysterious, between the height bees build their hives from the ground and the amount of snow the winter is going to bring. When the sun goes down and the wind drops, roosting turkeys will point in the direction the wind is going to come from next. It can be a matter of life and death to them not to be facing the wrong way when an ice storm cakes sleet up underneath their feathers and they freeze. It seems that animals know things we don't know – they have certain things to teach us. Little wonder, then, that our ancestors revered the animals as teachers and guides to a world of mystery, thinking of them as creatures of power. The first myths were about the powers and intelligences of animals. What the animals knew was considered sacred.

The sacred

In Leviticus, chapter 25 these words are put into the mouth of Jehovah. Every seventh year, says the Lord, "you shall not sow your field or prune your vineyard ... you shall not reap ... you shall not gather; it shall be a year of solemn rest for the land." Keep these statutes, the Bible adds, and the land will nourish you, "and you will dwell in it securely." Here good theology is good ecology. There is a practical wisdom in these verses that is best to apply, not question. Let the field lie fallow. The relationship between working the land and resting the land is kept sacred. The more you know about it, the more you will be tempted to try to win big, taking short-cuts that push the land to the very brink of "sustainable development" from which the land might not recover. Then you are manipulating the situation to personal advantage, not conceding the overall advantage to the land. For this reason, the patterns of relationship of the Earth were couched in a sacred language, which is myth. Each ecological locale was marked by gods or spirits who kept each place sacred, the sacred being best defined as something that prefers not to be talked about.

The terms for a definition of mythtelling involve a concept of ecological patterns which elude, or should elude, human manipulation, and are therefore coded as sacred. This understanding gets us away from the gods and goddesses of myth in its literary or decadent phase, who clutter the landscape with their frozen statues, testaments to some half-remembered relationship that condensed in them when the gods were uprooted and their worship became more important than the relationships they originally sanctified. I will give an example from Mediterranean mythology. One of the stories of the goddess Demeter tells how Erysikhthon and twenty of his men cut down a sacred forest belonging to this goddess. He used the lumber to build his new banquet hall. Demeter, in her form as the priestess of that sacred grove, asked Erysikhthon gently to stop the cutting – Demeter is always spoken of as the gentle goddess. Instead, he waved his axe in her face. Then the goddess in her own form put a curse upon him. It was the curse of perpetual hunger. The more he ate, the hungrier he became. Finally there wasn't enough food for him in the banquet hall. He ended up eating filth in the streets. It is an apt fate for Erysikhthon, whose name translates as "earth-tearer." The urge to win big is a hunger that can never be satisfied.

It seems that the most generous definition of myth involves a sense of mystery, a concealed knowledge about relationship that is available only in story. Myths are not stories about the gods in the abstract; they are about "something mysterious," intelligent, invisible and whole. The word "whole" comes from the Germanic word *halig*, from which we also get the word "holy." "Something mysterious" – a colleague of mine,

Ron Evans, a Métis storyteller, says this is the best translation you can give to the Ojibwa word *Manitou*. Rather than a Great Spirit, like the tiresome Gitchi-Manitou of Longfellow's "Hiawatha," one might think of *Manitou* as meaning "something mysterious." In the Ojibwa language, the word *ba* means a strait, a narrowing in the river. The Canadian province called Manitoba derives its name from a narrowing in a river where the presence of mystery is felt. "There's something mysterious happening at this narrowing of the river; there's something mysterious going on around here."

The song of the place to itself

Out on the rainforest coasts and islands of the Pacific Northwest, there is a mysterious relationship between the coming of the fair-weather clouds and the gathering of the salmon in the rivers. In the autumn when the berries are ripening on the mountains, something mysterious is happening in these rivers. Autumn weather, salmon, the headwaters of the rivers: these are the elements in an eerily beautiful knowledge of a power of fertility that comes from the deepest sea and, imbued in salmon shapes, is given to the rivers to guard. Altogether, the spawning of the salmon in the fall is one of the great mysteries of fertility which human life depends on out there. Other people depend on it too: the bears, the eagles, the mink, and many others. The coming of the salmon is the focus of much of the human and animal and bird life of the West Coast.

For the Haida and their neighbors this was one of the most sacred mysteries of all. Salmon are people, rather like us. They are people who have put on their salmon forms. When they die, their spirits return to their human shape. That is why when you kill a salmon, you are careful to put its bones back into the sea, so the salmon can become a person again and come back another time. And this relationship is guarded in each river by a Woman of Power, or what we would call a goddess.

They are the *Qaasghajiina*, the Creek Women. In each of the headwaters of the major streams the Creek Woman lives. She watches over the salmon people who congregate there. Her lover is *Sghaana*, the Killer Whale. He cruises out to sea, just by the reef, watching the river mouth. Having knowledge of the weather, he sends the fair-weather clouds, which means the fish are coming to the headwaters. Then they will be guarded by the Creek Woman. There is a complex web of patterns, a deep mystery going on in these rivers, figured in a sexual relationship between a goddess of the river and her mate, the whale, a being of power in his most powerful manifestation. All the stories say that you don't want to mess with these people.

These stories convey the warning bluntly. They are negative example stories, like that of Nanabozo – but far more solemn: this is something you just don't do. In its variations the basic plot of the story involves a gang of boys. They paddled out one day to a creek. There they carried on like juvenile delinquents at a beach party: they were hauling in the salmon as if they owned the creek. The boys had put a salmon on the fire and were watching it roast. Suddenly, a frog hopped into the clearing. The frog glowed like copper (copper is what the gods wear). It stared at the leader of the gang. Those huge, unblinking, lidless eyes. The boy was full of mischief; as told in Haida by Job Moody of the Sttaawas Xaaidaghaai, he is literally "without ears." The boy put the creature into the fire, piled the fire on top of it, then led the boys in the laughter. He should have remembered that the Frog is the totemic familiar of the Creek Woman; she calls the Frog "my child." And the Frog, the talisman of wealth, is especially the companion of the most senior of the creek goddesses, of the spirit of abundance felt in those headwaters. Her name is Jilaquns: she is the wife of the Raven.

There are various accounts of what happened next. This is Job Moody's account:

> On top of it they piled up the fire and laughed at it. After some time had passed, the frog exploded. The hot coals were scattered all about, but it sat in its place just as before. It was not burnt. Again they heaped hot coals upon it, and built the heap up large. Again they put it in. After some time had passed, it exploded, and sat in its place as before. Now they heaped the fire up high, and they put it into it. Again it exploded, but, as before, it sat in the same place. Then they went to sleep. When it was day, they went down along the creek. They came out and launched the canoe. Then they got in and picked up their paddles. But when they had paddled a while, and were off some distance, some one called after them from Singgil Point, "Ho, there! Stop until I have given you directions!" They stopped at once in surprise, and looked at him ... "The foremost one in the canoe on the right side will die at Point Ttsii. The one on the other side will die at Point Laaghanaus. The next one will die at Point Squaghaus. The next one will die at Point Qqaaighanttiis. Only the one in the stern will be saved; and when he gets home, and has finished talking about himself, he too will die." As this person stood at Singgil Point, they could see the ground through his body.

They died as he had foretold. One died first at Point Ttsii. One died at Point Laaghanaus. One died after that at Point Sqaughaus. After that, one died at Point Qqaaighanttiis. It happened as he had foretold. When the survivor came home around Point Sqqaaxunans, the people felt strange about it, and the people of Jigwa moved at once. They came down to meet him, and, as they stood beside his canoe on shore, he gave a rough account of what had happened. After that, when he had entered the house, he again told what had happened. He related everything from the beginning. When he had finished telling it, he acted like people who fall asleep.

In several stories of this type, Jilaquns herself appears, amidst evidence of a volcanic eruption, to become the patron of the one survivor of the town, a girl ordained to be the ancestor of several families. As Job Moody tells it,

> ... after the town had burned awhile and stopped, Jilaquns came and stood above her. She held a cane the lower part of which had the carving of a frog on it. The upper part had the carving of a cormorant [some say, duck]. Her hat had the design of a frog on it. Then she struck the butt-end of her cane upon the ground, and began a crying-song. There she sang awhile. Then she went away, and the town stopped burning.

It is an ominous myth: it remembers something sacred about the reefs and headwaters of the Queen Charlotte Islands, something which is dreadful to forget.

The myth of the Creek Woman tells how to behave in the sort of reality we now call ecological. But myths, especially hunter-gatherer myths, have more to say. That is Jilaquns' creek. She was brought from the mainland in mythtime by Voice-handler himself, and placed in the creek called Ghauquns, in the west arm of Cumshewa Inlet, where the boys fished. The goddess is inseparable from the locale and from the story: she is the mystery of the headwater itself.

Since every salmon stream in the Islands of the Haida has a woman guarding it, a presence of female fertility and renewal, each myth remembers a particular part of the land as story. That is the creek and those are the four headlands where the boys died. The events that happened there were compelled by greater-than-human powers, the powers which intersect with our world at various points, which send us the fish we eat, yet prefer to remain invisible. The myth teaches that these sacred places are to be respected for their own sake, not for what human beings can make of them. Myth, in its most ecologically discreet form, among people who live by hunting and fishing and gathering, seems to be the song of the place to itself, which humans overhear.

Wisdom about nature, that wisdom heard and told in animated pattern, that pattern rendered in such a way as to preserve a place whole and sacred, safe from human meddling: these are the concepts with which to begin an exploration of myth. Of these, the notion of the sanctity of place is vital. It anchors the other concepts. The stories remembered by the mythtellers were pictures of the flow of life and information from special places on the earth where that energy was felt most keenly. Once the power of the place is lost to memory, myth is uprooted; knowledge of the earth's processes becomes a different kind of knowledge, manipulated and applied by man.

As I write this, I am alarmed to hear that the year's population of salmon has not come back to the rivers of British Columbia. For the first time in memory, the fish were not there when the fair-weather clouds rose over the Pacific. There is an explanation for this. It involves the abuse of fishing practices in the north Pacific by driftnet trawlers, dragging their immense nets through the ocean, guided to the salmon by sonar. And there are the abusive logging practices which have silted in the salmon streams. But let us not forget the myth which tells us who the salmon belong to, for that myth is in effect a whole ecology holding itself in place in a part of the world, and expressing itself through the storytelling of local humanity. Ghauquns, the creek of the most senior of the Creek Women, is on the east coast of the southern island of Haida Gwaai, near the site of the ancient village of Hlqinnuhl, which was Job Moody's village once. Now the creek is a polluted drainage ditch through slash left over from an old logging clearcut, where the spawning beds of the salmon are filled with mud that has eroded from the riverbanks, no longer held in place by the roots of trees. This is a descriptive account of what has happened here – but there is also a narrative account, in which it is just as true to think that the Salmon People have not returned because of an insult done by modern hunters and collectors to Jilaquns, the wife of the Raven in his form as the Killer Whale, and, by extension, an insult done to all the *Qaasghajiina*, the Women of the Creeks who are her sisters.

CHAPTER TWO / MAPS

Skaai of the Qquuna Qiighawaai. Skidegate, October 1900

Aanishau tangagyangang, wansuuga.
L xitghwaangas, Xhuuya a.
Tlgu qqaugashlingaay gi la qiingas.
Qaudihau gwaayghutgwa nang qaadla qqaayghudiyas
lagu qqaughaayghan lagha xiidas.
Aa tl sghaana qidas yasgagas giinuusis gangang
lagu gutgwi xhihldagahldiyaagas.
Ga sghaanagwaay ghaaxas la ttista qqaa sqqagilaangas,
tlgwixhan xhahlgwi at wagwi a.
Ghaadagas gyanhau, ising ghaalghagang, wansuuga.

[Nangkilstlas nagha ghahau tadl tsigha'awagan.
Singghalghada l qaaxuhls gyan l kindagaangas.
Sta la xitkkuudahldajasi
gyan gaguu la qqaughaawas guxhan la qqaugingas.
Gyan nang qqaayas taaydiyas gam lagwi qiixhaganggangas.
Qaudi ising ising l qaaxuhls gyan kindaagangas
gyan sta la kkuugwijaasi gyan l qqaaugangas.
Gangang la suugang.
Qaudihau ghaatxhan l skujuu dayasta la kyanangas:
«Jaa, gaasintlau daa suuganggang 'aa,' kilstlaay?»

«Gam hau hla guudangangghi suuganggangga.
Sghaana qidas tsiiyahlingaay gaawun diigi suuwus.
Ghaagaanhau hl suuwugangga.

Gyan han la la suudas,
«Hla tlguhlghaasang.»]

...

RAVEN TRAVELLING: OPENING SCENE

Translated from the Haida by Robert Bringhurst (1994)

Hereabouts was all saltwater, they say.
He kept on flying, Raven did,
looking for land that he could stand on.
After a time, beyond the Islands, there was one rock awash.
He flew there to sit.
Like sea-sausages, gods lay across it,
putting their mouths against it side by side.
The newborn gods were sleeping, out along the reef,
heads and tails in all directions.
It was light then, and it turned to night, they say.

[Loon was living in Voicehandler's house.
One day she went out and called.
Then she flew back in and sat waiting,
right where she usually sat.
An old man lay there, not looking up at her.
She went out a second time and called
and hurried back in and sat.
She kept saying the same thing.
After a time, with his back to the fire, the old man said,
«Tell me, Great Speechmaker, why do you keep on talking as you do?»

«I am not talking only from my own mind.
The gods tell me they need places to live.
That is why I have been speaking.»

And he said,
«I am going to make some.»]

Now when the Raven had flown a while longer,
the sky in one direction brightened.
It enabled him to see, they say.
And then he flew right up against it.
He pushed his mind through and pulled his body after.

There were five villages strung out in a line.
In the northernmost, the headman's favored daughter
had just given birth to a child.
When evening came, and they were sleeping,
the Raven peeled the skin off the newborn child, starting at the feet,
and put it on.
Then he lay down in the child's place.

Next day, his grandfather asked for the child
and they passed him along.
His grandfather washed him.
Then, he pressed the child's feet against the ground
and stretched him up to a standing position.
Then he handed him back.
Next day he stretched him again
and handed him back to his mother.

Now he was hungry.
They had not yet started feeding him chewed-up food.
Then evening came again, and they lay down,
and when they slept,
he raised his head and looked around.
He listened throughout the house.
All alike were sleeping.
Then he untied himself from the cradle.
He squirmed his way free and went outside.

Something that was half rock, living in the back corner, watched him.
While he was gone, it continued to sit there.
He brought something in in the fold of his robe.
In front of his mother, where the fire smoldered,
he poked at the coals.
He scooped out a cooking spot with a stick,
and there he put the things that he carried.
As soon as the embers had charred them, he ate them.
They slithered.
He laughed to himself.
Therefore he was seen from the corner.

Again it was evening and they lay down,
and again he went out.
He was gone for a while.
Again he carried things back in the fold of his robe,
and he brought them out
and roasted them over the coals.
Then he pulled them out and ate them, laughing to himself.
The one that was half rock watched him from the corner.
He ate them all,
and then he lay down in the cradle.

When morning came, all five villages were wailing.
He could hear them.
In four of five villages, each of the people was missing an eye.
Then one of the old people spoke, they say.
« The newborn baby of the favored child goes out.
I have seen him.
As soon as they sleep, he gets up and leaves.»

Then his grandfather gave him a marten-skin blanket
and they wrapped it around him.

His grandfather whispered and someone went out.
« Come bring the baby of the favored child outsi-i-i-ide.»

And as soon as the people had gathered,
they stood in a circle, bouncing him up as they sang him a song.
After a while they let him fall,
and they watched him go down.
Turning round to the right he went down through the clouds
and struck water.
Then as he drifted about, he kept crying.
After his voice grew tired, he slept.

He slept for a while, and then something said to him,
« Your father's father asks you in.»
He looked all around.
He saw nothing.
Again, when he had floated there awhile,
something said the same thing.
He looked around.
He saw nothing.
Then he looked through the eye of his marten-skin blanket.
A pied-bill grebe appeared.
« Your father's father asks you in.»
As soon as he said this, he dived.

Then he sat up.
He was floating against a two-headed kelp.
Then he stepped onto it.
He was standing – yes! – on a two-headed stone housepole.
Then he climbed down it.
It was the same to him in the sea as it was to him above.

Then he came down in front of a house,
and someone invited him in.

« Come inside, my grandson.
  The birds have been singing about your borrowing something from me. »

  Then he went in.
  At the back an elder, white as a gull, was sitting.
  And he sent him to get a box that hung in the corner.

  As soon as he had it,
  he pulled out the boxes within the box, totalling five.
  In the innermost box were cylindrical things,
  one colored like mother-of-pearl and one that was black,
  and he handed him these as he said to him,
« You are me.
  You are that, too. »
  He spoke of some slender blue things becoming black
  on top of the screens forming a point in the rear of the house.

  Then he said to him,
« Set this one into the water, roundways up,
  and bite off part of the other and spit it at this. »

  But when the Raven brought them up,
  he set the black one into the water
  and bit off a part of the one like mother-of-pearl.
  When he spat that at the other,
  it bounced away.

  He did it the other way round from the way he was told,
  and that is the reason it bounced away.

  Now he went back to the black one
  and bit off a piece of it,
  and spat that at the other.

Then it stuck.
And he bit a part off of the one like mother-of-pearl
and spat that at the other.
It stuck.
That is how trees started, they say.

When he set this place into the water,
it stretched itself out.
The gods swam to it, taking their places.
The mainland did the same,
as soon as he set it into the water roundways up.
...

MAPS

Mythic centers

Long after encounters with other cultures ought to have dissolved in Europeans their pride in being alone at the center of a world, maps hold that pride in place. Controlling the world through visual maps is a long tradition. For the Romans, the Mediterranean was *Mare Nostrum*; beyond was *Terra Incognita* with its cherubic zephyrs and other decadent traces of myth haunting the margins of the maps. Following such maps as these, the explorers came, then the traders, then the settlers; capital cities flourished at the intersections of the trade routes, and soon politics linked up all the centers of power with which we are familiar: Rome, Paris, London, Washington, Tokyo.

If there were maps of the invisible realm of the powers that are greater than human, what would those maps look like? There wouldn't be a unified map, of course, because there is no singleminded order to mythtime. Instead, there would be places of local meaning where mystery is felt – this narrowing in a river, this headwater where the salmon come during the time of the fair-weather clouds, this cave at Altamira or Lascaux. Then there would be the regional mythic centers of larger civilizations where power wells up like vapor from subterranean hot springs. One could mark on a worldly map these and other sanctuaries where the gods and goddesses spoke to men and women: Knossos, Delphi, Eleusis, Stonehenge, Sinai where the Ten Commandments were given, innumerable temples dedicated to a newer religion while drawing ancient power from the sites they stood on, each laden with myth: Ephesus, Chartres, Glastonbury. And Cuzco, Tenochtitlan, Kitwancool, Pisaq – not to mention the Cambodian temples like Angkor Wat, the great rivers of India, the cliff drawings in the Kimberleys, Arnhem Land, Cape York and elsewhere in Australia, and also sacred drawing sites throughout southern Africa. Places where a continuing mythic tradition in some form is still going on.

I live near one of these spiritual centers. Tourist maps identify the power site as the Peterborough Petroglyphs – but the Anishnabe people call it Keno-mah-gay-wah-kon, "the rocks that teach." They are said to be one of the most extensive single set of rock carvings in North America. There are over 300 clear drawings – hundreds more obscure – of herons and cranes and ducks and deer and snakes, and shamanistic figures with sun's rays extending from their heads, figures in canoes being carried to the spirit world, and the image of a woman giving birth, and of a turtle with her eggs – Turtle who carries the world of time and space on her back. And the hare, one of the favorite forms of the trickster Nanabozo. The artists who inscribed these rocks came here to meet in dreams the animal ancestor, the god, whose children are given to the humans to be hunted.

Certainly, when you see the carvings on these teaching rocks, you see figures that seem to hang in spiritual air. They almost dance on the surface of the crystalline limestone. They are the spirits of particular animals, this creature as it exists and is encountered in dream. The young boys of the surrounding tribes would come alone to this rock, where the water gurgles – almost speaks – underneath. Dry-mouthed and taut with hunger after a prolonged fasting, light-headed from sleeplessness, the boy would be filled with the vision of a being of power come in its animal form. The animal god would teach the boy its power song. That being would be the boy's helper in adult life, the one animal which the man could not kill. The girls met the powers of the earth a different way. Entrusted up to the time of their first menstruation with the task of picking and sorting berries (these they could not eat while working – the injunction taught a certain respect), the girls were isolated during their first menses. That may have been, in a tribal society, the first time in her life when a girl was thoroughly alone – alone with the songs of the plant-beings. And this entry, through aloneness and humility into the physical and spiritual presence of the plant or animal god, was linked to the special place which that god favored.

In Australia, this link with the spirits of the land goes back a long way in time. On the Arnhem Land plateau, in what is now Kakadu National Park, there are rock paintings dating back as far as 23,000 years. At Burrunguy, the painters distinguish between images of animals like wallaby, turtle and so on, and images of beings like Namargon, the owner of lightning, and Barginj, his wife. The Aborigines say the animals were drawn by humans – but the gods *put themselves on the rock*.

These paintings are so precise that a herpetologist was able to identify the image of a particular turtle species, *Carettochelys insculpta* – not known in Australia (it is commonly found in New Guinea), until the painting prompted a search for the turtle and it was discovered living in Arnhem Land. In the area around Burrunguy, there are equally clear paintings of *Thylacinus cynocephalus*, the so-called "Tasmanian tiger" (in fact, a wolf-like marsupial, not a feline). Yet paleontologists say *Thylacinus* has been extinct on the Australian mainland since about 1500 BC. But this is apparently just a start. Other images in the paintings have been identified as *Zaglossus*, a long-beaked echidna still found in New Guinea but reportedly extinct in Australia for some 18,000 years; *Palorchestes*, a tapir-like marsupial altogether extinct for 18,000 years; possibly *Sthenurus*, an extinct genus of kangaroo; and *Thylacoleo*, another extinct marsupial carnivore. And there are paintings of large birds, also long extinct. There is archaeological evidence of the presence of humans in the area, and the use of pigments, for at least the last 20,000 years. And the people have been redrawing some of the images when the paintings become faint from standing in the open air. While some paintings clearly have not been touched for decades or centuries, others have been periodically renewed. It is hard to escape the deduction that out of loyalty to some Late Pleistocene story, still continued in a whisper beyond the range of modern hearing, people have been maintaining some of these images for 20,000 years. Of course, parts of that story have become blurred, parts forgot – but the forgotten parts are held up by the remembered parts in the incalculably complex interweaving that is Aboriginal narrative in Australia. What holds the whole elaborate structure of stories fresh in memory is the likeness of the patterns of story to the life of the land. The centers of life-giving energy found on the Arnhem Land plateau are the source of myths: nodal points of narratives that link together, providing an acoustic map of all the patterns of life, past and present, in that region.

Songlines, mythlines

Thanks to a generation of Australian anthropologists working in the mid-twentieth century, and thanks to the elders who spoke with them, we now have a sense of the complexity of this oral mapping. Australian song and myth retell the adventures of the first day of the world, when the First People – supernatural beings in human or animal guise – shaped the landscape, each leaving a trail of narrative where it travelled, singing through the land. Each traditional Aborigine is given a specific section of these mythical adventures to hold in memory. Reciting the myth, the tribesperson is re-enacting the particular "walkabout" that the god made, following the particular track he took, singing the poetry he sang. These are the Songlines. At least, that is how they are popularly known, from the title of a bestseller by Bruce Chatwin. I prefer the term *mythlines*. It is the term Theodore Strehlow uses, and comes from his time among the Aranda-speaking peoples. Mythlines – they crisscross the whole continent of Australia.

This is as far as anyone can safely generalize. Every descent-group in every locale has its own account of what seems universally referred to as the Dreaming, and some of these chanted myths have "outside" versions (for public ceremony within Aborigine society) and "inside" versions (for private rites, like initiations), the latter in some cases being recited in a special sacred language. Depending on the story and the part of Australia it comes from, the ancestors emerged from the mud to begin reshaping the landscape, or they came as discoverers – but the end-point of their adventures was usually to "put themselves in spirit," that is, to become for a local Aboriginal descent group a permanent source of information and energy emanating from the particular feature of the landscape each supernatural being had changed itself into – this tree, this waterhole, this sand-ridge, this ochre deposit. In so transforming themselves, the First People initiated a realm of sacred time that was concurrent with secular time. In that sacred time – timelessness is a better word – every aspect of the landscape is already named; each has an event associated with it. That heap of boulders over there – that's where the Rainbow Snake laid her eggs. That lump of reddish sandstone – that's the liver of the Red Kangaroo when he was speared. All along the mythlines – the tracks of a semi-nomadic people more or less constantly on the move – these episodes in the sacred chant tell the people what to look for next. The trails of the ancestral myth-beings who crossed the Western Desert meander for hundreds of miles, across the territories of diverse peoples divided by dialect and differences in social organization. Strehlow has traced a mythline involving the honey-ant ancestors, who in the Dreamtime travel from the country of the Pintubi, through the areas of the Kukatja, the Western and Northern Aranda, and the Unmatjera, as far as Iliaura territory on the Sandover River. All of the landscape is held in narrative and is made present by it.

Important to an appreciation of this Paleolithic mapping is the special place along the mythline that provides meaning for the local descent-group or totemic clan. For the Aranda people, these sacred sites (*pmara kutata*) are where specific myth-beings originated out of the ground and populated the surrounding countryside. One site is the originating place of the honey-ant men; another, the place of the ancestral possums; another, of the pigeon women, and so on. All of these personages of mythtime, together with the songs and traditions they sanctify, are believed to be in a state of sleep at their respective *pmara kutata*, from which they send out nourishing Dream energy. The members of the descent-group gather for rituals at these places from which their totemic clan derives its identity: the possum men, or the honey-ant men as the case may be. These sacred sites located along the mythlines are places where the potency of an ancestor is present at once as spiritual energy, music, and seed power – the latter a kind of vibration left in the earth. Native Australians call it the Dreaming of a place.

A.E. Newsome, a wildlife biologist, in consultation with Aboriginal elders, gives a detailed sense of what the mythlines meant to the Krantji Kangaroo clan. They are an Aranda clan living to the north of the Macdonnell mountains of central Australia. This is the country of Krantjiringa. He is the ancestor both of every red kangaroo and of every member of the Kangaroo clan. The god takes his animal form by day and his human form by night. The place where he emerged into the world during the time of the Dreaming is a small spring, called Krantji. He is said to be still there. He exists in part in slabs of rocks below the spring, from which he sends out reproductive energy. It is here that he is worshipped by his human descendants, who always approach the spring with their eyes closed and their weapons left some distance away, indicating they have not come here to hunt. No red kangaroo can be killed at the place of the Kangaroo Ancestor.

From this sacred site radiates the energy of life; it fans out with the mythlines that travel outwards from this spring, and from other sacred sites. The footprints made by the animal ancestor during his original walkabout are also trails of seminal ideas left by the ancestor, each idea ready to come into the world in the form of a particular animal when the circumstances are right. These ideas are hidden in the rocks. When chipped in a sacred way, the ideas may fall loose, to be quickened into life by the next rain.

The trails are also the paths followed by *Marcopus rufus* as it forages outwards seeking the particular grass eaten by kangaroos. During the rainy times, the red kangaroos graze in the foothills of the Macdonnell ranges. During the dry times, they fall back in groups to river beds where the grasses can be found. Because these springs and rivers are the sources of sacred energy, the kangaroo cannot be hunted in what is, in fact, its prime habitat. Accordingly, the mythlines preserve the species which children of the human side of the Kangaroo Ancestor are kin to and which they depend on for food. The local mythlines, in effect an oral map of the grazing patterns of the red kangaroo, are also the means by which the species is allowed to build up its local populations at the particular sanctuaries where Krantjiringa is worshipped.

Realms of Being

> *Hereabouts was all saltwater, they say.*
> *He kept on flying, Raven did,*
> *looking for land he could stand on.*

After a time, beyond the Islands, there was one rock awash.
He flew there to sit.

When John Sky recited this story for John Swanton, he indicated to the anthropologist that the first rock to appear at the beginning of creation was down at the south end of Haida Gwaii. It is still there now, the one physical reference-point in a myth about the deepest fecundity of those Islands.

To speak of this myth as a map stretches the imagination, because there is not one but three worlds in the narrative, interpenetrant as in a hologram. First, there is the undersea world of the old man who is white as a gull. He is Taangghwanlaana, the One in the Sea. It is his thought that becomes the world; the Raven makes that thought real. However, the Raven could not become the agent of creation until he was prepared for that role. When first mentioned at the beginning of the story, he is just *xhuuya*, an ordinary raven. He is flying along in what is to become our middle world; he rests on a rock on which the gods are clustered; then, suddenly, he finds the sky brighter and for some reason is compelled to fly right through it. "He pushed his mind through and pulled his body after." According to Job Moody's clarification, it was the Old Man's thoughts that took him there. The One in the Sea heard the crying of homeless gods in the Loon Woman's voice – if you listen to a loon's call, you will know what I mean: the loon's call is full of the cries of the gods. "The gods tell me they need places to live," she says. And the One in the Sea says, "I will make them some." That is why the Raven finds himself in a third world, the world of the Sky People, where the tops of the clouds resemble the ocean lapping at the feet of the villages. The Raven, once chosen for his mission, has to be reborn as one of these beings of power. Perhaps he has to steal omniscience from them before he can be given the work of creation. Then he is dropped down through the clouds to the ocean and, from the water surface, enters the world at the bottom of the sea.

The myth therefore speaks of three worlds – the world beneath the sea, the world above the clouds, and the world in between – and it shows the exchanges among them. When energy or information is borrowed from one world for the sake of another, there is a loss to that providing world. In four of the villages of the Sky People, every person has lost an eye.

It is more ecologically complicated than that, of course. The myth is concerned with a source of fertility and wealth which is found at the bottom of the sea. That power flows out like an immense potlatch from the Old Man to all the resident gods and, through them, to living things. But the One in the Sea is not that wealth itself – rather, he stands in relation to it as a tribal elder. The image of wealth is a being called the Snag – his name in Haida is Ttsaamus. He is the stone housepole that rose from the sea floor even before creation. Each of the islands of Haida Gwaii is held up by a housepole, each a form of Ttsaamus. The Raven, after his reincarnation, finds himself standing on this figure of awesome power – "yes! – on a two-headed stone housepole." The moment in the story is charged with mystery: the Raven and the Snag in conjunction is a central theme in Haida mythology, to be found on memorial poles, rattles, speaker's staffs, throne and box carving. The symmetry of the pillar that supports the world is pronounced; it is emblazoned on the features of the Sea Grizzly, the intelligence and foundation of the pole. Thus, there are three personages in the myth: the One in the Sea who provides the patterns, the Snag who holds worlds together, and the Raven who carries power between worlds. In a biological perspective, they seem to represent, respectively, the memory of pattern, the consistency of structure, and a force of restless trial-and-error innovation (those are cylindrical gambling sticks which the White Elder gives the Raven). Other myths of the

Haida suggest the dynamism of this three-way relationship. Bringhurst notes that it is one of hereditary kinship. The Old Man's nephew and heir is the Snag; the Snag's nephew and heir is the Raven. And the Old Man is the Raven's grandfather on his father's side: "it fits together snugly: three generations of males who all belong to the Raven side [of Haida civilization]. Each is entitled to say to the other, I am you." The myth moves as nature moves, as creation is recreated anew with each surge of power from the sky and from the bottom of the sea into the land. The One in the Sea is due to die, for the gods are not immortal in Haida mythtelling. But through the power of kinship the paternal grandfather is reincarnated in the grandson. And the process continues.

— *The wisdom of plants and seasons*

All but erased beneath the Homeric hymn to Demeter, as we have it, is a fine map of ecological relationships among the agricultural and seasonal and animal life cycles of the Mediterranean. The perceptions are encoded in the subtle language of mythtelling and rendered sacred under the name of the "golden-haired goddess swaying with the wind," who brings fertility to the earth (through her Latin name, Ceres, she gives us the word "cereal"). We remember the myth in its obvious sentimental form. Persephone, Demeter's daughter, is destined to spend seven months of the year under the earth, with Hades, the god of death. That is because of the seven pomegranate seeds she ate after she was abducted by Hades, who had planted a poppy bush to enchant her on the morning she was playing in the poppy fields of Enna. And so, the suspended animation of Persephone – she is like the seeds she ate in Hades' realm; and the sorrow of Demeter who withholds fertility from the land each part of the year her daughter is away. But the myth remembers more than that.

For example, poppies. They often grow among the wheat stalks in the Mediterranean. Poppyseed bread is common in that part of the world. The myth is also aware of the narcotic properties of the red flower. Persephone, the poppy goddess, is to be feared – her name means "she who brings destruction" (from *phero* and *phonos*). In a full rendering of the myth, we meet Hekate, the goddess-witch of the moon. Demeter goes to her for advice, and she seems to watch over Persephone like an aunt while the girl is in the land of the dead for seven months of the year. She ensures the terms of this arrangement are kept. The mythologist Robert Graves observes that the farmer has to wait seven lunar phases between the planting of the seeds and the appearance of the first green wheat-shoots in the fields. In Persephone's other name, Kore (transposed to her from her mother), there is a relationship involving swine, which she protects. Evidence suggests Demeter was once a sow goddess, but with the beginnings of agriculture her beneficence was transferred to the fields. One of her myths tells of how, drunk, she slipped outdoors during a wedding feast of the gods, and slept with Iasion the Titan on a thrice-plowed fallow field. The thrice-plowed field of her love-making sanctifies the sensible practice in Attic Greece of plowing a field first in the spring, then crossways lightly after the summer harvest, then again in the original direction in autumn to prepare for the sowing. Woven into the myth are perceptions of other patterns among bird behavior and the seasonal cycle. Some of these are lost memories now; some are obvious by etymology. King Keleos of Eleusis, ruling a place of pronounced agricultural mystery where Demeter stays for awhile, may once have been an animal god, or a shaman who took his name from one: his name could mean "woodpecker" as well as "sorcerer." Askalaphos, who hoots the evidence of Persephone's eating of a pomegranate from the orchard of the dead, is the harbinger of her annual disappearance. The short-eared owl (*ascalaphos*) is noisiest in November, at the year-end. These and other shifting relationships among the food cycles are mapped by the myths of Demeter.

The topography of story

Where a people have lived in the same locale for centuries, the stories of the land multiply. A ritual journey of only a few miles at the base of Ayer's Rock (Uluru) in Central Australia is marked by sacred sites remembering the names of 38 separate spatial directions. Later on, when the original oral map is forgotten, incidents are invented to account for a place name whose original power is still felt. The topography is dutifully remembered, each named place being the site of a sub-story, and each sub-story branching out, like a spur line on a railway system. This effort to re-root a story in the land is common as well in ancient Irish tradition. The effort is focussed on certain natural and man-made hills called *sidi* (*sidhe* in modern Irish) as well as passage-graves like the one at New Grange. They are associated with the exploits of the gods remembered generically as the Tuatha Dé Danaan, the "clanspeople of the goddess Dana," the Earth Mother who is herself identified with the two rises near Killarney called "the paps of Anann." There is a story here. And the story that begins the next chapter of this book, "The Wooing of Étaín," will tell of the god Midir of Sidh Brí Leith, an elfmound west of Ardagh in County Longford. Brí was Midir's broken-hearted daughter who was kept from marrying Liath, her lover. Because she was his lover by her own consent, the burial place bears both the lovers' names. The story of Midir and Étaín also mentions the Brugh na Bóinne, the mansion of the Boyne belonging to the love-god Aengus after he tricked his father the Dagda out of its possession. The stories seem to link hill to hill. And there are narratives more recent than the so-called Mythological Cycle which are also invested in the landscape. For example, no tribesperson travelling from Connacht to Ulster in pre-Christian Ireland could fail to intersect with the original route taken by the armies of Queen Maeve when she rode against Cúchulainn and his northern kinsfolk. The journey is recorded, probably as it was recited, in the *Táin Bó Cuailnge*, the main part of the Ulster cycle of heroic tales. Written down in the eighth century, they have a continuous oral existence from the Iron-age civilization of the Celts.

✔ *The Monday after Samain they set out. This is the way they went, southeast from Cruachan Ai:*
> *through Muicc Cruinb,*
> *through Terloch Téora Crích, the marshy lake bed where three territories meet,*
> *by Tuaim Móna, the peat ridge,*
> *through Cúil Silinne, where Carrain Lake is now —*
> *it was named after Silenn, daughter of Madchar,*
> *by Fid and Bolga, woods and hills,*
> *through Coltain, and across the Sinnan river,*
> *through Glúne Gabair,*
> *over Trego Plain, of the spears,*
> *through Tethba, North and South,*
> *through Tiarthechta,*
> *through Ord, 'the hammer,'*
> *through Sláis southward,*
> *by the river Indiuind, 'the anvil,'*
> *through Carn,*
> *through Ochtrach, 'the dung heap,'*
> *through Finnglassa Assail, of the clear streams ...*

This is the oral narrative of a heroic age, of a people who lived by farming and fighting. In the glitter and clash of warfare, the tale has lost some of its memory of the animal ancestors. But not all of it. As its title, *The Cattle-Raid of Cuilgne*, indicates, the epic is compelled by the memory of an earlier tale of a raid by one group of tribes on the territory of another. Indeed, the heroic substance of the story seems draped over a rather simple Stone-age plot-line. At the center of the epic — the prize that the battles are fought over — is a totemic animal, Donn Cuailnge, the Brown Bull of Cooley, whose homeward wanderings after his killing of a rival bull are recited by the bard at the end of the story:

> ... He headed toward his own land. He stopped to drink at Finnlethe on the way. He left Finnbenach's shoulder-blade there — from which comes Finniethe, the White One's shoulderblade, as the name of that district. He drank again at Ath Luain, and left Finnbenach's loins there — that is how the place was named Ath Luain, the Ford of the Loins. He uttered a bellow at Iraird Cuillenn that was heard through the whole province ... He came to Etan Tairb and set his brow against the hill at Ath Da Ferta — from which comes the name Etan Tairb, the Bull's Brow, in Murtheimne Plain. Then he went by the Midluachain road to Cuib, where he had dwelt with the milkless cow of Dáire, and he tore up the ground there — from which comes the name Gort mBúràig, the Field of the Trench. Then he went until he fell dead between Ulster and Uí Ecach at Druim Tairb. So Druim Tairb, the Ridge of the Bull, is the name of that place.

The narrative of Iron-age warriors has submerged the sacred chants of Stone-age hunters in *The Táin*. Yet the bull wanders freely across the story as a memory of some earliest form of animal reverence — as if he had just stepped off the cave wall at

Altamira, where he was drawn at the height of the Magdalenian Stone Age around 12,000 BC. Donn Cuailnge, himself a kind of god, is the memory of an animal ancestor, as well as the impulse for an oral narrative map of a landscape touched everywhere by footprints of the supernatural.

Sacrifice

At the nodal points of oral maps are places sacred to the animal ancestor who sends his children into the world and permits each one to die, when the time of death has come for that god's child. Lined up in the sights of a bow or stumbling into an animal trap, that creature has given its life because its ancestor wills it. When the creature dies, its spirit returns to its ancestor — to the world of Dream. The ancestor may then dream another spirit into a physical body to enter the dimension of the hunter. That is why the hunter always tells the animal ancestor that it is respected, and that the animal people it watches over will not be killed lightly. Thus the obligation by the hunter to respect the animal god is focussed towards an ecology of living and dying beings of the same species. The place where the ancestor's spirit is felt most strongly may mark a center in that actual ecology, as with Krantjiringa, the Great Kangaroo, who dwells beneath the spring called Krantji, and by extension in the other waterways where the red kangaroo forage in the dry season. The place of the god is the focal point of a principle of sacrifice and the promise of renewed life of a species. It is also one of the points of passage between the Otherworld of Dream and this world of physical embodiment, a point marked by death and the obligation to remember through the telling of stories. All this and more is contained in the term *sacrifice*, which in its fullest understanding has less to do with the killing of a victim in order to please a god and more to do with the process of becoming or making sacred (*sacrum facere*). The Celtic chieftain Brennus is said to have remarked at the sacrificial site at Delphi: "The gods have no need for treasures because they shower them upon men." In the perspective of Brennus, a sacrifice was a transformation of being, a change from one state of existence to another between this world and the spirit world.

Joseph Campbell has written a great deal about sacrifice in relation to the cult of the bear, found everywhere in regions around the north pole. Whether the myth of the bear was diffused with the migration of the animals from Old Europe across to Siberia between 70,000 and 40,000 BC, and then across the stretch of land that once linked Asia and America – Campbell was decidedly a diffusionist in such matters – or whether similar myths started locally, there is no denying the resemblance a bear holds to humans, especially when the animal is standing upright on its hind legs. The bear displays to the hunter a human form and intelligence, the same way the seal suggested to the coast-dwellers of Europe an elderly human-looking fairy. The bear is kin to the human in practical ways too; he provides much of the human's food and clothing. In all places where he is respected, he is the animal ancestor who has permitted the death, for the sake of the human hunter, of one of the children of his family.

Death marks the passage of the spirit back to the supernatural. That is why the hunter at the moment of the kill takes care to skin the animal-being with ceremony. The ritual of the killing and skinning tells the bear ancestor that the hunter is aware that one of his children has been given. The spirit of the slain creature can return in dignity to its father out of time. With this gratitude upon it, the spirit of the animal goes back to the Otherworld hunting grounds, to come back again one day, if the bear ancestor pleases. Campbell says, "Now, when we sit down for a meal, we thank God for giving us the food. These people thanked the animal." Millennia later, when myth had been displaced by Christianity in Europe and people remembered the old ways through the fairy tale, there is still a sense that the kindness done to an animal, however small, will not pass unrewarded. When the fairy-tale hero or heroine gives their last morsel of food to a mouse simply because the mouse is hungry, the act speaks of an instinctive reverence for the divine ecology of life, for the interdependence of all existence in a sacramental world where the life of one animal is possible because of the death of another. That fairy-tale mouse usually has some good advice to give the heroine in return. In many fairy tales, the mouse helper appears just when the hero or heroine is at a danger point between the world of the ordinary and the world of the supernatural. The mouse, like the spider in African stories, is a creature of the threshold, and marks that part of the landscape that is sacred to other-than-human beings.

Myths sing a map of the landscape of the hunter, but they are sung from the landscape's point of view. This otherness of myth ensures that the impulses of the hunter are tuned to the overall balance of life of the region. In fact, myths often tell of a loss of balance that is righted by the initiative of a supernatural being in his or her animal form. The sense of a mutual relationship advantageous to both animal and man is then woven as story into tribal custom, with the supernatural patron serving as the ancient kinsperson of the clan, the one who gives it special favor. The god's image is carved in the position of honor on the memorial pole and worn on the ceremonial head-dress of the chief.

There are countless stories of a woman who marries a bear – countless, because new stories are being made by present-day mythtellers in dozens of languages. I am going to refer to one story, a Nishga story told in 1947 at Kincolith on the Nass River, just south of the Alaskan border by the Nishga mythteller Agnes Haldane of the Wolf clan of Gitkateen. She told it to the Tsimshian anthropologist Gwisqqaayn (William Beynon) of the Wolf clan of Gitlaan. The story has all the elements of myth: the mapping of a specific bioregion, the retuning of a discordant relationship between the animals and humanity, the willing sacrifice of a child of the animal god, the courtesy extended to the body of the animal at the time of its death, and the obligation to remember an event that has given special power to the tribe, in this case, the Wolf clan whose chief was Nega'on ("Long Arm").

"The people were living then on the Nass River at Lax-angida," Mrs. Haldane begins. "Here they were catching the sockeye, as it was the salmon season; and the people were very busy setting and drying it. It was also the time of year when the salmonberries were ripening." There is one of high family, a girl, and she tells her companions that it is time to go up into the mountains to pick the berries. "Then, the next day, the young women assembled together and went to a mountainside which was known as Laxanhluu ('Landslide Place') near Walxsyaqhakwdaak ('Place where they go to hang bows'). This was the territory of Nega'on, chief of the Wolf clan."

Once the framing map is established in this fashion, the mythteller begins the story that will give that frame meaning. The princess of the tribe is picking salmonberries. It is not a task she enjoys very much – she, a princess, one of a high family, gathering berries in the woods along with the other village girls. But all the young women have to do it. She suddenly steps on some bear scat that just happens to be lying on the trail. "The bear that made this was a dirty beast and heedless of where it sits," the favored woman exclaims. She goes on in this way while she is within earshot of her companions, shouting angry remarks about the bear and muttering to herself.

And so she wanders farther and farther away from the other girls until she is good and lost.

I said the bear scat just *happens* to be lying there on the trail. To anthropocentric readers, which means most of us, brought up as we are on human-centered literature, events in a myth often don't make much sense. We like to follow the destiny of the human protagonist. However, with myth it is a good idea to assume that the story is told from the viewpoint of the supernatural. Some myths, like the events they recount, are given to humans by spiritual beings. In this respect, a myth is the power of the place speaking. Therefore, each happening in the story is predestined. We may attach our sympathy to the heroine – she is human like us. But we listen, if we can, for more. We overhear with the Bear People the abusive language that is directed against them (animals are very sensitive to spoken insult). We think with the Bear People how a trap might be laid for that woman. Could not that bear scat have been put there for the over-proud princess to step in? Certainly, she deserves this, and everything that follows. Her sense of superiority to the bears signals an imbalance in the relationship with nature that needs to be righted. So many narrative coincidences turn out to be patterns of circumstance initiated by an animal god, who sees more than human pride will allow.

But let us allow Mrs. Haldane to continue the story – it is her story.

After she had filled her basket, she started on the trail down to the shore where the canoe was. She had not gone far when the strap of her basket broke and her berries were spilled. She gathered them up again and started off. She called out, but no one answered. Her companions thought she had gone on, when actually she was all by herself, and they were at the beach waiting for her.

When she had refilled her basket, she went on and had not gone far when the strap broke once more. Her berries spilled and went all over, and she began to pick these again. After filling the basket, she travelled on, and she had not gone far when two handsome young men approached her, and one of them spoke to her. "Princess, we were sent to help you. You are having trouble with your pack. Let us take it for you and lead you, so no harm may happen to you."

She did not recognize these men, but found them most handsome, especially the man who seemed to be the leader. She failed to note that the trail was not going down to the canoe but away into the mountain. They followed a very good trail, and she went along, laughing all the time.

And so, her carelessness turning to a mood of carefree abandon – there is a warning in this too – she follows them, laughing.

Before she knows any better, she is being proclaimed as daughter-in-law to the chief of the Bear People. In the house, there are bearskins hanging on pegs: when the Bear People go outdoors, they put their bear-form on. This is the way Agnes Haldane tells of passage from the spirit world to the physical world. The princess tricks the people into believing she is a woman of power. The Mouse Woman suggested that trick to her, for the girl had been kind to the elderly person behind that squeaky little voice at her side. Ksemwittsiin – Mouse Woman that was. The girl gives Mouse Woman some mountain-goat tallow; Mouse Woman, in return, tells the princess to put pieces of her copper bracelet on the latrine after she has used it. Then the bears will think she is a *naxnox*, one of the supernaturals. They treat her better after that, and she is about to be married with great ceremony into the family of the Bear

People – they are *mediik*: Grizzly Bears, the mythteller adds at this point in the story:

> The Bear chief's guests who came in were other Bears from distant parts of the country, and the chief spoke. As he did, his wife opened her eyes, and she saw that among these were many human beings. Her own breasts were the heads of human beings and they were alive and moving about. Bright rays of light came from her eyes.
>
> Then the great chief spoke to his guests, saying, "I am showing you my daughter-in-law, who is with me. You will all know her; and whenever you see her in any danger, you will guard her and protect her. Her children will be my grandchildren. Now I will give the food, much food, which she has brought here with her."
>
> When he finished speaking, there was a great murmur of approval from all the guests, and large balls of mountain-goat fat were brought out. These had been made from the cosmetic fat she had given to the little Mouse Woman.

When it is the season for the bears to hibernate, she goes with the Bear chief's son to a cave above a rockslide. This is the rockslide in the hunting territory of the Wolf clan, just above Laxangida. So she is close to her village now. But she is pregnant. There, at the top of a steep hill, in a cave, she waits to give birth to her children.

The men of her village kill many bears that autumn, the storyteller goes on to say. It becomes sad for the Bear People. They are afraid of being killed off entirely. Things are badly out of balance. And as the hunters from the village get closer and closer to the cave, the Bear husband senses his fate. "I know now that I will soon be killed," he says. "Your brother is the one who will kill me." His concern is for the two bear cubs he has fathered. They are clever and grow fast, and the father begins to teach them the ways of the Grizzly Bear People.

When the day of his killing is come, the Bear husband gives his instructions:

> "I have not long to live, for my brother-in-law has found me." For a time the princess was moved, as she had begun to love him. Yet she was lonesome for her own people ...
>
> When they came close, the Bear prince called his wife, "Let me go into my inner den. They will smoke me out, and I'll be helpless. Do not let them drag my carcass or mutilate me. After they have skinned me, tell them to burn my bones so that I may go on to help my children. At my death they shall take human form and become skillful hunters. Now, before I go to my den, listen as I sing my dirge song. This you must remember and take it to your father. He will use it. My cloak he shall don as his dancing garment. His crest shall be the Prince of Bears." Then he went into his den, and there he lay in wait for his brother-in-law who was to kill him.

Then, as the hunters pick their way up the rockslide, he begins to sing his death-song. The spear is guided into the bear's heart by his own hand. At the moment of his death, his wife takes up the death-song, singing it while her brother skins the body and burns its bones. Carrying the body with honor, they go back to the Nishga village, where the woman's father is overjoyed to see her, and as well the two grandchildren who have now taken human form.

The princess related to her father what had happened, and said that her Bear husband had given him the Bear garment. The great chief, who was Nega'on, now called in all his people and had his house-front decorated to represent the young woman's adventure.

As for the twin children, they were always restless. Their mother went to her father and said, "Why do you not erect a pole upon which my children may climb? They are getting out of hand." They were awkward in their walking; and whenever they went out they wore their bear robes. They journeyed with [the dog] into the hills, and the mother would hear the dog howling at the Bear. So the people, on going out, would find a grizzly or a moose or deer. This happened every day, and soon the chief's house was full of food, and he had many skins. He became very wealthy. So he gave another feast, at which he erected a long pole. Upon this his grandchildren climbed, and it was called "the play-pole of the Bear." On this pole, the two cub brothers, children of the princess, would climb and, looking away into the distance, call out, "There is the smoke of our grandfather's village, away into the mountains." Whenever they felt lonesome for their father, they stood upon the pole and gazed at the distant smoke.

Every day they travelled into the hills, and soon their grandfather became the wealthiest man in the country. The mother was very proud of her twins and took good care of them. When the grandfather died and another chief succeeded him, the young brothers took their bear garments and went into the hills. They kept travelling until they reached the village of their grandfather, the great Bear chief. There they stayed forever.

The myth affirms the *kinship* between human beings and animal beings. Kinship does not mean relatedness by blood. Kinship in the full original sense is deep with obligation, responsibility, and reward. Both worlds benefit from it: the bears, because they will not be hunted to extinction by the humans; the humans, because they have the providence of the Bear Ancestor. In this way, the myth safeguards an ecology. It maps the ecology in space – at Laxanhluu in the territory of the Wolf clan where the relationship between animals and humankind was ordained. It preserves the ecology in time – for no hunter of the Wolf clan can forget his patronage from the marriage between a human woman and a son of the chief of the bears. The story of the two bear children raised by the Wolf clan is remembered on totem poles, and carved just as sharply in stories. "This happened in Nega'on's territory on the Nass River," the storyteller concludes, "and the tradition belongs to the Wolf house of Nega'on at Laxangida."

This Nishga myth shows more clearly than the others in this chapter the balance of exchanges that is necessary for life to coexist in a locale. That balance is felt even in the symmetry of each world tricking the other – the Bear Chief with his bear scat, the human princess with her own. However, for there to be an exchange of any kind, whether it is an exchange of trickery or of wealth, there must be a boundary between the worlds across which the exchange can be made. The mythtellers are always careful to map this boundary which guarantees the autonomy of worlds and which is the whole essence of myth.

84

CHAPTER THREE / BOUNDARY

FROM: TOCHMARC ETAINE:
MIDIR'S SONG TO ÉTAÍN

A Bé Fínd, in ragha lium.
a tír n-ingnadh í fil rind.
is barr sobairci folt and.
is dath snechta for corp slim.

Is ann nád bí mui na tui.
gel ded and dubai a brai.
is lí sula lín ar sluag.
is dath sion and gach gruadh.

Is corcair muighi cach muin.
is lí sula ugai luin.
cídh cain deicsiu Muíghe Fail.
anam iar ngnais Muígi Mair.

Cídh cain lib coirm Insi Fail,
is mescu cuirm Thíri Mair.
amrai tíre tír asber.
ní théíd óc ann ré sén.

Srotha téith millsi tar tír.
rogha dé midh fín.
daine delgnaíde cen ón.
combart cen pecadh cen chol.

86

FROM: THE WOOING OF ÉTAÍN: MIDIR'S SONG TO ÉTAÍN

O Fair-haired Lady – will you come with me
to a land wonderful with music?
Hair is like the blossom of the primrose there,
bodies smooth and white as snow.

There, it is neither yours nor mine;
bright are teeth there, dark the brow.
The eye's delight the number of our hosts –
in every cheek the hue of foxglove,

in every neck the hue of the pink flower.
And blackbirds' eggs for the eye to see.
Though Ireland is fair to see,
it is desolate beside the Great Plain of the Gods.

Though strong the ale of Inis Fáil,
more powerful by far is the ale of the Great Land.
A wondrous land this land I tell of:
there, youth does not perish to old age.

Warm, sweet streams throughout the land,
the choice of mead and wine;
the people elegant, and without blemish,
conceived outside of lust or sin.

Atchiam cach for cach leath.
nicon aice nech.
teimel imorbuis Adaim
dadonarcheil ar araim

A ben dia ris mo thuaith tind
ia barr oir bias fort chind.
mil fin laith lemnacht la lind
rod bia lium and a Be Find.

We see everyone, wherever they may be –
no one sees us.
The darkness of the world that fell with Adam –
that is why we cannot be discerned.

Woman – if you come to my radiant people,
a crown of gold shall be on your head;
honey, wine, fresh milk for the drinking
you will have with me there, Fair One.

THE WOOING OF ÉTAÍN

There was a king of Ireland of the race of the goddess Dana, and his name was Eochaid Ollathair, which means "father of many." But he was also called the Dagda – the good god, for he it was who worked wonders with the weather and the crops for his people. And one day, the Dagda came to Boand, the goddess of the river Boyne, while her husband Elcmar was away. Elcmar was sent away on errands by the Dagda – nine months he was away, but it all seemed one day to him, on account of the Dagda's magic. And the Dagda slept with Boand there, in the elfmound north of the Boyne, and the son they had in secret was called Aengus. But Boand named him the Mac Óc, which means "the young son" – for she said: "Young is the son who is conceived at the break of day and is born even before the evening."

Now, the Dagda sent him to the elfmound of Midir at Brí Léith to be fostered. And when he was nine years old, the boy asked that his true father acknowledge him, and that lands be given him as befits the son of a high king. And so Midir brought the Mac Óc to the Dagda's place at Meath in the very center of Ireland, from which the land stretches equally, to south and north and east and west. And there before the assembly, the Dagda acknowledged his son, and by trickery won for him the elfmound to the north of the Boyne, which had been Elcmar's mansion.

That is where Midir came, at Samhain time a year later, when some youths were fighting during the day that should be a day of peace among the men of Ireland. Midir broke up the fight in Aengus's stead, for Elcmar, on his mound at Cleitech to the south, was watching. But Midir lost an eye in the peace-making. The compensation he demanded of Aengus for the loss of an eye was the sight of Étaín Echraide, the most beautiful maiden in Ireland, and her hand in marriage, and a chariot and a mantle besides. Aengus, with the help of the Dagda, arranged all that – and so Midir took Étaín as his wife.

Midir and Étaín slept together in the elfmound of the Boyne. The mantle and chariot were given to him in the morning, and Midir was pleased with his foster-son. He spent a full year there at the Boyne with Aengus. It was a year from that day when he returned to his own mound at Brí Léith, to his own land, and Étaín with him. On that day he left, Aengus the Mac Óc said to Midir, "Take care of Étaín – for there is waiting for you a woman of terrifying druidcraft: she has all the cunning of her people, and on top of that she has my protection against the powers of the clan of Dana." This was Fuamnach, Midir's wife, from the family of Beothach, son of Iardanél, learned in the powers of the gods, for she was trained by Bresal the Druid who raised her before she was betrothed to Midir.

And this Fuamnach made her husband welcome. "Come, Midir, and I will show you your house and lands so that Étaín may see them also." Midir travelled around his lands with Fuamnach and Étaín, and then he took Étaín back to the house. But Fuamnach had slipped before them into the sleeping-chamber, where she had these words ready for Étaín: "The place of a good woman you have taken." Then, as Étaín took her seat on the chair in the middle of the house, Fuamnach struck her with a wand of scarlet rowan-tree and the girl turned into a pool of water on the spot.

Fuamnach lived with her foster-father Bresal, then. And Midir left the house to the water that Étaín had become. From that time, Midir was without a wife.

But the heat of fire and the heat of air and the heat of the sodden earth turned the pool of water into a chrysalis. And that chrysalis became a fly. And sweeter than flutes and harps and horns was the voice of that fly and the humming of its wings. Its eyes were like jewels in the dark, and its radiance and fragrance could take hunger and thirst away from any man. And she shed from her wingtips a spray of droplets that could cure sickness in anyone she went with. It was Midir she went with, following him in his travels throughout his land. He knew it was his Étaín, and during the time she was with him in the shape of a fly, he was nourished and never took a woman. He used to fall asleep to the humming of her wings, and if someone who did not love him came near, she would awaken him.

Fuamnach came. She brought three of the gods with her to obtain her safety. They were Lugh of the Sword of Light, and Ogma the Wise, and the Dagda himself – children of Dana. And she brought as well powerful incantations from Bresal the Druid to separate Étaín from Midir. And so she called up a wind that blew Étaín from the elfmounds of Brí Léith, and that wind endured for seven years with no tree or hill or height in all of Ireland where Étaín could rest – just the rocks in the sea and ocean waves. She flew about all that time until she found Aengus on his mound at the Boyne River.

The Mac Óc folded her in his cloak, and he carried her to his house, to a sun-bower with bright windows for going in and out. Aengus slept every night by her side, comforting the little fly until the lustre of happiness returned to her again. That sun-bower was full of the fragrance of herbs, and Étaín grew stronger in the aroma of them.

Fuamnach heard of this – she heard of the affection that Aengus gave to Étaín – and she said to Midir: "Let your foster-son come here, and I will make peace between you. And I will try to find your Étaín." But then, when Aengus left to speak with Midir, Fuamnach stole into the Mound of the Boyne. There, she summoned up the same wind as before so that the fly was carried out of her sun-bower and lashed about the sky in misery and weakness. —

In a house in Ulster, people were drinking. Étaín settled there, on the rooftree of that house. She fell into the golden cup that was before the wife of King Étar, and Étar's wife swallowed the fly when she drank from the cup.

Afterward, she gave birth to a child, and the child was a girl and she was called Étaín. And they say it was a thousand and twelve years from the first begetting of Étaín until her last begetting by Étar.

She was brought up at Inber Cíchmaine, and fifty maidens, the daughters of chieftains, with her. And they attended Étaín always. One day, all the maidens were bathing in the estuary there. They saw a horseman coming towards them, entering the plain. A broad brown horse, curvetting and prancing, curly mane and curly tail. The green cloak that the gods wear, a red-embroidered tunic, a gold brooch reaching across to either shoulder. A silver shield rimmed with gold hanging over his back, a strap made of silver, a buckle of gold. And in his hand a five-pronged spear, pure gold from haft to socket. Bright yellow hair hung over his forehead, held back by a band of gold. He halted on the river bank, the horseman did, and he gazed at Étaín, and all the girls loved him. Then he uttered this poem, and when it was finished he was gone, nobody knew where:

> *So this is Étaín – here this day*
> *at the Mound of Wisdom west of Ailbe!*
> *Here among maidens is she*
> *on the boundary of Inber Cíchmaine.*
>
> *She it is who healed a king's eye*
> *from the well of Loch Dá Lig;*

she it is who was swallowed in a drink
from a cup by the wife of Étar.

Because of her a king shall chase
the birds off the plain of Tara.
Because of her he will drown two horses
in the waters of Loch Dá Airbrech.

Because of her there will be much warring
with Eochaid, King of Meath;
the mounds of the gods will be destroyed
and many thousands will battle.

She it is who will be sung of throughout the land.
She whom the king is seeking.
She we called the Fair-haired Lady –
now, our Étaín.

When Aengus went to speak with Midir, he did not find
Fuamnach there. The Mac Óc returns to his house, and the
crystal sun-bower empty. Then he follows Fuamnach's trail
to the house of Bresal the Druid, and he takes her head there
and brings it home with him.

Eochaid Airem was the High King of all Ireland, and the
five provinces were subject to him. And the year he became
king, he held the crowning ritual at Tara, the dearest of his
strongholds, where the taxes and tributes were to be
reckoned. However, the chieftains of the land had the same
reply for Eochaid: "Unless you yourself have a queen, we
will not take our wives to Tara." So Eochaid sent envoys to
each of the five provinces of Ireland to find the fairest
maiden in the land. And it is said they came to Inber
Cíchmaine and found Étaín there. And Eochaid married her
– she who was his match in beauty and form and ancestry.

There is a poem that tells of how he first saw the goddess
in her human form, washing her hair in the sun by a well
near the elfmound of Brí Léith:

A woman
with a comb of silver   adorned
with gold   washing
at a silver basin.
Red the jewels
in that basin rim,
and four birds sat on it.

A hooded cloak she wore   stiff with green silk
beneath red embroidery of gold,
clasps of gold and silver
over her breasts   and on her shoulders –
bright gold against green silk flashing in the sun.

Her hair parted
in two golden-yellow tresses,
and each tress braided
in four strands,
at the end of each a little ball of gold.

And there she was
loosening her hair to wash it,
arms white as snow   cheeks red
as the foxglove   eyes
blue as the hyacinths –
it seemed to Eochaid that she
was from the elfmounds.

And it was said of her: as beautiful
are all women   until compared
with Étaín.

"What are you named?" said Eochaid, "and who is your
father?"

"Étaín is my name, and a king is my father. And I have
waited here with a child's love for the high tales of your
splendor – and now it is you I have found!"

"You shall have welcome," said Eochaid. "And for you,
every other woman shall be nothing to me, and I will live
with you only."

And Eochaid paid the bride-price and made Étaín his wife
and queen.

Now Eochaid had a brother, and his name was Ailill. And
Ailill fell in love with the queen at the Assembly of Tara.
And Étaín ministered to him in his lovesickness until he
confessed his love for her. And then they arranged to meet
on the hill above the court. But at the hour of the tryst Ailill
was still sleeping. The man Étaín saw there was Ailill in
form, and the words Ailill would have wished to say, those
were the words the stranger spoke. But when Étaín came
back to the house, there was Ailill, awake and sorrowful.

"Why are you sad?" she asked.

"That I made a tryst with you and did not keep it."

"One day follows another," she said.

Three days Étaín went to the hill, and Ailill was not there.
Instead, the same man who had the form of Ailill.

"Who are you that comes to meet me? The man I am
intended to meet here, it is not for sin nor for hurt –
only to heal the sickness of one who has the makings to be
a king of Ireland."

"It were more proper you come instead to me," said the stranger, "for I am your husband."

"What is your name?" said she.

"I am Midir, King of the Elfmounds of Brí Léith."

"And what was it that parted us?"

"The druidry of Fuamnach and the spells of Bresal Etarlám – that is what parted us."

And then Midir called her *Bé Find* there, which means the Fair Woman – and he sang to her of the joys of the world of the gods, and asked if she would go with him.

"I will go with you," said Étaín, "if you obtain me from my husband. If you obtain me not, I will not go."

Then she went back to her house.

"Good it is that we meet here," says Ailill, "for now I am healed and you are not dishonored."

"It is well, this outcome," said Étaín.

After that, Eochaid was glad to find his brother healed, and he thanked Étaín for ministering to him.

It was another time – on a beautiful summer morning – that King Eochaid arose and climbed the heights of Tara to look out over the plain of Breg rich with color and blossom of every hue. And there was a stranger on the height beside him – a young warrior. A purple tunic about him, and golden-yellow hair to his shoulders, and his eyes were perfectly grey. He held a five-pronged spear in one hand, a white-bossed shield in the other, with gems of gold on it. Eochaid was silent, for he did not know of the warrior being in Tara the night before, and the doors of the court were not yet opened at this hour. But since he came under the protection of the king in any case, Eochaid welcomed him:

"Welcome, here – though we know not who you are."

"I know you, however," said the stranger.

"What is your name?" said Eochaid.

"Midir of Brí Léith – not a famous name. But I play chess."

"I am good at chess myself," said Eochaid.

"Let us put it to the test," said the visitor.

"The queen is asleep," said Eochaid, "and the chess-board which is hers is in the house with her."

"I have a chess-board," said the stranger. "It will do."

True enough that was – for the chess-board was silver with pieces made of gold, and in each corner of the board was set a precious stone that shone with light, and a bag of plaited bronze for the pieces.

Midir arranges the pieces on the board. "You begin," he says.

"I will not play except for a stake," Eochaid says.

"What stake?" says Midir.

"It is all one to me."

"You shall have from me," said Midir, "if you win my stake, fifty horses out of Faërie – dark grey, with dappled heads, blood-red ears pricked high, chests broad, nostrils flaring, feet thin, strong, keen, spirited, and broken with fifty enamelled bridles that go with them."

Then they play. Midir's stake is lost. He leaves, taking his chess-board with him.

When Eochaid awoke next morning, he went up to the heights of Tara at sunrise, and his opponent coming towards him. And there! Fifty dark-grey horses with enamelled bridles.

"What is promised is fulfilled," said Midir. "Shall we play?"

"Gladly," said Eochaid, "but for a stake."

"You shall have from me," said Midir, "fifty boars out of Faërie – curly-mottled, grey-bellied, blue-backed, and a vat of blackthorn to hold them in. Moreover – fifty swords with hilts of gold. And fifty red-eared cows with red-eared calves, all white, and on each a bronze spancel."

Each fifty was won on its own day by Eochaid.

Then Eochaid's foster-father asked the king where he had got all this wealth.

"I would take care," said his foster-father. "It is a man of magical powers you are up against. Wager hard tasks for him."

That was how the famous tasks were laid on Midir: Meath cleared of stones, rushes put on Tara, the causeway over Móin Lámraige, the planting of the trees of Bréifne.

"You lay too much upon me," Midir said.

"Not at all," said Eochaid.

"Then grant me this request," said Midir. "Let no one under the king's protection be outdoors tomorrow."

"It is granted," said Eochaid.

But Eochaid commanded his steward to go out and see how the causeway was being made over the bog, and it seemed to the steward that all the men in the world had come there. From their clothes they made a mound, and Midir sat on it. Into the base of the causeway they put trees from the forest, trunks and roots and all. Then earth and gravel and stones on the bog. You would have thought every man in the world was there, making that tumult – and Midir standing there and urging them on. The men of Ireland used to yoke their oxen across the forehead; now the People of the Mounds were putting the yoke across their shoulders. And from that night, Eochaid did the same – that is why he is called Eochaid Airem, which means Eochaid the Plowman, for he was the first in Ireland to yoke the oxen in that fashion.

The steward comes to Eochaid and describes what he has seen. He says there is not in the chariot-pole of the world a greater power than what he saw. Then, while they are speaking, Midir is coming towards them, and an ugly look on him.

"Cruel and pointless it is of you to lay such toil and suffering upon me. And would I not have undertaken more to please you – but now I am of an angry mind."

"I will not repay anger with anger," said Eochaid. "The thing that is in your mind to choose, let that thing appease you."

"Accepted," said Midir. "Let us play chess now."

"To what stake?" asked Eochaid.

"The stake that either of us shall wish."

That day, Eochaid's stake was taken.

"What will you have from me?" Eochaid said.

"Two arms about Étaín, and a kiss from her," said Midir.

King Eochaid was silent, then. But finally, he said:

"Come a month from today, and what you ask will be given you."

After a month had passed, Eochaid called together the best of the war-bands of Ireland. They assembled, each ringing another around Tara, and the king and queen in the middle of the house, and the court-doors locked: it was a man of great power who was coming. That night, Étaín was pouring the drink for the chieftains. And while they were talking, they saw Midir coming towards them. He was beautiful always – but more beautiful than ever was Midir that night. The hosts fell silent. Then the king gave him welcome.

"It is this I have come for," said Midir. "This, and what was promised me – let it now be given. It is a debt until a promise is due, and what I promised you was given."

"I have not had second thoughts about it," Eochaid said.

"It was promised by Étaín that she would come away from you," said Midir.

At that, Étaín blushes.

"Let there be no blush upon you, Étaín. No wrongful marriage-feast is it for you – for I was a year seeking you with the most beautiful treasures that are in Ireland, nor do I take you without the permission of Eochaid. It is no gratuity to me if now I obtain you."

Then Étaín replied: "I have said that I will not come to you unless Eochaid gives me up. To my mind, you may take me with you if Eochaid gives me up."

"Never will I give you up," said Eochaid, "but I have promised to let him place his two arms around you, here as you are standing in the middle of the house."

"That shall be done," said Midir.

Then he took his weapons in his left hand, and he put his right arm around Étaín, and he carried her up through the skylight of the house. The chieftains rose from their seats about the king. And they saw two swans ascending over the plains of Tara, toward the Mound of the Gods at Femun, which we call Síd Ban Find, the elfmound of the fair-haired women.

BOUNDARY

A biological analogy

Where do we come from? Where do we go when we die? The mythtellers address these questions, and in a way that preserves respect for an overall ecology of life. The respect is enforced by the element of boundary. Always the mythtellers speak of a boundary between the Otherworld where life has its source and this world where life has its manifestation. And they speak of how this boundary may, and may not, be crossed.

In nomadic societies a boundary marks a sacred site where the being of power dwells, where its power is strong and its children are protected. These sacred locales and sanctuaries are everywhere in Aboriginal Australia. In societies where village life is more rooted, there is a tendency to situate the boundary between nature and culture. In either case, this separation of the mysterious and the familiar has a practical advantage. It segregates the world of mystery from the world human beings have some control over. Without that boundary, the world of mystery does not stand apart from the world of human making; each world contaminates the other. On this side of the boundary, a space needs to be held open for ordinary human ingenuity and predictability: it cannot become dense with superstition. On the other side of the boundary there must be freedom for intelligent nature to behave in all its wild unpredictability: that realm can never become uniform with the human capacity to remake the environment, as on the maps of explorers and colonizers. The societies that have not survived are the ones that have not respected boundary or that have had their sense of boundary obliterated.

• Boundary is vital to the whole structure of myth, where it seems to function, among other things, as a principle of balanced exchange. To understand this balancing function more fully, it is useful to think about the phenomenon of boundary in biological nature. The mythtellers understood that the natural world is full of discrete beings, each entity differentiated from the rest of the world. They knew, probably better than we do, that a living thing acquires its energy by means of exchanges across a boundary, so that the living thing remains distinct from its environment, yet interacts continuously with it. The lining surrounds the cell; bark surrounds the tree; skin surrounds the animal. These membranes act in a selectively permeable way, allowing nourishment in, keeping poisons out, expelling wastes or, in the case of the nursing mother, expressing food. Wherever there is an exchange, there is the crossing of a boundary. This is as true of the chemotactic exchanges, of, say, a snail with its surroundings as it is of the exchange of gifts marking the passage of a marriage partner from one clan to another. Boundaries are the magic points where worlds impinge.

If one thinks of the human body as a bounded entity, one has an idea of what boundary permits and does not permit. Exchange with the world is made at the mouth, nose, ears, eyes, anus, sexual organs, and the skin itself. These exchange points are accentuated in Haida carving, with animals in the act of eating other animals, animals caught in the eyes of others, animals joined to the tongue of others or emerging from the anus. Grotesque as it may seem to someone used to a static kind of visual expression, the art makes graphic a basic insight about nature. Creatures consume each other and nourish each other. Life is bounded; life is in continuous exchange with other life.

Boundaries can also be crossed invisibly. They can be crossed by words, by thoughts, and by spirits. Oral cultures are sensitive about these forms of exchange. The sensitivity is summed up in a sense of respect for the bounded otherness of someone or something, which we call courtesy. Just as an inappropriate exchange at one of the orifices of the body causes injury or death, the inappropriate use of words can cause insult. Words can kill. They can cause a change in the spiritual balance of life. This verbal power makes mythtelling a sacred art, in which the listener is virtually transported by language into the invisible world. Exchange across a boundary is effected in myth because words can convey the thoughts of the spirits.

Much of this sense of a shamanistic journey into the realm of mystery remained for a long time in Celtic mythtelling. The language of Irish formal narrative shimmers with the elegant perfection of the Otherworld. The earliest Celtic myths were probably about human raids on the world of the gods to steal a sacred object or reclaim a mortal princess. The mythteller, raised in the Druid schools, was then a spiritual guide and companion on a *real* trip of the imagination into the realm of the sacred. The old Welsh word for story (*cyfarwyddyd*) means something like "guidance," "knowledge" or "direction." The stem of that word (*arwydd*) also meant "omen," "miracle," "manifestation." It derives from a root that means "to see," suggesting that the storyteller was also a seer. The etymology proposes that myths were not merely flights of the imagination; they were flights of the spirit, with the narrative acting as the conduit of supernatural energies summoned and made present by story, and the mythteller acting as the conductor of the souls of the listeners to the Otherworld and back again. Hence it is vital for the mythteller as the guide across boundaries to know where particular worlds begin and end. If the listener doesn't get back, there is a spiritual imbalance. The storyteller always takes care to mark the boundary in myth.

Boundaries are marked differently in different mythtelling traditions, but they are always explicit. To a hunting society, they are physically explicit. Beyond the stillness of village life is the edge of the forest. You must be careful out there. Anything can happen beyond that boundary. Just as provoking to a fishing people is the surface of the sea. You put your hook through that surface; who knows what you'll find? The world beneath the sea teems with life in all its forms. Bringhurst speaks of the Haida sense of boundary, *xhaaidhla*, which he translates as "membrane": it stretches "skin-tight and resonant over everything in the world of Haida myth." The metaphor of the resonating drum-skin is deliberate. The shaman beats on a drum to summon the animal powers. The effect of a membrane is also felt in Haida box carving where the faces of the gods seem to push against the two-dimensional surface of the box. Still more creatures of power well up and press out at the viewer. They might almost burst through. Presumably the mythcreatures exert that same almost-bursting-through effect on the membrane of language during the telling of myth.

The sundering of a membrane boundary is pronounced in the portion of the Haida Raven epic containing the account of the creation of a world for the gods. Here the Raven bumps up against the sky, then penetrates it to find himself in the world of the Sky People:

> *And then he flew right up against it.*
> *He pushed his mind through and pulled his body after.*

To the Sky Beings, the top of the sky ebbs and flows like an ocean. Their boundary is conceived in the image of the sea surface which the Raven descends through later in the story.

In this way a central boundary makes other boundaries possible in myth, often creating a complicated hierarchy of realms.

These supernatural Otherworlds are ascribed to parts of the created world that humans cannot see or reach easily. The realms are in the sky, across the sea or under it, under a river, at a mountain top, or beneath the earth. At the Peterborough Petroglyphs, the realm of the gods is under a crystalline limestone rock, reachable by spirits through natural fissures in the limestone made by water which can be heard gurgling underground. Here the Snake is a prominent inscription. He is the one who slips through holes easily, linking two realms. In Celtic myth, these holes have become bigger: they are located in the mounds, called tumuli, that rise at the tops of so many hills in the British Isles, the hills themselves thought to be hollow. The story of Étaín takes place at several of these elfmounds sacred to the gods who dwell underneath them, and it takes place at Tara, their spiritual center. Focal points of a matriarchal mythology, the hills are sometimes vulviform or mamilliform. Glastonbury Tor, in southwest England, is both − it is called "the tit" by pilots from RAF Yeovil nearby, who take a bearing from it. From one of these mounds, the horse goddess Rhiannon rides out in the first story of the Welsh *Mabinogi*, the hero having been told that if he sits there, on the top of Gorsedd Arberth, he will get one of two things: "wounds and blows, or else his seeing a wonder." Later, displaced into superstition by Christianity, these mysterious hills contain, not the gods, but the fairy people: poor relatives of the gods, ruled by a King of Elfland. Yet going to his subterranean court is still a dangerous business in the fairy tales.

The mountain top, offering passage to the stars, is prominent in many myths that draw together the realms of earth and sky. The Greeks put their temples there. It was from one of these places of sacrifice that Psyche was carried to the court of the Snake God, Cupid. The Egyptian step pyramids, like their counterparts in America, are artificial mountains. After his death, the Pharaoh ascends a stairway to the world of the gods, to be judged by Osiris, called "the god at the top of the staircase." Where two worlds come together at a boundary, the point is sacred, often becoming in later ages the focal point of organized religion.

The conditions of hunter-gatherer life do not permit the luxury of specialized priest classes and formal religious worship. For such societies, the threshold to the realm of the spirit creatures is nearby, as close as the forest edge or the shoreline where the sea throws up strange things. If there is no physical marker, there may instead be a small ritual act that transports the seeker into Dreamtime. In one myth of the Samit people of Lapland, the hunter walks three times around a fir tree, then turns into a bear. He probably has to walk in one direction, not the other, to make the transformation. It is like the hundreds of silver prayer wheels in the mountain temples of Nepal: one spins the wheels, just as one walks around the circle of wheels, clockwise; otherwise all the prayers that have come before will be undone. In the English fairy tale, "Childe Roland," a sister unluckily circles a church "widdershins" and then is snatched away to Elfland. "Widdershins" means contrary to the sun's direction. The Celtic corn goddesses were careful not to grind the wheat that way: the circular millstone must grind in motion with the millstone of the Earth turning about the polar axis, grinding the cosmic wheat into stars. Similarly, the housepole that carries the shaman's spirit out the smoke-hole is related to the housepole that holds up the sky-tent. You have to be careful to rub the god in the housepole the right way if you want his cooperation. The flight of the shaman's spirit into the world of the animal powers is the model of passage into the Otherworld in myth. At its most simple, this journey is begun when the hunter prepares himself for the hunt by ingesting drugs that sharpen his awareness.

In its more complicated forms, the journey is made by the spirit of the shaman, while the shaman is in a trance, to the realm where the gods look after the ecology of death and rebirth. In either case, the way to Dreamtime lies through the seeker's own unconscious or semiconscious state. This mythic principle is remembered in Greek and Roman literature and in later medieval dream vision poems, where the speaker meets the god or goddess in dream. It is remembered as well in the nineteenth-century story of Alice, who descends down a rabbit hole to a wonderland of imperious talking animals in the one story (originally titled *Alice's Adventures Under Ground*) and passes through a membraneous mirror in the other.

Once in the Otherworld, the seeker may find that everything is, in Alice's words, "contrariwise." It is a place where things are done backwards. This is a dramatic way for the mythteller to mark the Otherness of the spirit world. In the Nishga myth of the woman who marries a bear, the captive girl notices that the Bear People gather water-soaked sticks from the bottom of the river for the Bear chief's fire. When she contributed dry sticks from the forest, the sticks hissed and the fire went out. "Remember," says Mouse Woman, the goddess who helps adventurers cross the boundary, "never use dry wood: only green wood or water-soaked logs from the bottom of rivers. That is the best wood for fires." In a Haida myth, a young man presents his new wife, one of the supernaturals, at the door of his father's house. "Lady, come in!" "She declines to come in," the husband says. "She is given to doing things backwards." A similar contrariness – or at least a departure from normal time – distinguishes Otherworld behavior in the *Mabinogi*. In "Branwen," the tale that makes up the second branch of this myth, a being gives birth at the same time she conceives; at the end of a month and a fortnight the baby has grown into a warrior, fully armed. In the first tale of the *Mabinogi*, a human hero is instructed about how to deal with an adversary he will encounter in the lower world: "And only one blow you must give him; he will not survive it. And if he asks for another, do not give it, even if he pleads with you." Pwyll does what he is told. Moreover the whole year he is down there he never sleeps with the wife of the Otherworld king, even though he has been given that king's body, and the wife is the most beautiful lady he has seen. The mythtellers say you must never take anything of the Otherworld's. You don't accept the food of the gods, as Persephone did in the realm of the dead, or help yourself to otherworldly treasures. The archaeologist, poking about in the ruins of an ancient temple, has to brush away with the cobwebs a lingering inhibition about taking something that belongs to the gods.

There are beings of the boundary – like the Mouse Woman of Haida and other Northwest Coast mythtelling, who gives advice to travellers between worlds and keeps the energies of the worlds reconciled. The Mouse Woman is a boundary marker too. Her counterpart in Irish myth is Gráinne, the reconciler of the gods. In *The King of Ireland's Son*, Padraic Colum's reconstruction of myth and folktale, this goddess likes to take the form of an old woman in a run-down cottage outside of town, who makes a living by telling people their dreams and solving problems people bring her way. Her most secretive messenger is the corncrake, a bird that hides in the middle of a wheat field and gives its strange croaking call – you can never tell where the bird is or what direction the sound is coming from. Its role to Gráinne is like that of the crane to Hermes, another being who knows the laws of boundaries. In the Welsh stories, birds are sacred to the goddess Rhiannon, and sing the music of the Otherworld. Branwen, in her story, trains a starling to talk and carry a message from the Otherworld to her kinspeople in this world. In the Haida mythworld, the messengers are the loon and the pied-billed grebe, birds of good omen. Birds disappear mysteriously during their migration; they reappear with the renewal of fertility; some are at home in the worlds of ocean, land and sky; they fly across boundaries like the shaman. In much of Aboriginal Australia birds are the messengers of the unconscious part of creation, signs of shifting energies in the Dreaming.

Transformation

These few examples suggest the care taken by mythtellers to keep the ordinary and the supernatural worlds distinct from one another. The care is necessary: Otherworld personalities resemble human beings in their thinking and behavior, and they burst spontaneously into the normal world, just as human individuals are always stumbling into the Otherworld. Partly to differentiate these encroaching worlds further, the mythtellers emphasize a change that happens to whoever crosses the boundary between two realms. This change is an important and almost universal event in mythtelling. Since the boundary separates one state of being from another, any passage across a boundary involves a temporary sacrifice of an essential part of the self in the interests of communication. That change is, at the very least, a physical transformation; at the most, a death in one world and rebirth in the other.

These moments of transformation hold an awe for the mythtellers. They may, to modern ears, seem casually stated or understated in a story, yet they are events of profound mystery. That is because transformation implies, not an existence in one world and then in another; rather it implies existence in both realms simultaneously. The shaman may beat on a drum in order to summon animal helpers, and then the body of the shape-shifter may go into a lifeless trance. The body is still here in the physical world of time and space, but the mind of the traveller has shifted fully into its spiritual state and is moving in the world of the gods, an animal spirit among animal spirits. The Raven makes that shift in the Haida creation myth quoted earlier. Evidently picked out by the One in the Sea to be a shaman, the bird-being has to enter the realm of the Sky People in order to steal their knowledge. There he has to be reborn as a sky child. But he is still the Raven. For the mythtellers, life happens at the boundary between two worlds where energies are transformed. An ideal of Haida art is to capture the Raven *in transition* between his Raven and Human forms, in that "moment that can not be seen" – "that instant of movement between two states of being." Similarly, in the Irish myth, "The Wooing of Étaín," the goddess who does not have a world to make for herself is transformed into a fly, a creature who emblemizes her restlessness of spirit. Swallowed by a mortal, she is reborn as a human child, to become the wife of King Eochaid of Ireland. There she enjoys the pleasures of mortality – but she gives back the gifts of fertility before she is recalled to the world of the gods. These examples, and others like them in fairy tale as well as myth, teach that death is not a final end. Where the prior and enduring form of existence of beings is in the spirit world, beings do not die; they take off their body-masks. This hunter-gatherer metaphysics elaborates the event of transformation found in the earliest Stone-age tales, where the shaman, assuming the form of a totemic animal, travels to the spirit world to gain a knowledge of the gods or to rescue a human spirit who has been taken from a body before its time.

The myths speak of such journeys as dangerous adventures. One of the dangers is to be trapped in the realm which the traveller does not belong to. A goddess can dwell on the earth with a human mortal, as Étaín does, but eventually she must go back. The human princess who marries the son of the

Bear chief must return to her father's village. In the *Mabinogi*, Branwen is treated poorly in the Otherworld. Over and over again, the myths tell of the discomfort of beings who are not in their primary world. There is always an urgency or tension felt here. The time spent out of their proper element must be brief; otherwise, beings fall subject to the laws of their adopted world. Often there is no going back, as Adam and Eve, having learned the secret pleasures of mortality from a snake, cannot go back to Paradise. In the later agricultural myths there are dying and reviving gods like Persephone and Adonis, but their transformations, if automatic, are not easy, involving a shattering death like the vegetable forms they represent, then a gloomy suspended animation under the earth like a waiting seed. In some versions of the Adonis myth, the effigy of the god is torn to pieces and scattered on the land or thrown into the sea at the end of harvest. The virgin or the image of the virgin representing the spirit of the dying and reviving corn is similarly sacrificed, as can be seen in the myths collected by Sir James Frazer. According to Christian teaching, these customs are anachronisms – the sacrifice has already been made, but the sacrificial role in this case falls on the Man-God whose body and blood are ritually divided up and consumed by the community and whose transformation at the threshold of eternity involves a spectacular agony and death. Even Christian teaching remembers the difficulty of a God out of his proper element.

Frames

What is fascinating about boundary in mythtelling is not simply the beautiful narratives of adventure it permits, but the way it functions to keep certain kinds of knowledge separate from each other. Thus, the forest-edge, the sea-surface, the

sky, the holes and caves in the earth, the transformation rituals, the boundary goddesses – these are all epistemological
frames, markers of categories of knowledge, saying in effect:
"Beyond this point is a zone where ordinary human thinking
cannot go. You must make the shift to another kind of thinking. You must think like an animal now. Enter at your peril."

The idea of shifting to a wholly different overall mentality
in certain situations is difficult for the modern person to grasp.
We are not capable, or at least we do not think we are capable, of switching deliberately to an unconscious kind of deci-
sion-making – thinking, say, like a bear when we are in bear
country. We forget that in fact most of our thinking at any
time is happening at unconscious levels. And because that
thinking is going on at unconscious levels, it is inaccessible to
investigation while we are engaged in it. There is evidently a
boundary at any moment between what it is functionally useful to know and what it is not useful to know. We do not
bother to question all the cognitive and sensory processes at
work when we have an experience. Indeed, it puts the experience at risk to question the mechanical processes that make it
possible. Swimmers, while they are swimming, do not stop to
ask what enables them to swim – otherwise they would sink.
Much of our ordinary life is made up of tiny unaware acts of
faith in what we are doing, and a functional separation of
categories of awareness and knowing seems essential to un-
confused behavior. A similar efficiency is served by the function of boundary in myth. The knowledge and processes appropriate to one realm of human activity in nature are then
uncontaminated by the knowledge and processes appropriate
to the other. Ingenuity is free from the density of superstition.
Mystery is safeguarded from intrusions of conscious purpose.

In this respect, it is important to hear what the mythtellers
say about communicating across a boundary. Generally, there
is an injunction against it. That is why a shaman is often re-

garded with suspicion and dread by his people. He is a necessary transgressor of a world of structured existence. If the supernatural is to be spoken about, that speaking is done in the language of the supernatural; the shaman, possessed by a spirit, speaks in the frenzy of that power. One does not tell of the help given by a supernatural power, or that help is lost. A Buryat story from the Lake Baikal region of Siberia puts this injunction into focus. A hunter helps the Snake Ancestor out of a jam; in return the Snake People offer the hunter this choice: "If you want, we will give you gold and precious stones, as much as you can carry. Or, if you want, we will teach you seventy languages so that you will be able to understand the conversations of the birds, the animals, and the fish. Choose!" Being a hunter, the man chooses the seventy languages. He is not interested in surplus value. "Better to choose the gold and precious stones," the Snake God warns. "The person who knows seventy languages does not find it easy to live." This, as it turns out, is an understatement – for the first voices the hunter hears when he gets to his village are the neighbor's dogs complaining about how they are treated by a stingy owner. Having done some good here, the hunter returns home to listen to his own dogs crying about how his wife beats them while he is away. It then becomes very hard for the Buryat hunter to keep the secret of his gift of languages, harder still when he hears his bull boast: "There goes our kind master who can't get along with one stupid wife. I have many wives, and they all obey *me*." Suspense mounts as the wife uses every trick she knows to find out the secret that cannot be spoken about. It ends happily for the hunter. After all, he has chosen what a hunter – not a farmer or a herdsman – would choose: knowledge of the speech of the animals. Yet it is a knowledge that cannot be mentioned.

Why not? Ostensibly, because it is sacred knowledge: the Snake People warn that the price of revealing it is instant death. But there is also a practical advantage to the hunter in keeping such knowledge privileged. He must hold his peace: he cannot talk, he must listen. The hunter is someone used to finding what he cannot see. There is a special power in tuning oneself to the singing of the forest. To know the seventy languages of the forest is certainly a useful gift.

Polyphony

But how does one listen to seventy languages simultaneously? And there are still other languages, though they do not issue from beaks or throats or the drumming of feet. There is the language of smells, like the dank smell of the north side of trees. There is the language of wind and weather and seasons of the year. There are all the languages of wilderness. The answer is that the hunter is open to something there are no words for – the music of pattern: relationships of relationship in states of change. Altogether, they make up a polyphony, with each voice, each being, singing its own song or story – each speaking its own poem at its own rate, picking its way through the poem of the whole which it helps to create. This polyphony is a coherent yet endless and unresolving music composed of simultaneous but distinct individual voices. A change – a hesitancy – in the overall pitch of the forest is likely to mean as much to the hunter as a particular theme played within it. "There's a predator out there!" And to hear this shifting music more keenly, the hunter cannot afford to be aware of it consciously. He carries the whole music of the forest in his soul. He cannot break it down for objective analysis or filter it through fixed frameworks of conscious purpose without losing the feel of it altogether. And usually, the less he has to say about what he feels, the better. The power to read nature is internalized deeply as a skill, and skill by and large is an unconscious activity – a body language that goes beyond words and cannot be too conscious of its own processes.

I know a little of what skill means for the artist – it is a playful inner power that seems to know its own mind, yet cannot speak of what it knows except by acting itself out fully. But I can hardly dare to think what such skill consists in for the hunter. Uncle Bul, the Aborigine elder, told Robert Lawlor that he could tell where the animals are by dreaming them. He joins his dreams to theirs. Evidently, what Uncle Bul sees are not the physical forms of the animals, but their spiritual forms. He explained that when he is in a trance vision he sees them hanging on a "web of intersecting threads" together with scenes of the physical world, dreams and prophetic insights. Here, even the term "spiritual forms" is inadequate. Other elders who have been willing to speak about these things say that what they apprehend is a kind of music. They perceive the animal ancestors as fields of resonance or vibration. These gods are thought to speak their dreams of the plants or animals by naming the specific vibratory pattern of each. That is how they create life. Drawing vibratory energy out of themselves, they name that energy – the inner name is the potency of the form or creature. What the aborigine elders see, or rather hear, in their trances, then, are the acoustic signatures of each of the animals. I imagine this skill to be a developed prescience – like the prescience bird-watchers have: they get the feel of the terrain and the weather, then they have a premonition of what they are going to see or hear – and then there it is! But Uncle Bul says more than this, and it vulgarizes his dreaming to imagine it as merely a heightened prescience. Our prescience may, rather, be a tiny, inadvertent dreaming. For what Uncle Bul says he sees is the life of the landscape interwoven in a web of threads. His unconscious (if we can use that term) is continuous with nature's. In some way, he is so open to the various signs and songs of the world that he is aware of them in their simultaneity as pure abstract pattern. Aboriginal visual art shows this abstraction. A painting of the Dreaming of a kangaroo – that is, the energy field out of which an actual kangaroo emerges to the human eye – is like a dance of colored pattern. There may be nothing resembling what we know as a kangaroo in the painting at all. (The animals are said to have been put into the paintings later for the sake of the tourists.) Instead, there is in the patterns emerging out of fields of energy a quality of *vibration* – vibrations that represent the original Dream-songs of the animal-being on the day the world was made. Other hunter-gatherer people also seem to be able to apprehend the energy of their surroundings as music. The Bibayak, a tribe of the Pygmy People near Minvoul, in Gabon, chant what they call "dialogues with the spirits." These ceremonial chants are believed to have the power to engage the spirits of the jungle in a dialogue. The art of vocal projection is mastered in these ceremonies. In practice, the vocal projection is used as a means of echolocation in the dense jungle, where the hunter cannot see but can hear, for example, a precipice hidden on the other side of foliage. By listening to the subtle changes in echo and pitch as he turns his head from side to side while singing, the Bibayak hunter can gauge his position in the jungle. And then there are the *tabla* performers of India, in whom an ancient feeling for energy as music still survives. For these drummers, everything is felt to be composed of an order of vibration – of wave forms that take on the appearance of light, and are fragrant, and give the *illusion* of the surface texture that we experience with our senses. With practice, the drummer can learn to isolate the particular *rag*, or mode, of his surroundings and so be involved in the most direct communication with what is. Then the drummer is recreating a certain part of the universe. All *tabla* rhythms are held by different families of players, where they are passed down from father to son. There is, for example, a rhythm specific to the evening which is said to imitate the sound of wildlife at dusk on the Deccan plateau in the winter. Such rhythms make up the thousands of rags, each with its own purpose. One cannot begin to describe the polyphonic complexity of the *tabla*, or of any developed oral tradition. I have used external descriptive terms merely – energy, rhythm, memory, skill. Somehow the experience they describe comes together in the unconscious. It is easy to imagine that with the internalization of particular related sets of skills, particular more-or-less autonomous minds develop in the unconscious with them. With a loosening of the restraints of the self, one or more of these minds may start speaking and having visions. The shaman must have an unusual degree of discipline not to be carried away altogether by a dream-vision. This brings us back to the necessity of boundary.

However we are to regard these instances of extraordinary consciousness, it is clearly a function of myth to bracket off one kind of thinking for the sake of concentrating on the other. One type of thinking cannot be allowed to contaminate another type. There is a boundary here. The Buryat story suggests this epistemological segregation. Indeed, it suggests it is not easy to possess both discourses simultaneously. The story also suggests that, for the hunter at least, the prior discourse is the singing of the animals. In the beginning was, not the word, but the music. By music, I mean a non-verbal discourse that protects its integrity from human possession and control. Open to the most subtle gradations of difference in the natural world – in fact, formed on those shifting relationships – this discourse of pattern is the primal associative power that we share with the animals. The mythtellers say it was given to us by the animal helpers. In so ascribing itself to a source beyond men and women, myth, by a strategy of circularity, keeps its frames of knowing in order within an overall kinship with nature.

Change, and the boundary beyond which change cannot go

Myth structures itself so as to preserve its own levels of knowledge, yet it is an epistemology that is remarkably sensitive to patterns in states of change. The framing of types and qualities of knowledge means that nature is apprehended in her variety, in her distinctiveness, in her unpredictability, with energies crossing boundaries continually. Boundaries are permeable, and the Raven is always crossing them, causing exchanges, making things happen. In the first part of *Raven Travelling*, he passes through different worlds, through different kinds of consciousness, and in the whole epic, as in Haida mythtelling generally, the myths are arranged in suites for performance so as to allow the different worlds of forest, sea and sky to be mapped together. There are social boundaries just as there are natural boundaries. Haida civilization is divided between its Eagle and Raven halves, with exogamous marriage the crossing of a boundary into maturity. Human beings themselves are spoken of by the gods as "common surface people." The islands are called by the old people "The Islands at the Boundary of the World." Everywhere there is a sense of exchange across a boundary as being a source of energy and information. Boundary is the place where change gathers and releases itself.

Yet there is a point beyond which change cannot go without imperiling the whole epistemology. What must be kept intact is the basic double-phrasing that ensures a separation of conscious purpose from the unconscious apprehension of reality. All the finer modes of thinking and etiquette are based on it. For this reason, the mythtellers are especially sensitive to the theme of a human intrusion on the realm of the sacred:

knowing too much about the natural powers can imperil the whole process of fertility.

The myths warn particularly of the consequence of excessive curiosity about what is on the other side of the membrane. That is forbidden knowledge. Prometheus who stole fire from the gods; Adam and Eve who stole consciousness; Tiresias who stole the carnal knowledge of woman; Daedalus who stole the knowledge of flight – all show there is a price to be paid for making nature's thinking the property of man. The ideas and emotions of the earth should be inaccessible to human manipulation. Too much knowledge of them will alter the whole ecology. In each of the myths just cited, the seeker reaches for some bigger part and as a consequence loses the whole. It is a kind of gamble. The myths do not always say it is categorically wrong – they simply state that acts of human ingenuity have consequences. Prometheus gave man the secret of how to domesticate fire; Adam and Eve of how to domesticate knowledge. There is a Haida myth told to John Swanton by Skaai's colleague, Walter of the Qaayahllaanas, himself a master storyteller. A human being falls in love with a goddess whom he sees bathing naked in a pond, with her goose-skin off. Equipped by an old shaman with certain technical implements like a marlin spike and wedges, he follows the trail taken by his mate to the sky world. Mouse Woman helps him through the boundary. As is usual in myth, the human does not like it there in the world of the gods, and in this myth he says so. Soon the man is a nuisance to these courteous beings. They wonder about how to return him to the surface world. The Loon cannot carry him through the clouds. Neither can the messenger Grebe. Finally, a Raven does, depositing the man like a piece of carrion on a strand. There, in the last image of this oral poem, he is left to wake up, with a lone herring gull screaming in his ear.

Ironic? In negotiating a dialogue with nature, the mythteller safeguards a balanced and flexible exchange between two kinds of knowledge: one approached through ritual, skill and dream, the other through some form of consciously purposeful behavior. The continuing exchange between these divergent modes of knowing is crucial to a mythtelling society.

CHAPTER FOUR / DREAM

THE EARTH-SHAPERS

By Ella Young, told by Alice Kane

In Tir-na-Moe, Brigit was singing. Aengus, the Ever-Young,
Midir the Haughty, Ogma the Wise, the Dagda, and the
others of the Dé Dananns were listening. This is what she
sang:

> *Now comes the hour foretold, a god gift-bringing.*
> > *A wonder sight.*
> *Is it a star, newborn, and splendid up springing*
> > *Out of the night?*
> *Is it a wave from the Fountain of Youth, that is upflinging*
> > *A foam of delight?*
> *Is it a great immortal bird that is winging*
> > *Hither its flight?*
>
> *It is a wave, high-crested, melodious, triumphant,*
> > *Breaking in light.*
> *It is a star, rose-hearted and joyous,*
> > *Risen from night.*
> *It is a flame from the world of the gods, and love runs before it,*
> > *A quenchless delight.*
> *Let the wave break, let the star rise,*
> > *Let the flame leap.*
> *Ours, if our hearts are wise,*
> > *To take and keep.*

There was silence in Tir-na-Moe after Brigit finished
singing. And then Aengus spoke:
"Strange are the words of your song. And stranger still the
music. It was as if the voice of strange worlds was breathing
on my face while you sang. And yet, though the sound came

closer and closer and you were singing, it was not you who was singing. Who was singing?"

"The Earth was singing," said Brigit.

"The Earth? Is not the Earth in the abyss? Is not the Earth in the darkness of the void? Who has ever stayed to hear the Earth – to hear the sound of it, or to see the darkness of it?"

"I have stayed," said Brigit. "I have stayed to hear the Earth. I have stood and watched the writhing, monstrous life of the Earth, that devours itself. I have stayed and heard, and I have shuddered in the adder pit of hell."

Uroburus

"Why do you not forget it? Why do you not forget it?" said Ogma. "Forget it, and let it be a dream that has passed away. Let it be forgotten like a dream."

"Hear one thing more," said Brigit. "Hear one thing more. The Earth has cried all night. It has wailed all night long because it has dreamed of beauty."

"What beauty? What beauty?" said Ogma.

"The Earth has dreamed of the white stillness before dawn. The Earth has dreamed of the star that goes before the sunrise. The Earth – the Earth has dreamed of beauty."

"I wish you had never sung it," said Aengus. "I can't get it out of my mind! I can't think of anything else. I wish I had never heard it. I wish I had never known of it."

And Brigit said, "Aengus, Aengus, you clothe yourself in all the colors of the sun. You clothe yourself in all the colors of the sunlight; why should you not want to let some of that beauty come to Earth, which is crying for it?"

"No, no," said Aengus. "No. I would not go to Earth. I would not want to shudder there. I would not want to see it."

"But I would," said Midir, "I would." He stood up, he tossed his long mane of golden-red hair till he was surrounded with brightness like the daylight, and he said, "I would go. I would like to go and see what is there."

"Well," said Brigit, "because the Earth has dreamed of beauty, I am going to throw my mantle around it. Would you come with me?"

"Yes," he said, "I'll come with you. I'll follow you. I'll make a way for you. I'll make a space for your cloak."

"And I'll come too," said Ogma.

"And I'll come," said Nuada.

"I would come," said Aengus. "I would come if you were taking the Sword of Light with you."

"We will take the Sword of Light," they said. "We will take the Sword of Light, and the Cauldron of Plenty, and the Spear of Victory, and the Stone of Destiny. We'll take them all. We'll take them with us."

So Brigit set off, and Midir followed her. He carried the Sword of Light. And Nuada carried the Spear of Victory. And they brought with them the Cauldron of Plenty, and they brought with them the Stone of Destiny, and all the gods followed. And they dropped – they dropped down to Earth like a shower of stars down towards the darkness.

But when they came near the great, moving, horrible, self-devouring darkness that is the Earth, they all drew back, shuddering, away from it. All except Midir. Midir dropped right into it. Taking the Spear in his hand he went down and he trod out that darkness – that monstrous darkness – the way a man treads out grapes in a vineyard. He walked here and he walked there, and it moved and he made a path through it. And he held up the Spear, and he waved it this way and that. He waved it around, and it made a path through the dark.

And he turned and he said, "Cast your cloak, Brigit. Cast your cloak, for I have made a space for you. Throw your cloak into it. And let there be beauty, and music, and lavish-heartedness upon the Earth."

And Brigit took her cloak and she cast it – all silver-grey, with a little flame at the edge of it. And she cast it upon the Earth. And where it fell, a great soft mist spread over the Earth. Everywhere the darkness was driven away by that little sliver of flame that was at the edge of the cloak.

It moved farther and farther, and it spread over, and it would have gone on spreading like that for a long, long time. But Aengus – Aengus, the youngest of the Dé Dananns – couldn't wait. He leapt down into it, and began treading back and forth and playing like a child, and calling – calling, and crying back to his fellows. And they dropped down with him, and the drifting silver mist closed round them, and through it they saw each other like images in a dream.

And then the Dagda, the Great God, took the Cauldron of Plenty, and he put his hands into it, and he said, "O Cauldron of Plenty that gives to everyone what is meet for them, give me now a gift to give the Earth." And he drew both hands up out of the Cauldron, and in them he had a great, green fire which he threw down over the Earth. And everywhere it spread there was a greenness like grass – a greenness like grass over everything. And Aengus ran about joyously in that greenness, and he played in it the way a child plays in sand. He built it up into hillocks, he dug it out into little hollows, he dug it into long lanes.

And then Manannán – Manannán Mac Lir who is the ruler of the seas – he saw that now that the cloak had spread over almost everything, he could see this great life rising up on the other side of the cloak to look over and see what was happening. And Manannán reached for the Sword of Light. And he lifted it in his hand, and he raised it above his head, and he waved it. And the great, monstrous life drew back, back in one enormous wave, dark green and high, and it went back, back, back into the sea. And he waved it again, and this time it was a smaller wave, violet and blue, and a softer green and very gentle, and it drew back. He waved it a third time, and this time it was a small wave, white-crested and gentle. And the Three Great Waves of Ireland drew themselves into one, and broke on the shore.

They looked at it. They looked at it all as it lay there. And then Brigit said, "I am going to lay the Stone of Destiny in the Earth and let it stay there, that the Earth may have power." And she laid the Stone of Destiny on the top of the Earth. And it began to sink in, and when it sank down into the Earth, music sounded. And as the music sounded, up from the great waves there flowed water. And it filled all the little pools that Aengus had dug until every pool and every river and every lake was full of water.

And then, then Aengus looked at it and he said, "I want to stay here. I want to stay here – I want to build things, I want to make things. I would like in this pool to make a little pool like the Well of Connla. I would like to make little fishes, silver fishes and gold fishes, and I would like to make an orchard full of golden apples like the ones in Tir-nan-Oge."

But the other gods said to him, "No, no, no! Earth is new. Do not make in Earth the things that there are in other places. Not the things of Tir-na-Moe, not the things of Tir-nan-Oge, not the things of any other place at all. Let the Earth make her own things, till she is all full of beauty."

"Yes, yes," said the others. "Yes. And let us stay here. Let us stay here all of us, and fashion the things for Earth that she needs, until there is nothing in the whole Earth that is not beautiful. Yes," they said, "we'll all stay here."

"Except for me," said Brigit. "I have to go. There are things that I must see in Moy Mell, and Tir-na-Moe, and Tir-nan-Oge, and all the other worlds. They are mine to care for."

"Well," said Ogma, "if you must go, before you go, tie a knot of remembrance in your mantle so that you may always remember this place. And tell us – tell us before you go what we shall call it.

And Brigit looked at the Earth, and she saw it. As she lifted the mantle they saw that they were standing on a green island covered with grass. And the grass was studded with flowers, little flowers – yellow ones, red ones, purple ones, blue ones, all kinds of flowers. And it was altogether beautiful. She said, "You shall call it the Green Island. And its other name shall be the Island of Destiny. And its other name – its other name shall be Ireland."

And then Ogma tied a knot of remembrance in Brigit's mantle. And that is the story of the creation of the Earth.

Each has its own Dreaming

Though a piece of literary mythmaking, the story of Brigit –
cloaked like a shamaness, separating an actual world from
dream – tells us something about the universe of the mythtellers. It is, of course, a metaphysical universe. The animals and
plants and rivers and stones of nature are not physical entities;
they are spirit people shifting in and out of bodies. But even
this is still a mis-characterization – for the mythtellers often
seem to be speaking of creatures in relation to galvanic fields
of energy, audible at the moment when a creature appears.
Myth vibrates with this energy of life which is felt to be mental – a kind of brain-wave – and it is to that larger mental energy, or Dreaming, that I attach the term "metaphysical." No
disservice is done to the term to say that the language of the
mythteller is a language of images, not concepts. "The Earth-
Shapers" is told in images and in the exalted voice which even
for literary Celts like Ella Young belongs half to the writer
and half to the Otherworld.

Everything in myth says that this is so – mentality is prior;
nature is like a playground of minds. Each entity sends out its
energy-voice to mingle with all the others to create infinite
layers of songs which humans drift through never hearing
each detail consciously. Myths are cross-sections through the
interweavings of nature where various points intersect or are
amplified. Storytelling interprets these mental energies of nature. And the normal state of these mentalities is Dream. That
is why Brigit overhears the Earth dreaming of a new form of
itself. The dream unfolds as song in the goddess's unconscious, and she gives the dream words – words of a kind of
shamanistic chant. When pressed to explain the song, she says:
"The Earth has dreamed of the white stillness before dawn.

The Earth has dreamed of the star that goes before the sunrise. The Earth – The Earth has dreamed of beauty." Then the gods descend to the abyss, taking their talismans with them. They fear that monstrous writhing darkness with all the fear that a newly emergent agricultural people can muster. Those mental beings "rising up on the other side of the cloak to look over and see what was happening!" To an aboriginal people, this darkness rife with intelligence would not be so frightening – but the clanspeople of the goddess Dana are deities of recognizably human order, and so their first act is to divide this formless potential from the actual earth itself, studded with the forms of things we know. The flame burning at the edge of Brigit's cloak marks the boundary. It is a boundary between Dream and an externalization of that Dream, between potential and actual, between spirit world and this world, between darkness and light.

Dream, then the actualization of that dream – it is the sequence followed by any artist. But since intelligent life is already potent in a dream, the act of creating is a sort of remembering. This is true also of the opening creation scene of *Raven Travelling*, the Haida epic of the Raven. Here, according to Job Moody's narrative miniature, it is given to Loon Woman to overhear the voices of the gods wailing. She expresses that music as song:

> *I am not talking only from my own mind.*
> *The gods tell me they need places to live.*
> *That is why I have been speaking.*

Then the One in the Sea says that he will fashion a world for the homeless gods. But he does nothing. At least, he *seems* to do nothing. He lies there facing the wall with his back to the fire. Of course, he is not doing nothing – he is dreaming. Eventually, the Raven, having been initiated into the spirit world, is summoned in, to find his grandfather still dreaming. The dreams are potent in a talismanic box which the old man gives him. If the box is like the Haida boxes I have seen, it has the faces of the gods carved on the outside of it, with gods inside the eyes of other gods, faces inside other eyes. Five boxes, like a set of Chinese boxes – consciousness within consciousness within consciousness, a symbol of memory. From memory the world of the Haida was made.

Australian aboriginal myth shows the full complexity of this process of translating dream into physical form. The supernatural ancestors wandered nomadically across a formless landscape in the days when the world was made. Dreaming their quests before setting out, like hunter-gatherers, they made from their dreams the animals and plants and springs and rocks and mountains. Then, exhausted, the ancestors disappeared into the earth and the sky, where they continue to dream. Their nourishing dream energy is felt around the places where the ancestors fought and made love and tricked each other during the days of creation. It is also felt as a vibrational residue in every member of every species that exists. This spiritual potency of a creature is its *totem-pattern*. The term refers to the energy – at once idea and seed and song – which the ancestors left behind.

We lack the intellectual qualifications to approach a metaphysics in which, for example, the particular plant is felt to be the dreaming of the seed, and that seed itself is the dream-idea left by the plant's ancestor. We can try to focus this metaphysics in tangible ecological circumstance. Myself – I think of the exhausted Pacific or Coho salmon, heaving themselves upriver at the ends of their lives to spawn. Their decaying bodies will provide the nutrient which the hatchlings will eat when they emerge from their eggs. The whole river is made rich – it is made sacred – by the wealth given by the ancestor, who is not dead but is still alive in the place and in her children. Alive as music, as seed, and as mental energy. The equation between these gifts of the gods is remembered as late as "The Wooing of Étaín" when in Ella Young's version of the myth the three crowns are put on the land – "the crown of plenty, the crown of victory, and the crown of song," the departing goddess saying: "Tonight you have heard the music of Faïrie, and echoes of it will be in the harp-strings of Ireland forever." The equation is embedded in the language of the Haida, with *sghaana*, the word for "gods," sharing its root with the word *sghaalang*, one of the words for song.

Dreaming: conscious and unconscious

Dreaming suggests a state of the unconscious, but there is difficulty in reducing Aboriginal dreaming to what Freud termed "primary process." That difficulty comes from the way we regard the unconscious. In Western thinking and habit, we feel the unconscious to be active mostly during sleep, when it throws up dreams out of the repository of daily experience. For mythtelling societies, however, the unconscious is continuously awake and aware, and not merely in the individual but in nature as well. It might best be thought of as a dimension that transects the physical realm at every point and that, whether we are aware of it or not, is present in any object and event. In contrast, what we call "consciousness" is for the mythtellers merely a tiny moving arc – a sort of pencil beam – among the myriad dreaming processes that make up reality. The existence of beings in their physical forms can be caught in that arc of consciousness: they flash in and out of it like animals caught in a headlight beam at night, just as, in the larger unconscious Dreaming of the world, the animals flash in and out of existence. But their enduring mode of being is in the spirit, which is to say the state of dreaming.

The state of dreaming is similar to the state of pattern, if by pattern we mean what was described in the first chapter of this book – something invisible yet making its presence felt in visible forms, something that behaves as if it had properties of mentality, something that occupies no time and space. These are all aspects of information, technically defined as organization or relationship. We do not really see organization except in the particulars that are organized. We do not see a relationship except in the behaviors of two things or beings brought into one. What we see, scientifically speaking, are matter-and-energy processes which are the bearers of pattern, just as the notches on a key convey the differences that make up information. The differences have a potential to make a pattern. When they meet matching differences on the tumblers of a lock, a pattern is formed. Similarly, the patterns that are remembered in the arrangement of amino acids in the life-molecule DNA are themselves invisible and potential – they are the enduring Dreams; the particular form that is printed out in time is a visible child of that Dreaming. Matter-and-energy processes therefore invite a different level of explanation from that of informational processes, and it is an unending headache for a Western thinker to reduce the latter to the former.

The metaphysicians of the Stone Age did not make that mistake. From their first initiation rites on, everything in their training was intended to awaken experience of the prior reality of pattern. An anthropologist provides evidence of how complete this experience was. Showing an Aborigine tribesman a row of nine matches, all evenly spaced, the anthropologist took one match away from either end. The Aborigine saw no difference. The end matches were removed again – still no difference. And again – no difference. Then the row of nine matches was restored, and the anthropologist took one match away from the right-hand side. The Aborigine exclaimed: "Everything is different, the balance is gone."

Dreams are one portal to the realm of pattern; there are others, involving everything from the correct use of language in the presence of spirits to drug-induced trance. But dreams are probably the easiest way that we in the modern world can appreciate the shaman's ability to be fully awake and aware within a subconscious state of mind. Louis Pennishish, storyteller of the Omuskigo or West Main Cree people, spoke to me about a point during deep sleep that arrives about four in the morning – it sounds therefore like what we know as a phase of REM sleep – when the dreamer's mind, entirely lucid, detaches itself from the body and goes for a look-around. The body, immobile, is as if left behind. That is only a small instance of what was possible to the shaman.

It seems that even if we suspend them in inverted commas, the terms "conscious" and "unconscious" lose their usefulness in approaching a shamanistic metaphysics. For this is a way of knowing in which even ordinary practical consciousness is charged with an unconscious resonance that vibrates sympathetically with the wave-lengths of unseen realities. It is a knowing in which the hunter drops lucidly and purposefully aware into unconscious states of mind. Perhaps it is better to discard the terms altogether, and wonder instead at a universe that is everywhere and at all times mental. Such a universe enjoys through each of its beings a myriad of constantly changing modes of awareness – in each, a shifting of mental energy, across a boundary, from Dream to a physical objectification of that dreaming, then back again to Dream. The seed has a mind; the mind is full of ideas about becoming a tree; the tree flourishes as the dream of the seed, and then takes up that Dreaming itself. The mental pattern in the seed fluctuates into tangible existent form, then becomes seed-energy again. A fluctuation of mental power therefore defines life itself, which moves from the unborn, to the living, to the dead – with the dead active as another kind of potency no less tangible and alive than the unborn or the actually living. These are all mental states – aspects of the shifting of thought to and fro between inward Dream and outward objectification. The initiation rites and other intellectual training of hunter-gatherer peoples was directed towards the private mapping of these shifting states of mind in the various beings of nature. The mapping, as I suggested earlier by the use of the term *polyphony*, was largely acoustic. For the Native Australians, the momentary formation of energy and thought in a particular physical being has its virtual counterpart in the way vibrations of the air, issuing for example from the instrument called a *didjereedoo*, are stabilized, held for a moment as song, to echo back again to the mothering power-field of latent patterns, to become at another time another song.

Knowing: things and states

In trying to understand how early humanity thought, we find ourselves applying modern concepts which we then have to discard after they have taken us a little way into the mythtellers' world. Such was the fate of the dualism "conscious and unconscious." A similar fate now awaits the terms I make recourse to in the section title above, my hope being that the concepts "things" and "states" may at least elucidate Stoneage knowing a little before they betray it. Remember – these concepts are offered by a modern language that objectifies entities against a background of space and time. And when we speak, in our modern languages, of space or time, we mean distance, not event. The English language uses the demonstrative pronoun "this" to indicate something near, and "that" to indicate something far. The Inuit have some thirty different words to express different kinds of location: "that in there," "that high up in there," "that – unseen." The language of the Aranda peoples of Australia, consistent with the understanding that particular existences are sung dreams, does not distinguish between things and activities or states. There are available to the Aranda verb nearly a thousand combinations of suffixes. Thus, by a complex synthetic process, the basic verb _atakererama_ ("to spread out roots") may be built up into _atakeritakerereperelatanguna_ ("to remain rooted down firmly for all time"). In these – not words, but holophrases – the thing or entity named is gathered up into the energy of the agglutinative verb; the object is not allowed to stand apart from a process. The cliché about the many Inu words for snow is partially explained by the fact that distinctions between qualities of snow are also travel and weather condition advisories. Hard-crusted snow – it gives under one's steps (_katakartanaq_) – _is_ different from melting snow – difficult to traverse (_aumannaq_). Hunter-gatherer specificity, when measured against a modern vagueness about the conditions of a thing's location, shows the degree to which Western thinking has lost its reference points in the real, and so floats free in abstract space and abstract time.

That said, it may still be useful to see in the thing-in-process holisms of ancestral knowing a distinction between two orientations of seeing. The first of these I will call the knowledge of things as states; the second I will call the knowledge of states as things.

Our orientation towards objective things is to some degree physiological. Aspects of the world seem thing-like to us because we have appendages such as an apposable thumb, plus overlapping fields of vision, that have predisposed us to manipulate reality. Our finger and language skill – our articulation – co-evolved with mental processes that are relatively specialized and isolated from each other. In contrast, say, to the cerebral cortex of the _Cetacea_ (dolphins and whales),

138

where hearing, touch, vision, taste and motor areas are clustered together in a paralimbic lobe, the sensory functions of the human being are dispersed in the brain. Each function is bordered by an interpretation area that deals with its respective sensory mode. The physical structure of humans is eye- and hand-oriented, and an evolutionary history of using tools and moving in cluttered environments has perfected a habit of making figure-ground separations. We were once the kin of fast-moving treetop mammals in a setting full of objects and choices. We needed to distinguish the tree from the forest when making our first mental leaps.

How it came about that human beings evolved specific sounds to stand for these objects and choices is one of the mysteries of language. The sea otter will dive to the sea-floor and come up with a shell in its paw and a rock for smashing the shell against under its armpit, and the otter is smart enough to put the rock on its chest while it floats tummy-up and to hold the shell in its paw. That way, it will not lose the shell. But I doubt if the otter has a specific sound for rock or shell. As sociable as a human, the creature undoubtedly does have a specific body language with which to imitate this acculturated tool-using. However, that body signal is not as variable as human speech, in which thought categories have evolved from states of the body. In Homer, perception is a kind of breathing – the two words are related etymologically in Greek: thought is like breath moving in and out of the lungs. The linguistic skill of humans presumably emerged in the capacity of the sensory functions, relatively dispersed in the human brain, to map one interpretation upon another simultaneously. This brings us back to the concept of *frames*.

The concept of frames is what allows the mythteller to keep certain types of knowledge and certain ways of seeing relatively apart from each other, so that one modality of knowing will not contaminate another. Framing is therefore an excluding principle. Like the frame around a picture, it says "Pay attention to what is inside the frame; ignore what is outside the frame." One obvious frame will give you a picture of reality; another frame imposed on top of that first frame – say, the frame supplied by the occasion of being in an art gallery – will make you more certain of what you know. A third frame – for example, the signature of the artist on the painting – introduces even more precision. A fourth frame, supplied by an exhibition catalogue or guide book, yields another mutually confirming overlap. Thus identifying a thing is a function of how much potential meaning is excluded by added qualification. It is like using the computer to reference a desired title in a library. The more information we bring to bear on it – the more redundancy we introduce – the more the item gains clarity as alternative meanings are excluded.

Yet the more words we deploy in longer and longer messages – the greater the overlap of frameworks – the less we are actually certain about what it is we are so certain about. This is true of the picture in the gallery, where one feels the experience is lost in the process of identifying it. In the ironic condition of modern language, mental frameworks themselves have taken the place of physical objects in our orientation to things as states. Consequently, goals, ideals, guiding concepts, objects of reverence are all mental objectives – ideas treated as if they were objects. Their pursuit involves an increasing focal vision, held in place and ultimately submerged in an excess of loquacity.

Historically, this degree of abstraction has many causes. Foremost among them is the ascendancy of the written text, and a corresponding loss of faith in the oral. It is not just the case that the act of writing something down as an aid to memory is basically a decision to forget it, as an enlightened king tells the god of writing in one of Plato's dialogues. It is that the text, as a framing device, allows an item of consciousness to be held in place long enough for an endless array of further frameworks to be positioned on it. So it is that the first recorded texts of a culture immediately attract a tradition of commentary, as one sees with the texts of Homer and with the trigrams that became the *I Ching*. To the mythtellers, frames marked permeable boundaries. The boundary – the membrane – is the place where truth is felt, truth being the nourishing exchange of energy between everyday life and the supernatural. With literacy, that permeable boundary is hardened. In effect, the boundary is as hard as the written page.

I turn now to the second modality of knowing, the orientation to states as things. By "states" I mean complex totalities, like the state of a river-mouth during the moon of the sockeye salmon, or the state of the world above the clouds, or the state of being alone at the rock where Dreams are given. By "things," I mean the sense that such states are intelligible entities. It will be seen that what I am talking about again is *pattern* and the ability to perceive it as directly as possible.

Our orientation towards pattern is as basic as our animal bodies. The mythtellers say pattern is what the animals and plants know better than we do, and to find out something about pattern you have to enter the spirit of one of the animals or plants. Scientifically considered, pattern knowledge has its origin in a fundamental capacity in the nervous systems of animals to weave together the sights, sounds, smells, tastes and textures of an environment into intuitive wholes. In animals, the skill is second-nature. In humans today, the skill is probably just as strong, but because it does its work at semiconscious levels we are not aware of it, except in subliminal messages like "The feeling in this room is bad," or "I think I can trust this person." These are all intuitions of states. And often they have to remain as intuitions of states. They cannot be directly or immediately framed by words because then the intuitions slip away. That is why unconscious perception, especially when it is reinforced as a skill, is awkward when it tries to talk about itself. That skill, once self-conscious, is awkward for all people who are accustomed to use their bodies to see and feel – artists, lovers, athletes, hunters, anyone who knows how to do a job well. "How did I know to be in the right place to receive this pass seconds before the play veered my way?" "How did I know where to find this animal?" "Why did I use this perfect word in just the right place in the poem?" Such questions cannot be answered easily, and, indeed, it often seems like bad luck to press the question. There is a boundary between focal knowing and tacit knowing, between the ability to transfix entities purposefully by framing them with words, and a playful pattern-thinking in which states are allowed to stand more or less in their indigenous frames. The taciturnity of the hunter speaks volumes about this ability to read the patterns of things through the body, to be open to the polyphony of existence in states of change – this particular falter in the music of the forest canopy, this particular sound of a twig breaking, this feeling of the hairs starting to rise on the back of your neck: "There's a predator out there!" To the sixth sense of the hunter, it is not a particular event that he can name, but the overall relation among various events, which signifies the animal who cannot be seen. It is the *state of pattern* that does the naming.

States as things cannot be named easily. But this does not mean they cannot be expressed. The shifting patterns of nature are caught in an organ of perception that is as various and changing as sunlight on the forest floor. That organ is the feelings, which themselves obey a kind of ecology. Feelings are always mixed, and even in their absolute outspoken state contain subdominant voices in their overall register. "Excess of sorrow laughs. Excess of joy weeps." Being in the significance of love, yet being ignored; enjoying a festive dinner yet feeling far from home – these are mixed states. To express them, we involve ourselves in a thought-play that emphasizes the *relationship* or *pattern* among the feelings. To frame them, we point to another frame which is like them. We think analogically: "This is similar to that in the same way that some other is similar to something else." That form of thought-play is called *metaphor*.

Metaphor is a type of thinking and expression oriented towards wholes as things. The word comes from the Greek "to carry across," and in metaphor one set of patterns is, as it were, carried across to another set in the mind, and in a way that safeguards the integrity of relations of the whole that cannot be spoken about directly. Thus metaphor allows patterns to come to light by a process of self-framing. Say, we are feeling the elusive and complex experience which words frame as "love." No quantity of words can trap into definition the hopes and fears of that glorious yet insubstantial, permanent yet fading, enticing yet thorny experience. We cannot reference these complexities by translating them into simple verbal frames. Nor would we want to. There is something sacred about our feelings, something that prefers not to be talked about. "It's too big for words!" Instead, we can point to a rose. "There – that is how love feels." The rose acts as a metaphor, catching the difference in relationship that resonates on the strings of feeling.

In order to pluck that chord in the feelings, metaphor emphasizes the relationship more than the actual related particulars. It is not "love" or "rose" that concerns the speaker who intuits an analogy in these terms; it is a set of feelings involving differences in the state of love. Elusive as these differences are, they can implicate as well time and change, the most elusive of phenomena. And so the metaphor hears, in love, strains of a process – rich yet painful, glorious yet insubstantial, permanent yet fading. With this extra dimension, the relationship of relationships that sounds in metaphor has a better power than the objectifying name to map a state or condition. Metaphor lets a sense of time into our seeing in a way that naming, for all its power to be precise, does not. (Here I am speaking of spontaneous metaphoric perception rather than figures of speech that have become cliché.) But I am merely talking about particular words used metaphorically – not intonation or inflection or body-language or physical context or all the other events that surround the speech act. These paralinguistic events come into their own most truly in music, where the relatedness of existence is embodied for the mythteller. Especially that relatedness is embodied metaphorically in the music and rhythm of the spirit-song, which the mythteller feels is given to him by the beings in nature.

The orientation towards states of pattern that goes on at the most discreet levels of perception escapes manipulation by purposefully chosen words. It does so by virtue of its different kind of coding. But the price human beings pay for that different kind of coding is difficulty in making the perception of pattern accessible. We live in the interplay of two modes of knowing, the one chattering like a monkey yet powerless to mean, the other meaningful as a sunset yet powerless to name.

Double knowing

Myth takes the condition of human double-mindedness and raises it to a special power. It enhances the condition by means of an economy of signs. Where human speakers are caught at any moment between a volubility that stacks frame upon frame for a greater precision of reference, and an economy of expression that allows entities to sound in their own space and time, myth favors the latter. That favoring begins by conceding stories to the land. Myths give themselves to the mountains and forests and ocean and sky for safekeeping. According to this naturalization, the wilderness becomes the reference system, and everyone in the particular mythtelling culture knows the places and beings mentioned. A Tlingit elder speaks of her Taku River, at the top of British Columbia, as *wé àxh i shagûn khuwdzitìyi yé*, "the place where your history came into being"; the river tells *wâ sáyú ikawdayâyi*, "what happened to you in your past." But the messages must be listened for and told again and again, because patterns are only information, as vulnerable to effacement as writing on the sand. With stories entrusted to the Dreaming and re-Dreaming of the land, the mythteller can be sparing in her naming. The best mythtellers usually are. John Sky has this tacit focal framing. He is always careful to evoke the power of a god before naming him, and quite often he does not name the god at all. When Sapsucker is drumming his beak against a barkless spruce tree, Sky says ineffably:

> *something said,*
> *"Your father's father asks you in."*
> *He looked for what had spoken.*
> *Nothing stood out.*
>
> *When it said the same thing to him again,*
> *he looked inside the hollow of the tree.*
> *Something shrunken and sunken, white as a gull,*
> *sat at the back.*
> *And he stepped in.*

This affectionate familiarity is possible when a landscape is permitted to speak its own stories. Then the *state* of being enfolds the being. Like the God of the People of Israel, who refuses accommodation to a name (Exodus 3:14), the Raven is often mentioned by the Haida mythtellers as if he were, not a person, but a process: "it-is-the-one-it-usually-is." Similarly, she is both the feeling of plenitude in the headwaters and she is Jilaquns, seniormost of the Qaasghajiina. He is both the energy of the Bear God in the land and the particular bear who has been speared. It is both the right flint tool hidden in the quartz rock, and the whole Dreaming process that has prepared that tool in Dreamtime, making it ready for the Aborigine who finds it.

This economy of naming happens also at every level of mythtelling above the level of language. Its effect is to orient the listener to the pattern world. Haida myths are told in precise arrangements, like music, with one myth serving as the analogical frame for another. Then there is no need for titles and explanations – the process does the identifying. Within this loose structure, the individual myth has a freedom and flexibility unlike the notated concerto or the written story with its fixed conflicts, climaxes, resolutions and finales. Instead, it is a box of surprises. Since in an oral culture there is no official version of anything, the mythteller is free to combine pieces of stories within a sense of the rightness of the patterns they make. Structure emerges as if it were improvised on the spot, and the narrative shifts unexpectedly between the ordinary and the supernatural, from one satisfying recognition to another, making causal reasoning chase its own tail. This double-seeing accounts for the sly humor one hears in the native American mythtellers – also for their disarming vagueness about matters of formal belief. The anthropologist Jaime de Angulo, during his time with the Achumawi people in California, asked his native go-between, Wild Bill, if the natives believed their myths:

> "Listen, Bill, tell me ... do the Indians think, really think, that Coyote made the world? I mean, do they really think so? Do you really think so?"
>
> "Why, of course I do ... why not? ... Anyway ... that's what the old people always said ... only they don't

all tell the same story ... And then you hear the Paiutes
tell it different! And our own people down the river,
they also tell it a little bit different from us."

A vagueness about matters that cannot be fixed in frames
does not extend to matters that can be, and ought to be, so
fixed. It perpetuates a mistake made by a primitive generation
of linguists to think that because a people do not have a word
for something, they do not have the concept either. It furthers
that error in another form to consider that because a people
do not organize their narratives into plausible verbal sequences, they lack logical reasoning skills. An oral people are
no less capable of consequential reasoning than we are. They
are exceptionally circumspect about the results of, say, sitting
the wrong guests together at a feast. Here, care is partly a matter of practical diplomacy – but it is also a question of genealogy; for each person, like each being, carries with her her
own resonance from Dreamtime. The Tlingit elder whose
ancestry is encoded in the Taku River knows who she is. Mrs.
Elizabeth Nyman to her English-speaking friends, she is also
Sèdayà of the Yanyèdí, that is, a woman of her mother's clan,
Yanyèdí, of the Wolf side, and child of her father's clan,
Khàch.ádi yádi, of the Raven side. She knows the stories of her
parents, grandparents, great-grandparents and great-great-
grandparents. All this naming is held in pattern; it is really pattern that is named and does the naming.

To read the old myths is to feel this double-phrasing of the
being and its genealogy, the thing and the state, the physical
and the spiritual. Even the most discreet entity is volatized by
currents of power from its larger surround. But I have spoken
of this double-phrasing as if there were only two levels of existence to anything. In fact, this double-knowing extends
everywhere in a mythtelling tradition. The result is a mythology packed and bursting with different ways of seeing, each

frame a doorway that listeners step through into the various worlds of the mythcreatures, each world carrying its indigenous mode of knowing, undeniably whole and relevant but not verifiably true. Altogether, it amounts to an ecological nesting of types of consciousness with and within other types of consciousness, with energy and information exchanged at the membranes, and the whole open to a vaster surround felt as mystery. Myths, with their shifting epistemological frames, encourage in the listener a hesitancy in the prospect of an unnameable awareness, and a corresponding wryness about the knowledge which this larger awareness frames. Life inside such a box of stories would make a person as wise as the sage, and as simple as the fool.

CHAPTER FIVE / COMPLEMENTARITY

BRANWEN VERCH LLYR

Llyma yr eil geinc or mabinogi

Benðigeituran uab llyr aoeð urenhin coronawe ar
yr ynys honn. Ac arderchawe o goron lunðein.
Aphrynhawngweith yðoeð yn harðlech yn arðuðwy yn
llys iðaw. ac yneisteð yð oeðynt ar garrec harðlech
uch penn y weilgi. amanawyðan uab llyr y urawt
y gyt ac ef. aðeu uroðer unuam ac ef. nissyen ac
efnissyen. a gwyrða y am hynny ual y gweðei
ygkylch brenhin. Y ðeu uroðer unuam ac ef meibion
oeðynt y eurossyð ocuam ynteu. Penarðim uerch
ueli uabmynogan. ar neill or gweisson hynny
gwas ða oeð. ef a barei ðangneueð y rwng y ðeulu
pan byðynt liðyawckaf. Sef oeð hwnnw nissyen.
Y llall a barei ymlað rwng yðeu uroðer pan uei
uwyhaf yðymgerynt.

BRANWEN DAUGHTER OF LLŶR

Here is the second portion of the Mabinogi

Brân the Blessed, son of Llŷr, was king over us, and it happened that he was at a court of his at Harlech overlooking the sea. And they were seated upon the rock there. Manawydan of Llŷr, his brother, was with him, and the two brothers on his mother's side – Nissyen and Evnissyen were their names. And besides these, such other noblemen as is proper for a king to find company with. Of the two half-brothers, one was a good young man: he could make peace between warbands even when they were ready to battle – that was Nissyen. But the other – the other could make even the most loving brothers come to blows.

Now, they were seated there above the water, and they could see ships from the west running easily before the wind. Thirteen ships they saw, and fast approaching the land. "Those ships are making for a landing here," Brân said. "The men should arm themselves and go find what it is these people want."

The men of the court armed themselves and went down to meet the ships. And when they saw those ships up close, they were sure they had never seen anything as well fashioned as those ships were, with the bright pennants of brocaded silk that hung about them.

And one of the ships outreached the others, and there was a shield raised over the deck, point upwards in the sign of peace. Then the people put out boats and rowed towards the shore and greeted Brân – he could hear them from his place high on the rock.

"May the gods be with you," said Brân. "And a welcome to you here. Whose ships are these, and who is chief over them?"

"Lord," they said. "Matholwch the king is here, and these are his ships."

"What are his wishes? Will he make landing here?"

"Only if he is given what he has come to ask of you," they replied. "Then he will come ashore."

"What is it King Matholwch wishes?" asked Brân.

"Lord," they said, "the king wishes an alliance with you. And he has come to ask for Branwen, daughter of Llŷr. And if that seems good to you, he will unite the Island of the Mighty and his realm, and both will prosper."

"Bid him come ashore," Brân said, "and we will hold council on it."

This answer was given to Matholwch, and the king came ashore and was made welcome. And it was a great throng at Harlech that night with the hosts of the visitor and Brân's own following. And at daybreak, the chiefs of the Island of the Mighty held council. And the decision of the council was this: Branwen was to be given to Matholwch – and she one of our Three Great Matriarchs and the most beautiful woman in the world. This the council agreed to – but not Evnissyen: he did not consent to it.

The time was set for their lovemaking, and they started for Aberffraw where this was to happen. Brân and his party went by land, Matholwch and his people in their ships. And there they met and began the feast – in tents, because Brân was so big he could never be contained within four walls. This is the order of their seating: Brân, with Manawydan of Llŷr on one side, Matholwch on his other. Then, Branwen, daughter of Llŷr, sitting next to Matholwch. Thus, they ate and sang and talked, and when it was better to sleep than carry on further, to sleep they went. And that night Matholwch slept with Branwen.

The next day, they all arose and looked to the billeting of so many horses – for Matholwch's people had brought their horses with them in the ships. And the horses were quartered in every place as far down as the sea.

Now, Evnissyen, the quarrelsome one we mentioned, comes upon the horses of Matholwch. He asks whose animals they are. And feeling insulted in the matter of the giving away of his sister – for he had not consented to this union – he maims the horses there and then. What he did was this. He cut their lips through to the teeth, and their ears back to their heads, and he cut their tails off – and when he could get his hands around them, he cut their eyelids right back to the bone.

When Matholwch was told of this, he took to his ships at once. Then Brân heard that his guest had quit the court without formality. Messengers were sent to ask why this was so.

"Truly," Matholwch said to them, "had I known, I would never have come here. A strange turn it is that Branwen is given to me – and she one of the Three Great Matriarchs and daughter of Llŷr, King of this Island of the Mighty. And that I should sleep with her, and then be insulted in this way!"

The messengers replied: "In truth, lord, this insult was not Brân's doing, nor did any of his council consent to it. And if you think it an insult, consider how much more King Brân is affronted by that act."

"Even so," Matholwch said, "he cannot undo it."

When Brân heard this, he said, "It will do us no good if he goes away angry. You, Manawydan, and Heveydd the Tall, and Unig Strong-shoulder – go to him and say that he will have a sound horse for every horse that was maimed. And more: he shall have as his honor-price a silver staff as thick as his little finger and as tall as he is, and a plate of gold as broad as his face. Tell him what sort of man did that insult to him, and how it is against my will that such a thing be done. And tell him that it was my brother on my mother's side who did it – that is why it is not easy for me to put him to death. But bid Matholwch meet with me in person and I will restore peace on any terms he names."

Matholwch listened carefully to the messengers. Then he held council with his chiefs. The decision they came to was this – that they would suffer greater shame and lose a chance of greater reparation if they did not accept the peace that Brân offered. And so Matholwch and his people determined to accept it, and they came back to the court in peace.

The tents and pavilions were set up so as to make a proper hall, and they sat down to eat: as they first sat at the beginning of the feast so they sat now.

Brân and Matholwch begin to talk, but the visitor is listless and heavyhearted – before this he had been so merry. And Brân thinks it is the slightness of the reparation that is making him so.

"Lord – you are not so fine a talker tonight as you were before. If it is because the reparation seems too small, I will increase it to your liking. And the horses shall be made over to you tomorrow."

"May the gods bless you for that," said Matholwch.

"I will give you a cauldron," Brân said. "And the power of the cauldron is this: if a man of yours is killed today, put his body in the cauldron and tomorrow he will be as whole as ever – though he will not have the power to speak."

Matholwch thanked Brân for that, and felt glad because of it. The next day, the horses were made over to him – as many as there were tamed horses to be found; and then they travelled to another district of the cantrev and colts were given until the compensation was complete.

On the second night, after the colts had been made over and the kings were sitting together again, Matholwch asked Brân how he came to own the cauldron.

"It came to me," Brân said, "from a man who was in your realm, and I guess it was there that he got it. And his wife came with him: they had escaped from a house made of iron – the house was made white-hot around them, but they escaped from it.

"I find it strange you know nothing of this," Brân added.

"I know something of it," Matholwch said. "And what I know I'll tell you. I was hunting one day, and there is a sacred place in my country – it is a mound above a lake we call the Lake of the Cauldron. That is where I was hunting. And I looked down and saw a huge man coming out of the lake. Yellow-red was his hair, and on his back a cauldron, and the look of a chief about him – and his wife following him: if he was huge, twice his size she was. And they came up to me and greeted me. 'How goes it with you?' I said. 'This is how it goes with us,' the man said. 'In a month and a fortnight this woman will be pregnant. And in that same month and a fortnight she will bear a boy and he will be a full-grown fighting man armed to the teeth.' Well, when I heard that," Matholwch said, "I took the couple with me and looked after them. A year they were with me, and during that time I was happy enough to keep them. But four months into the second year I was beginning to wish to see the end of them, for they were making themselves a nuisance in the land, molesting and harassing everyone. Soon enough, my chiefs are meeting with me to persuade me to be rid of these strange folk, and the choice is this: my kingship or them. So I held council, asking what could be done with them, for the strangers were in no mind to go, nor did they have to – there was so much fight in them. But then it was thought to make a chamber out of iron for them. And when that house was built, the smiths came from all over the country with their hammers and tongs. They piled the charcoal to the very top of the chamber, and gave the strangers every kind of meat and drink until they were good and drunk. Then the smiths fired the charcoal and blew the bellows – one man to each pair of bellows placed around the house – until that house was white with heat. And the strange ones talked together there in the middle of the chamber-floor. They waited until the iron wall was white-hot and brittle; then the man charged that wall with his shoulder and through it he broke by sheer force, and his wife after him. Only he and his wife came through.

"Then, I suppose," Matholwch said, "he found his way to you."

"He came over here, sure enough." Brân said. "And the cauldron with him, which he gave to me."

"What did you do with them?"

"I billeted them here and there in the kingdom. And now they are numerous and thriving. Wherever they are, they defend the place – the best men and arms anyone has seen."

That night, they ate and sang and talked as long as it pleased them to do so. And when it seemed better to sleep than to carry on further, to sleep they went. In that manner they spent the period of the feast in mirth and pleasure. And when it was over, Matholwch departed for his country, and Branwen with him. Thirteen ships sailed out from Aber Menei; thirteen ships reached home. And when they made landing, there was great welcome and rejoicing. No chief or lady paid their respects to the daughter of Llŷr and left without the gift of a brooch or ring or precious jewel – it was a marvel to see those gifts received. No wonder, then, that Branwen spent that year in praise and companionship. And in that year she conceived and in the proper time gave birth to a son. Gwern, they called him, son of Matholwch, and they sent him to be brought up in arms and kingship in the very best place for men to be fostered in that realm.

But then in the second year – listen, a murmuring everywhere in that country as the people remember the insult done to their king in Wales, the maiming of the horses. Even the king's foster-brothers and the men close to him do not conceal their taunting, and there is such uproar in the land that there is no peace for Matholwch unless he redress the wrong. This is what they do to Branwen – they drive her from her husband's chamber and make her work in the kitchen. When the butcher finishes with his cutting, he hits her on the ears every day. Then the chiefs of the court put a ban on every ship going to Wales so that Branwen's kinsfolk will not hear of this. That is the punishment they had for Branwen. For the whole year it was this way for her. But in that time she raised a starling – she raised it at the edge of her kneading-trough, and she gave it words and told it what kind of man her brother was. And she wrote a letter telling of her shame – this she fastened under the starling's wing and sent the bird towards home. And the bird came to our country, and it found King Brân at Caernarvon: the bird sat on his shoulder during the Assembly there, ruffling its feathers so the letter could be seen.

When Brân heard the letter read, he was grief-stricken. There and then he mustered the whole Island of the Mighty, all one hundred and fifty-four districts. In full assembly, he spoke of the suffering of his sister. Then they determined to set out for the other realm. Seven were to be stewards here: Caradawg, Brân's son, was their leader.

Brân the Blessed and the multitude set sail. In those days, the water was not so wide. Brân – he went by wading. He waded across with all of the harpists of Wales on his shoulders, and strode towards the realm of Matholwch.

Swineherds were by the sea one day, watching over their pigs, and what they saw on the ocean made them come running to the king.

"Lord Matholwch, we have news of a great wonder. There is a forest growing on the sea, and that is a place we have not seen a single tree grow before."

"Well, that is a wonder," said Matholwch. "And did you happen to see anything else?"

"Indeed, we did, lord. We saw a mighty mountain close to that forest, and that mountain is moving. And there is a high ridge on that mountain, and a lake on either side of that ridge, and the mountain and everything is moving."

"Well," said the king. "Only Branwen will know what this is about. Someone go ask her."

"Lady," the messengers said to Branwen, "what do you make of all this?"

"Lady I am not," she said. "But I know what it means. It means that the men of the Island of the Mighty are coming because they have heard of my disgrace here."

"What is the forest growing on the sea?"

"That is the masts of many ships, and their yardarms."

"What is the mountain beside the ships?"

"That is Brân, my brother – there was never a ship big enough to hold him."

"What is the high ridge with lakes on either side?"

"That is the face of my brother, Brân. And he is looking towards this place and he is angry. Those lakes are his eyes; the ridge between them is his nose."

Then the fighting men were mustered quickly from all over the island and its headlands, and a council was called. "There is no recourse," the chieftains said to Matholwch, "except to retreat across the Llinon and put that river between us and them. Break down the bridge that is on the river, and trust the load-stones at the river's bottom to prevent their ships from crossing."

They retreated across the river and broke down the bridge. Then Brân and his army came to the bank of the river.

"Lord," said his chieftains to him. "You see the problem with this river: no one can cross it and the bridge is gone. What is your counsel as to a bridge?"

"None," said Brân, "except that he who is a leader must be a bridge." (Then was that saying first spoken, and it is still heard among us as a proverb). "I myself will be a bridge." And saying that, Brân lay down across the river; frames were placed around him, and in that way his warbands passed over him.

Then even as he rises up – look, the messengers of Matholwch are approaching with greetings from the king, his kinsmen, and they are saying that nothing but good is intended by Matholwch. "And Matholwch is giving the kingship of his country over to Gwern, your nephew, your sister's son, and he will bestow the kingship in your presence for the wrong that has been done to Branwen."

"Indeed," said Brân, "if I do not take the kingship myself, I will at least hold council over this. Until different terms come, you will hear nothing from me."

Then the messengers replied. "The best terms we hear, we will bring them to you, if you will but wait for them."

"I will wait, if you return quickly."

The messengers went back to Matholwch and told him that Brân awaited better terms for peace.

"Chieftains – what counsel do you give me?"

"Lord – there is only this. Brân has never known the inside of a house. You might build him one in his honor. Make it big so that all the men of Wales can be contained in one side of the house, and your men in the other. And give your kingship and your service over to him. And for the honor of your making a house for him – for there never was a house that could contain him – he will make peace with you."

When Brân heard these terms, he determined to accept them. It was Branwen who interceded in this matter – she feared that the land would be laid waste.

The peace was arranged, and a house was built for Brân – vast and strong was that house. But the builders planned a trap, and the trap they planned was this: the house had a hundred pillars, and on each side of every pillar they fixed a peg; on each peg hung a leather bag, and an armed man in every one of them.

Evnissyen was the first to go in. He gave the house a hard firm stare – without mercy it was. And he saw the bags.

"What is in this bag?"

"Flour, friend."

Then Evnissyen felt with his fingers until he made out the head of the warrior within the bag, and he squeezed through the bone until he could feel his fingers meet in the brain. Then he left that one and put his hand upon another.

"And what is here?"

"Flour."

This Evnissyen did to every one of the two hundred. Then he sang an *englyn*:

> *In these bags a form of flour:*
> *Heroes, champions, fighters in battle*
> *warriors set for ambush.*

Then the hosts entered the house: the men of the Island of the Mighty on one side, the men of the other kingdom on the other. Then as soon as they were all seated, there was peace between them, and Gwern, son of Matholwch, Brân's nephew, was made king. Brân called the boy over to him. Then Gwern was embraced by Brân, and then by

Manawydan, and then by Nissyen, and everyone who saw the boy showed love for him. But not Evnissyen. "Why," said Evnissyen, "does my nephew not come to me?"

"Let him go to Evnissyen," Brân said.

And the boy went gladly to Evnissyen.

"Before the gods," whispered Evnissyen, "what I am about to do is something this household could not imagine." And he took the boy-king by the feet and threw him headfirst into the fire. When Branwen saw this – when she saw her son burning alive in the fire – she tried to leap into the fire herself, but it was too late for him. Brân seized her with one hand, his great shield with the other. Then they all rose up and reached for their weapons, and Brân protected his sister between his shield and his shoulder.

The men of the other realm started a fire beneath the Cauldron of Rebirth. The dead bodies of their people they threw into it – the next morning they would be reborn as whole as ever, through they would not have the power to speak. Then Evnissyen saw those corpses filling the Cauldron, with no room for the bodies of his own kin. "Before the gods I am shamed if I do not deliver the men of the Island of the Mighty from the desolation I have brought upon them." And he crept in and hid among the bodies of the other kingdom. Two bare-bottomed warriors came to throw him into the Cauldron as if he were one of them. Then Evnissyen stretched himself out inside the Cauldron, and it broke into four pieces. His heart broke also.

It was because of that act that victory came to the men of the Island of the Mighty – such victory as there was, for only seven came back from the other realm. These were the seven who returned: Pryderi, Manawydan, Glifieu son of Taran, Talyessin, Ynawg, Gruddyeu son of Muryel, and Heilyn, the son of Gwynn the Old.

Brân the Blessed did not return: he had taken a poisoned spear in the foot. This is what he said to his men who were left. He said that his head should be struck off. "And take my head and carry it with you to Gwynfryn – the White Mountain. And bury it with its face towards the east." And he said, "You will be a long time upon the road. At Harlech you will feast for seven years and the Birds of Rhiannon will be singing to you there. And the head will be as good company to you as it ever was when it was mine. Then after, you will be at Penvro eighty years and my head will not decay; only until one of you opens the door towards Aber Henvelen will you stay there. But when that door is opened, you cannot stay longer – then you must go east to the White Mountain to bury the head. But now – now it is time for you to sail home to the other side."

Then Brân's head was struck off, and they crossed the sea with it, these seven men and Branwen. They made landing at Aber Alaw in Talebolyon, where they rested for awhile. Then Branwen looked back towards the other kingdom, and she looked at the Island of the Mighty. "Alas that ever I was born – for two good islands have destroyed themselves because of me!" And with that she sighed and her heart broke. A four-sided grave they made for the Daughter of Llŷr, and they buried her there on the shore of the Alaw.

The seven men made their way to Harlech; the head was with them. On the road they met a throng of men and women fleeing.

"What news have you for us?" asked Manawydan.

"Only that Casswallawn has conquered Wales and they have made him king in London," they answered.

"But what of Caradawg, Brân's son, and the six stewards who were left with him to govern the Island?"

"Casswallawn fell upon them and killed all six. Then Caradawg's heart broke at the sight of it, and he

not discovering who did the slaying. You must know –
Casswallawn has a magic cloak, and no one can see him
while he is slaying; only the sword you can see. But his
sword spared his nephew Caradawg, his sister's son. And
Caradawg, the Chieftain of Dyved – he was with the six
when he was young – he escaped to the forest."

They went to Harlech, then, and a boundless feast awaited
them. As they began to eat and drink, there came three birds;
and the birds sang to them there, and all the songs the men
had ever heard were nothing beside this song. And the birds
were a distant vision over the sea, yet they seemed a presence
around them. And the men were seven years there feasting at
Harlech, with the Birds of Rhiannon singing to them.

Then, at the end of seven years, they made their way to
Penvro. There a wonderful hall awaited them – a royal hall
looking out over the sea. In that hall they found two open
doors – and a third door facing towards Aber Henvelen:
that third door was closed. "It is the door we must not
open," Manawydan said. That night they had everything
they wished for and in their joy they remembered nothing of
the sorrows they had suffered, nor of any other sorrow in the
world. And eighty years passed at Penvro, and during that
time they could not remember ever being happier. No one
could tell another that he seemed any older, nor was the
head of Brân any less company to them than when Brân had
been alive. And we call this story "The Assembly of the
Wondrous Head." The story of what happened in the other
realm we call "The Assembly of Branwen and Matholwch."

Now this is what Heilyn, the son of Gwynn did. He
gazed at the door that faced towards Aber Henvelen, and he
said, "Shame on my beard if I don't open this door to see if
it isn't true what is said about it." And he opened that door
and looked out over Aber Henvelen to the south and west.
And when he looked, every loss they had suffered came

flooding back to mind, and every friend and kinsman they had lost, and every misery that had come upon them – these sorrows all came back to them at once as if they were just now happening. And above all others the loss of their great lord Brân. From that moment there was no rest for them: they set out at once for the east to bury the head on the White Mountain. However long they were on the road, they reached Gwynfryn and buried the head there. And that burial we call in the stories one of the Three Fortunate Concealments. We call its uncovering one of the Three Unhappy Disclosures, for no plague ever came across the ocean to our land during the time Brân's head was hidden.

That is how the tale goes. That is their adventure – the men who came back from the kingdom across the sea – and we call the story "The Men who Went to the Other World."

In that other place, no one was left alive except five women in a cave in the wilderness – and they were pregnant. The women all bore sons at once. The mothers raised their sons until they became grown youths and began to think of wives. Then each slept in turn with the mother of each of his companions, and they ruled the country and settled in it, dividing it among the five of them. And they searched the land for where the battles had occurred, and found gold and silver lying there where warriors had fallen. And so they became wealthy.

And that is how this Branch of the myth ends, concerning the disgrace done to Branwen, which was one of the Three Unhappy Blows to this Island; and concerning the Assembly of Brân, when the hosts from all our districts went to the other realm to avenge that hurt; and the Feasting at Harlech when the birds of the Goddess came to sing; and the Assembly of the Head which lasted eighty years.

COMPLEMENTARITY

Hierarchy

The term hierarchy denotes an organization having distinct yet interrelated levels of activity or being. Borrowed from information theory, the term is useful to this chapter which is about how a myth contains within it a whole mythology and how that mythology constitutes an ecological vision. The term hierarchy is useful so long as one does not confuse it with the power pyramid spoken of by sociologists. In the power pyramid, all mind and control is concentrated at the top, like the eye of Reason surmounting the pyramid of Matter on the back of the American one dollar bill. In contrast, in a natural ecology no part of the system is in a position to control the rest of the system unilaterally. That is because the system is informational in character. It consists essentially of a circuit or loop of communication, with messages travelling around the circuit bringing the parts of the system together into an overall pattern of complementarity. Consequently, the behavior of any part of the circuit is partially determined by the results of its previous messages. An action by one part of the circuit, say, the organism, creates a difference in another part, say, the environment. The environment, being altered, constitutes a message sent back to the organism. The difference travels around the circuit as feedback. For example, in a wolf-deer cycle (to take one ecosystem) who runs the show? Is it the deer, who being too few in number act as a message to the wolves to cut back on their breeding? Or is it the wolves, who having cut back on their breeding cause there to be more deer? It is not as if wolves and deer alter their populations unilaterally. It seems as if the overall circuit governs their actions. It is as if the overall pattern thinks.

Ecologies exhibit this circular causation (to borrow another term from information theory). They are a network of causes-causing-causes-to-cause-causes. Mapping this poly-causality, hunter-forager myths and indeed Celtic visual and narrative art as well is typically complex at the center and open at the edges – all complicated middle with no pronounced beginning or end. Skaai commences to tell of the relationship of the young Red-headed Sapsucker and the old Spirit of a spruce tree this way:

> *Grass surrounded something round, they say.*
> *He travelled around it, Sapsucker did.*

And Skaai ends the story:

> *And he clutched the tree and drummed his beak against it*
> *just the way he did before.*

It is all process – unending. The later myths of organized agricultural humanity lose this openness to the circuits of meaning in wilderness, to copy instead the imposed order of the garden. Such myths must have "a beginning, a middle, and an end," Aristotle said. They typically organize their sequences toward an end-point which is often a point of explanation. Their causality is therefore simpler, the material causality of an arrow sent directly towards its target. Hunter-gatherer myths belong instead to the world of the boomerang.

This has been said before in the chapter on "Pattern." I say it again here because there is a tendency among those who write about myth to see all myths – hunter and agricultural – as having a closed structure and, within that closed structure, a logic of polar opposition – *this* as the opposite of *that,* rather than hierarchy's *this* as different from *that.* The concept of hierarchy allows one to escape this dualizing because the term denotes levels rather than opposites. And hierarchical reasoning insists that kinds of information be kept to the levels to which they belong. When reasoning in levels, instead of the oppositional drama of "either/or" choices and dilemmas, one begins to see in myths, even in myths exhibiting sharp dynamic contrasts, a "both-and" logic of inclusion. According to that logic of inclusion, there is always one level that is hierarchically superior to the other – superior in the sense in which an environment is superior to an organism because it contains both the organism's and its own greater complexity. Thus, consistent with a hierarchical thinking in levels, it is a mistake to speak of two equivalent states called "light" and "dark." It is an even larger mistake to speak of them as adversaries. Instead, light is an aspect of the prior and enduring state which is darkness. And so the state of light and the state of dark are present at the same time to the mythteller, like the light and dark phases of the moon.

It takes a while for Western readers to respond to this principle of hierarchical organization in myth. That is because Western cultural tradition is structured by an agriculturalist fascination with the gross alternations of nature. Looking upward from the intricacies of earth-bound life to the grand seasonal oscillations of dry and rainy, or looking outward to periodicities of day (for working in the fields) and night (when the spirits are out and about), the farmer privileges one set of values and debases the other. Light and dark are then restated as adversaries, with "the forces of light" friendly to the agriculturalist, "the forces of darkness" inimical. "Night, thou foule Mother of annoyance sad, / Sister of heavie death, and nourse of woe," says a speaker in a European Renaissance epic, echoing a literary tradition that goes back to Greek and Roman fear of the unconfined and uncontrolled. The Romans were a day people: for them, bright Mediterranean sunlight bathing the Roman forum. Julius Caesar in his *Gallic*

War seems bemused to note that the Celts "called themselves the sons of the god of night" and celebrated their feasts on the night before passage into a new season. A person born during the night was said to be able to see the spirits, who are active after sunset, invisible to the children of day. Among those spirits may be the spirits of relatives and ancestors. For the Celtic peoples, as for the original peoples of Australia, night was the element of the Dreaming. And for the Japanese too. Quoting from a Noh song, Hajime Nakamura writes: "No-where is there a shadow in which a god does not reside: in peaks, ridges, pines, cryptomerias, mountains, seas, villages, plains, and fields; everywhere there is a god." The gods inhabit the dark side of existence. Winter, the dark season when the animals are hibernating, is the season of the Dreaming. Accordingly, the time when life seems to have gone out of the world is actually the time of the greatest fertility because then the ancestors are busy dreaming up new forms of life for the spring. Winter is therefore the time to tell stories – ancestor stories that bring the living closer to the dead. The ancient Irish officially began their mythtelling at the year-end festival of *Samhain* on the eve of the first of November. In *The Voyage of Bran*, the poet Forgoll recites a story to the king of Ulster every night throughout the winter, "from Samhain to Beltain" (May 1st). The Algonkian storytelling period commences on the moon of the first snowfall, and it is a loss of faith with ancestral nature to tell the sacred stories out of season. The world of the gods is most active when it is least visible – this is the hierarchical understanding that lets one see an entire vision of complementary worlds articulated within a single myth.

One of the most haunting stories that Skaai of the Qquuna Qiighawaai told to John Swanton during the winter of 1900 is the story of the weather god of Hecate Strait. Called *Nangdldastlas* ("One They Gave Away"), the myth celebrates a covenant between a Haida village and the sea-god who sends the fish to the rivers in the time of the fair-weather clouds. Technically speaking, the story maps exchanges across the boundary between the world of "the surface people" (*xhaaidhla xhaaidaghaai*, that is, human beings) and the world beneath the sea. This concern with renewing the principle of reciprocity between the human and superhuman worlds is extended in the two stories that follow *Nangdldastlas* in an apparent narrative suite, which fills out the map with accounts of exchanges with the forest world and the world above the clouds. Thus a whole mythology is embedded in this triptych. As in so many myths about the righting of the balance of life, the overture myth tells of the returning of articles and beings that have been misplaced. Things have gotten on the wrong side of the boundary; there is a mislocation of power – power in the wrong place – which is dangerous to pluralistic harmony.

The power of the weather-god is decidedly mental. As a being of the dream side of existence, he can do things simply by thinking them. He can think thunder and lightning. He can lift and drop an entire Haida village with his mind. With the point of a feather he can think human travellers in the domain of the gods back to their village in two strokes of a paddle. This awesome mental power is concentrated appropriately in images of the head and headgear. In fact, the story begins when the son of the weather-god, borrowing a magic hat belonging to his father in order to go courting, leaves the hat on the beach of a Haida village as a gift for the father of a human girl he has taken away in marriage. That hat must be returned to its rightful owner, because it does no good for human beings to possess an object that can alter the weather and change the cycles of fertility:

Something encircled his hat.
It was white, they say.
It was breaking like surf, they say.
It was foaming and churning, they say.
And when they refused him,
    the earth became different, they say.
Seawater surged over the ground.
When they found themselves half underwater, the villagers
    feared that they might have to give him the woman.

The favored child of the village, who is taken to the supernatural world, is kept there in a cave by the sea-god until the hat is returned. She is in a state of suspended animation or, as Skaai tells it, the sea-god "thought grease into his son's wife's mind." So now there is a human princess – a vessel of fertility – on the wrong side of the boundary. Somehow she must be returned to her people and to the limited practices of power which they enjoy.

On the human side of the boundary, these practices of power are those of the sea-hunter. They are part shamanism, part a matter of using one's tools properly and keeping the gear clean and tidy. The story describes the quest of a shaman from the girl's village through the great membrane of the sea to find out where the girl was taken. Then, in another great cycle of adventure, the myth narrates the canoe voyage by a party of villagers to the sea-god's home, to give presents of shells to the god, and the hat on top of that heap of shells, for the return of the girl. The gods like shells – especially they like abalone shell, and, when the gift of tobacco is also offered, the proper accompaniment is calcined clamshell: this serves the same catalytic function with tobacco as the compacted ash chewed with coca leaves in the highlands of Peru. But quite apart from such aids to mental acuity, there is a sense in this story that the gods appreciate shells because shells are practical tools. Shells can be used for spooning up whale-flesh soup. The gods do not have a great treasure of shells and, for all their power, are reduced to offering their human guests the rotten shell of a horseclam for this purpose. How their eyes bulge when a guest – it is the girl's mother – is

> *unwilling to eat in this way.*
> *Reaching into her purse,*
> *she took out two horseclam shells and two mussel shells.*
> *Silence fell in the house.*
> *Even her host looked at nothing except the shells.*

The event tells something about the limited power in the realm of the practical of sea-spirits who are used to getting what they want by dreaming them. For all of their power to alter the patterns of things, for all of their power to change the weather and to bring spirits back to their physical bodies, the gods are curiously at a loss in the world of discrete objects. Can they not even open a horseclam? Must they wait for it to rot before it falls open for them? In contrast to this limitation on the part of the gods, the story emphasizes the inspired practicality of the humans, especially the resourcefulness of the shaman. He uses a sea-otter spear to guide his canoe to the world of the spirits. He throws it in front of him and when it wiggles its tail it tows the canoe along. Later, when he comes to the edge of the sky, where the sea and the sky open and shut as if on an immense hinge, he uses the spear to prop the sky open long enough to descend to the village of the gods.

There is a balance of kinds of power in this story, but the lesson of the telling is the dependence of these powers on each other. Each kind of power makes the other kind possible; the potentials of one compensate for the limitations of the other. Eventually, the weather-god releases the princess to her people – but she is released pregnant. In Haida tradition, the grandparent is incarnate in the grandchild. Nangdldastlas has found a way to renew his immortality through the marriage of his son to a human princess, reincarnating himself as her first-born son. The villagers let the god be reborn with due ceremony from the womb of their favorite child, and they will hand the baby on to the sea. In return, the god promises that he will send the fish to the rivers at the right time of year. Human surface-dwellers can please the gods by giving them gifts of tobacco and seashell – and from time to time a high-born maiden through whose womb a god can perpetuate his immortality. Otherwise, the creatures of power do not need very much from the world of human beings. Related at some fundamental level by marriage, and co-involved by the tricks each plays on the other, the two worlds pursue their separate concerns, like biological symbionts.

Exchange: the Celtic

The fullest elaboration of the complementarity of worlds in myth that falls within my experience (my experience is limited) is found in the Celtic *Four Branches of the Mabinogi*. The "Four Branches" refer to four separate tales of "youth" or of "the hero," depending on how one translates the Welsh word *mab* in the title. They present themselves as accounts of human heroism, but this is only the surface level of what is actually a narrative archaeological site, with stories told on top of the ruins of older stories like villages built on the strata of older villages that have crumpled in time. At the bottom of it all is a foundation in myth. Myth gives its form to later tellings, so that semi-historical legends of human warriors are virtually stories of the relationship between the humans and the gods.

Here the world of the humans and the world of the gods each has distinctive attributes. The worlds are divided by gender, color and location, like the Navajo myths which ascribe femaleness to points of the compass (south and west) and to the colors blue and yellow, while maleness is invested in a differing set of complements. For the matriarchal Celts, the world of the gods – the Otherworld – is decidedly feminine, its color white, its location beneath the physical world or across the sea to the west. The world of human power is correspondingly masculine. But there is a deeper set of attributes given to each of these worlds. The deeper terms of this complementarity appear to be psychological, and are felt first in the way the Otherworld typically thinks. And the way the Otherworld thinks is through patterns. Always, it thinks through subtle indirection. "This is similar to that in the same way that some other is similar to something else." It seems quite incapable of reasoning in the algorithmic lines which in the male human world run straight to goals and objects. For the Otherworld to bring a Dream to fruition, it must lay down complicated, playful, semi-random streams of circumstance. A human agent may stumble onto one of those far-reaching nets of thought-play and, without knowing it, find that he has been gently used to bring about some outcome dreamed of in the mind of the Otherworld.

An example of this analogical indirection begins the action of the *First Branch*. Arawn, a being of power in the Otherworld, has a dispute with another being called Hafgan. It is the sort of cosmological problem that concerns gods (Hafgan means "Summer Song" and Arawn is a ruler of the dark, unconscious half of the year out of which light arises). Arawn seems incapable of solving the problem himself. One often sees this powerlessness in myth-people. The Buryat hunter with his knowledge of the seventy languages of the animals was given this gift by a grateful Rainbow Snake whom he had helped in that snake's elemental battle with the Snake of Fog. In the *Mabinogi* this powerlessness is more pronounced. It may be so because the dispute involves territory and encroachment, matters the gods are innocent of. In many Celtic myths, the Otherworld, for all its omniscience, is strangely impotent in matters having to do with territory, ownership and war. So Arawn has to borrow an agent from the upper world to do his business for him, and the human he borrows is Pwyll (his name translates as "Sense"). It ought to be a simple matter of asking Pwyll to descend to the realm of the gods to undertake the simple task that will resolve the dispute. But nothing is simple to the Otherworld. Instead, Arawn tricks Pwyll into spending a year in Arawn's likeness – the year represents one complete turning of the cycle of fertility. The trick is this: Pwyll will be out hunting, and he will set his dogs accidentally on an Otherworld stag that magically appears. The stag is gleaming white – white means power, as it does in native American myth; Moby Dick was white (Melville knew about such things). Arawn, whose quarry this is, will appear to be offended. Pwyll will ask for the right to make amendment for the discourtesy he committed. Arawn will then name the terms of the reparation. It is all very subtle and complicated. The trap that the Otherworld king prepares for Pwyll to stumble into is like the one orchestrated by the Bear People for the princess who went berry-picking. But there is more to it than this.

Pwyll's sojourn in the Otherworld turns out for him to be a time of testing. Each night, in the form of Arawn, he sleeps beside his host's wife – "and of all he had ever seen to converse with, she was the most unaffected woman, and the most gracious of disposition and discourse." Yet Pwyll does not so much as touch her. For this courtesy to the world of the gods, Pwyll, in a second story – an unmarried king and therefore the focus of much anxiety in the realm – is given a supernatural woman as his wife. Her name is Rhiannon – the "Otherworld Maiden." She is herself escaping a problem of territorial possession she cannot solve: forced marriage to Gwawl ap Clud ("Radiance, Son of Light"). Thus each of the worlds, pursuing its separate ends, resolves problems by contact with the other. The myth suggests that this sort of reciprocity characterizes the human and the divine worlds when they are in their best inclination to each other. The product of this marriage, and the symbol of the cooperation of two worlds, is Pryderi, half god, half man. The Irish bards, who liked to group their stories according to theme, would have called this a *compert* or "conception" tale. Its setting is spring, when the fertility of the Otherworld is renewed in the world of human affairs.

The *Second Branch* is the part of the myth reproduced in this book as the tale of Branwen. The tale is set in summer, when the thoughts of a warrior culture turn to war. It is a sequence of stories belonging to the thematic category of *macgnímartha* or "youthful exploits." But the exploits in this case involve an attack by a human army on the Otherworld hosts. The tragedy came about this way. A lord from the Otherworld appeared on the shores of this world to ask for the hand of a favored princess in marriage. She is Branwen ("White Raven"), sister of Brân son of Llŷr ("Raven of the Sea"). Like the son of the weather-god who comes to the Haida village in a harbor-seal canoe (the seal is a totemic animal and its bones know the way to the kingdom underneath the sea), the Otherworld lord travels by magic boat. Like the Haida story, the myth invites a double-thinking. From the human, and human-centered, point of view we hear of marriage negotiations breaking down because of an insult done to the Otherworld visitors by Branwen's half-brother. (As in Haida society, descent in Celtic society is matrilinear: chieftainship passes from the brother to his sister's son, so a son that Branwen bears will force aside the claim by the son of the half-brother.) The Otherworld lord is finally appeased by the gift of the Cauldron of Rebirth. That is how the events stand in a human-centered listening to the story. But myths, as I have said, are double-phrased, and circumstances such as these find their place in a broader pattern when we think of the events from the point of view of the gods. In that perspective, not Branwen, but the Cauldron of Rebirth may have been what the gods were after in the first place. The Cauldron, with its power to regenerate life, plainly belongs in the world of fertility. Like the magical hat of the sea-god it is on the wrong side of the boundary. There is a lurking sense in the story, encountered hierarchically, that all of the confused events surrounding the marriage proposal are another of those elliptical chains of circumstance set in motion by beings who can get what they want only by thinking through pattern. Pattern is what names the object. At a truce during a later battle for ownership of this sacred cauldron, the gods attempt an ambush by hiding warriors in flour bags around the hall where the two armies join in banquet. Such ineptness is typical of the Otherworld; even in military tactics the gods cannot move beyond their primal thinking in terms of wombs and fertility. Yet a world that is short-sighted about tactics enjoys a very elaborate sense of strategy, and it is probably a strategy of the feminine Otherworld to keep the seven human survivors of this battle, all male, in a trance during which they cannot recall the Otherworld or speak of its mysteries. The trance lasts four score years. It is long enough for the five pregnant women, who are all that is left to the Otherworld, to bear sons – sons who "each slept in turn with the mother of each of his companions" (the Otherworld is innocent of boundaries) until the spiritual population is restored. Always the world of the goddesses looks out for a future harmony between the worlds.

That harmony is not recovered fully in the *Third Branch*, the *indarba* or "banishment" set of stories. The *Third Branch* is an account of the consequences of the loss of fertility to the human world: the land is waste and empty; people and animals have vanished; the heroes work at servile trades in a country under foreign occupation; Pwyll and Rhiannon have been snatched away to the Otherworld to do work in their totemic horse forms. Yet there is movement towards a restored bond with the goddesses at the end of this Branch, when a human king tricks the Otherworld into giving its fertility back to the world of time and space. Nevertheless, the mood of desolation carries into the *Fourth Branch*.

This Branch is hard to read as a fourth phase in an overall account of the relations between two worlds. Here the narrative archaeological site has collapsed inward upon itself; new structures have been added involving new personages. But in that rubble the original foundations of myth are clearer. Stories of rape, of the senseless death of Pryderi, of a lady made of flowers, of a tragic love triangle which this mirage creates, and of a shamanizing druid who sings the spirit of one of the dead lovers – a god reverted to his eagle form – back to earth: these are all stories of sterility and winter. They are consistent with what the Irish storytelling schools classified as *aided*, tales surrounding the death of a hero. Yet out of that cycle of death there grows a process of sacrificial initiation into Otherworld power on the part of a new hero who is half man, half god.

Birth, adventures, disappearance, death: these are stories, respectively, of spring, summer, autumn and winter. More specifically, they are accounts of the changing relationships between this world and the Otherworld in the four phases of fertility that Celtic agricultural societies honored. Unlike the Romans, who organized the year according to the apparent movement of the sun through its solstices and equinoxes, taking their meaning from a mythology of sky patriarchs, the Celts looked at life in relation to the periods of the Mother Earth's fertility.

According to this periodicity, two nights of special significance, referred to as the two great joints in the year, were the eve of the first of November and the eve of the first of May. These are times when the boundary between this world and the Otherworld becomes especially permeable, and there are all kinds of exchange between the realm of the living and the realm of the spirits. *Samhain*, the more foreboding of these nights, marks the end of the tangibly fertile half of the year and the movement of the earth to her dark, nascent phase – her Dreaming. Summer is returning to the under-realm. Then, when life seems to be going out of the world, when objective existence seems threatened, it is a time to remember the dead by lighting the ceremonial bonfires (originally, bone-fires) on the hilltops, the places of passage to the Otherworld. During this hibernation of nature, and her gathering of power for the new year, men and women retreat to their homes to reflect on the legends of their ancestors. This Feast of Departed Life on the eve of November is now taken over by Christianity which renames it "All Souls' Night" in dim recollection of the time at the end of the year when the horse-goddess Rhiannon is active, carrying the souls of the dead to the Otherworld. Correspondingly, May Eve (*Beltain*), the other great joint in the year, marks the earth's turning into her explicitly fertile phase, from Dream to objectification (in Ireland, May Day used to be spent mending fences, re-establishing boundaries). *Beltain* is also a time for wooings and betrothals. Between these two hinges in the year fall August Eve and February Eve – the one a harvest feast of the god Lugh (now celebrated in some Christian churches as the Feast of First Fruits, or Lammas), the other a feast of the goddess Brigit, marking the beginning of the agricultural year. In this way, *The Four Branches of the Mabinogi*, set in the order of the seasons, contains a whole mythology.

At the center of the mythology is the great complementarity between two kinds of power, the power of Dreaming and the power of doing. The superior of these is the power of a world to which the animals are sacred. Concerned with fertility, feminine in style, circuitous in its ways of knowing, this Otherworld can be invoked by human beings but can never be compelled. It demands the utmost courtesy before it chooses to appear at all. Free of the laws of time and space, and omniscient, it is curiously powerless in matters involving the division and possession of things. The inferior power is the power of a world constructed by men: aggressive, practical, tool-using, naming, active, purposeful – the world of time and space. For all its ability to measure and compare, it is in danger of ignoring the mystery of fertility on which it depends. Each pursuing its own end, the two worlds sustain each other mutually. While the world of the goddesses is prior, as process is prior to objectification, there is no sense that either of the worlds rules the other. In fact, the myth of Branwen speaks of such a state of affairs as catastrophic. With its vision of what seem to be speechless clones emerging from the Cauldron of Rebirth, the myth stands as a warning against the modern temptation to manipulate the principle of fertility, just as the Haida myth of the weather-god warns about the consequences of natural power in the wrong hands.

There is a need for an agricultural society, operating in the memory of the Paleolithic, to keep its relationships with nature in harmony. For a warrior culture, quick to take up arms in a cause, the need is even more acute. Therefore the myths as they evolved phrase and rephrase the reciprocity between subjective knowledge, or Dreaming, and objective knowledge, or purposeful practicality, keeping the complementarity in trim. This exchange in trust between the powers of the earth and the powers of humanity is ultimately the function served by the double-narrative of myth.

CHAPTER SIX / TRADITION

Κῆρυξ δ' ἐγγύθεν ἦλθεν ἄγων ἐρίηρον ἀοιδόν,
Δημόδοκον λαοῖσι τετιμένον· εἷσε δ' ἄρ' αὐτὸν
μέσσῳ δαιτυμόνων, πρὸς κίονα μακρὸν ἐρείσας.
δὴ τότε κήρυκα προσέφη πολύμητις Ὀδυσσεύς,
νώτου ἀποπροταμών, ἐπὶ δὲ πλεῖον ἐλέλειπτο,
ἀργιόδοντος ὑός, θαλερὴ δ' ἦν ἀμφὶς ἀλοιφή·
"Κῆρυξ, τῇ δή, τοῦτο πόρε κρέας, ὄφρα φάγῃσι,
Δημοδόκῳ, καί μιν προσπτύξομαι, ἀχνύμενός περ.
πᾶσι γὰρ ἀνθρώποισιν ἐπιχθονίοισιν ἀοιδοὶ
τιμῆς ἔμμοροί εἰσι καὶ αἰδοῦς, οὕνεκ' ἄρα σφέας
οἴμας Μοῦσ' ἐδίδαξε, φίλησε δὲ φῦλον ἀοιδῶν."
"Ὣς ἄρ' ἔφη, κῆρυξ δὲ φέρων ἐν χερσὶν ἔθηκεν
ἥρῳ Δημοδόκῳ· ὁ δ' ἐδέξατο, χαῖρε δὲ θυμῷ.
οἱ δ' ἐπ' ὀνείαθ' ἑτοῖμα προκείμενα χεῖρας ἴαλλον.
αὐτὰρ ἐπεὶ πόσιος καὶ ἐδητύος ἐξ ἔρον ἕντο,
δὴ τότε Δημόδοκον προσέφη πολύμητις Ὀδυσσεύς·
"Δημόδοκ', ἔξοχα δή σε βροτῶν αἰνίζομ' ἁπάντων·
ἢ σέ γε Μοῦσ' ἐδίδαξε, Διὸς πάϊς, ἢ σέ γ' Ἀπόλλων.
λίην γὰρ κατὰ κόσμον Ἀχαιῶν οἶτον ἀείδεις,
ὅσσ' ἔρξαν τ' ἔπαθόν τε καὶ ὅσσ' ἐμόγησαν Ἀχαιοί,
ὥς τέ που ἢ αὐτὸς παρεὼν ἢ ἄλλου ἀκούσας.
ἀλλ' ἄγε δὴ μετάβηθι καὶ ἵππου κόσμον ἄεισον
δουρατέου, τὸν Ἐπειὸς ἐποίησεν σὺν Ἀθήνῃ,
ὅν ποτ' ἐς ἀκρόπολιν δόλον ἤγαγε δῖος Ὀδυσσεύς,
ἀνδρῶν ἐμπλήσας οἳ Ἴλιον ἐξαλάπαξαν.
αἴ κεν δή μοι ταῦτα κατὰ μοῖραν καταλέξῃς,
αὐτίκ' ἐγὼ πᾶσιν μυθήσομαι ἀνθρώποισιν
ὡς ἄρα τοι πρόφρων θεὸς ὤπασε θέσπιν ἀοιδήν."

translated by Robert Fitzgerald

Now when the roasts were cut, the winebowls full,
a herald led the minstrel down the room
amid the deference of the crowd, and paused
to seat him near a pillar in the center –
whereupon that resourceful man, Odysseus,
carved out a quarter from his chine of pork,
crisp with fat, and called the blind man's guide:
«Herald! here, take this to Demódokos:
let him feast and be merry, with my compliments.
All men owe honor to the poets – honor
and awe, for they are dearest to the Muse
who puts upon their lips the ways of life.»
Gentle Demódokos took the proffered gift
and inwardly rejoiced. When all were served,
every man's hand went out upon the banquet,
repelling hunger and thirst, until at length
Odysseus spoke again to the blind minstrel:
«Demódokos, accept my utmost praise.
The Muse, daughter of Zeus in radiance,
or else Apollo gave you skill to shape
with such great style your songs of the Akhaians –
their hard lot, how they fought and suffered war.
You shared it, one would say, or heard it all.
Now shift your theme, and sing that wooden horse
Epeios built, inspired by Athena –
the ambuscade Odysseus filled with fighters
and sent to take the inner town of Troy.
Sing only this for me, sing me this well,
and I shall say at once before the world
the grace of heaven has given us a song.»

The minstrel stirred, murmuring to the god, and soon
clear words and notes came one by one, a vision
of the Akhaians in their graceful ships
drawing away from shore: the torches flung
and shelters flaring: Argive soldiers crouched
in the close dark around Odysseus: and
the horse, tall on the assembly ground of Troy.
For when the Trojans pulled it in, themselves,
up to the citadel, they sat nearby
with long-drawn-out and hapless argument –
favoring, in the end, one course of three:
either to stave the vault with brazen axes,
or haul it to a cliff and pitch it down,
or else to save it for the gods, a votive glory –
the plan that could not but prevail.
For Troy must perish, as ordained, that day
she harbored the great horse of timber; hidden
the flower of Akhaia lay, and bore
slaughter and death upon the men of Troy.
He sang, then, of the town sacked by Akhaians
pouring down from the horse's hollow cave,
this way and that raping the steep city,
and how Odysseus came like Arês to
the door of Deïphobos, with Meneláos,
and braved the desperate fight there –
conquering once more by Athena's power.
The splendid minstrel sang it.

                                And Odysseus
let the bright molten tears run down his cheeks,
weeping the way a wife mourns for her lord
on the lost field where he has gone down fighting
the day of wrath that came upon his children.

At sight of the man panting and dying there,
she slips down to enfold him, crying out;
then feels the spears, prodding her back and shoulders,
and goes bound into slavery and grief.

The storytelling act

The closer we get to the mythtellers, the farther they recede from us, as if safeguarding their integrity. We are then in the position of defining myth by the shape of its absence. Probably the most haunting absence in any popular account of myth is the oral tradition. With the text of an old myth encapsulated before us in print, we forget that the story is an encyclopedia of knowledge, dispersed, multitudinous, rooted in customs, deeds and genealogies, and in the common ways of human beings and animals. We will never know enough about this oral knowledge that compels the telling of myth, and the more we know about it in the abstract the further we are removed from experiencing a continuity which, like life itself, leaps from being to being in the most complex yet chancy of patterns. One can appreciate some of its resilience by studying the oral traditions of popular culture, and schoolyard, and family – but these media do not catch the startling mixture of authority and vulnerability in mythtelling. They lack the power of the moment in which mythological tradition is most active, the moment when its orders of knowledge are most focussed. That moment is the actual telling of a story. In the intense discretion of that moment, the mythteller reawakens a people's whole memory by an act of "handing on," which is what the word *tradition* literally means. That is when the oral tradition is most tangible, and that is where I propose to catch it in this chapter, which approaches the mythteller as the embodied power of oral culture. There are other ways in which an oral culture is transmitted – through dance, ceremony, song, oration, ritual costuming, mask-wearing, the carving of totems, the painting of bodies, the watching of tasks being done expertly – but the gathering-point of all of these activities is the told story. And the instrument of story is voice – the voice which speaks at the edge of the ordinary, carrying the listener into the unseen turbulent worlds beyond the stillness of tribal memory.

Voice

One spring day, a king and queen were walking in their garden. They were walking by a blue pool, and all around it the broom was yellow. And a white swan had come to the blue pool. The queen sighed, and she said, "If only I might have a daughter who showed the colors of this spring day – eyes blue as the blue pool, hair gold as the broom, and skin white as the swan. If I might have her, I wouldn't care if all my seven sons went off with the wild geese."

"Hush!" said her husband, "oh hush! You ask for a doom and a doom may be sent you."

And she shivered, and he took her home.

And that night, a servant said, "A grey man came and circled twice around the young princes, and said to them, *If it be as your mother said, let it be as she asked.*"

And before the spring came again, before the white swan came back to the blue pool, before the broom was yellow, the queen gave birth to a child. And it was a little girl. And when the servants came to tell the king the news, he turned to his sons and said, "Oh my sons – may you be with me always!" But even as he spoke, a great wind came and blew them out of the house, right across and outside the door and up the little hill outside, where they spread their wings as wild geese and flew away into the empty hills.

The king sent all his noblemen and all his servants out to search, but no one brought any word of his sons.

And the king and queen were left alone with just one child, a little girl whose name was Sheen – Sheen means "Storm." And they called her "Storm" after the storm that took her brothers away on the night that she was born.

This is the voice of the wonder tale, a kind of long, richly mythic and folkish fairy tale, which is about as close as literature comes to myth. Its voice is not the perfectly oral voice of myth, yet it rises off the pages to the ear, putting the listening reader in the ambience of the storyteller, in this case Alice Kane. Behind her is the voice of Padraic Colum, who wrote wonder tales, but did so with the inflections of the cottage storytelling he heard as a child in Ireland. And so, behind Padraic Colum are peasant storytellers who kept an oral tradition alive right into the twentieth century. To hear a voice like this is to be transported to a particular space between visual literature and oral literature. This is the space the wonder tale occupies. From that inbetween space, one sees, or rather, hears the difference between printed and told narrative, a difference marked in every detail and reach of story, in the quality of the pauses as well as in the rhythm of the overall composition. Without generalizing too severely, I would say that written narrative is conveyed within a relatively narrow acoustic band. Its range of sound is delimited by the individual who writes alone and silently, and by the purposeful self who sits with a furrowed brow on the shoulders of every writer absorbed in the task of presenting the illusion of a unity of consciousness achieved through properly constructed verbal sequences. In contrast, oral narrative is free of this arm's-length language. It is told with a voice in which many other voices sound with unexpected ranges and resonances, reverberating with tones here and tones there until the whole story starts to sing inside itself.

This open oral voice is most immediately the storyteller's. Yet the storyteller is engaged in a kind of dialogue with her or his listeners. Even if the listeners are totally silent, there is a dialogue going on. The listeners have heard that tale many times before. Each one of them could recite it with style. What makes the storytelling a performance that runs to the very edges of the body in each listener is the sympathetic resonance of the community as it listens, in effect, to its own oral voice. It is the listener's voice that is being orchestrated, along with the voices of all the other listeners in the audience, by the storyteller. In this respect, the storyteller is simply the one who speaks the myth on behalf of the listeners. The voice of the storyteller is the collective voice of the community.

This collectivity is realized at every level of the performance by a process of bonding that voice makes possible. Though we are unaware of it in quite this way, even ordinary conversation between modern everyday speakers constitutes a kind of performance. Psychologists have done frame-by-frame analyses of films of adults in conversation, showing that when human beings converse their bodies move in a precise rhythm with each other. Accompanying the speaking voice is a host of involuntary body signals – nods and blinks and sway-ings and gestures – so that both speaker and listener are "mov-ing in tune to the words of the speaker, thereby creating a type of dance. The rhythm or tune of the dance is the patterns of speech." A similar study of the communication between newborn infants and their parents shows this synchronization of sound and body language. It is "a sort of mating dance." Mythtelling, especially when the story is sung or chanted in its original sound as oral poetry to the beat of a drum or strum of harp, is also very much a bonding ceremony.

One of the voices we would hear in myth, then, if we ever heard it truly, is the voice of the whole community. I suppose it is also the voice of that community travelling through time.

After all, the story has been given richness and lustre by the performance conditions it has passed through in countless retellings. It carries its own performance history in it, echoing with each spiral it has made in time, like a conch shell. Moreover, the story is given inflection by the sounds of ordinary community life. These sounds make up a familiar oral pattern, the daily background music of community, which cannot fail to echo in the community's oral tradition. Here, for an example, is Tolstoy's account of the rhythms of work and song in oral Russia. It is easy to imagine how these rhythms and energies are embodied in Slavic song and folktale:

(e↗)

> The peasant women, with their rakes on their shoulders, gay with bright flowers, and chattering with ringing, merry voices, walked behind the cart. One wild untrained female voice broke into a song, and sang it alone through a verse, and then the same verse was taken up and repeated by half a hundred strong, healthy voices of all sorts, coarse and fine, singing in unison ... [until] the whole meadow and distant fields all seemed to be shaking and singing to the measures of this wild, merry song with its shouts and whistles and clapping.

Alice Kane speaks of the Irish childhood memories that color the stories she retells – the wash of the tide against the shore, the smell of newly-mown hay, the breeze that rises off the sea just before nightfall in the long northern summer evenings, the smell of baking bread, the shouting of children. To speak of these sensory memories as voices seems to be stretching a term, yet they reverberate within the voice of the storyteller, to be heard as an interwoven background music to the telling.

Beyond community, but not far beyond it, there is nature. For the oral societies that lived by hunting and fishing, nature was the very source of voices. It was like a huge, infinitely resonant drum. From it came the startling noises – the thunderstorms and howling winds imitated in the sounding of rattles and drums of village celebration, noises meant to catch the ears of the spirit world. There were also the animal sounds, danced and sung by humans, with different singers mimicking different powers. In "The Song of the Moon-Bone," each of the creatures of the lagoon where the Wonguri-Sandfly clan gathers speaks in the first person in the song. I have a recording of an African drum song that gives an experience of the interwoven voices of the animals. It is a shaman's chant. Gradually, the voices of several drums accompanying the singer pick up the chant, as if they have been summoned. Soon the drums are talking to each other more or less independently of the singer, who goes on summoning even more powers from nature, each one present in a particular drum tone and rhythm. The energy of the singer invokes energies in nature, which gather until the whole drum song hangs in a tumultuous and chancy kind of order, much like improvisational jazz. The Haida gods, denizens of a similar extravaganza, are often pictured as having several pairs of ears. They are not hearing words so much as musical patterns, and probably the best term to describe the many voices that sound together in myth is a musical term: *polyphony*.

A guiding statement about this equivalence of music and myth is made by the anthropologist Claude Lévi-Strauss, who pursued the analogy everywhere in his work: "Mythic structures prefigured later musical forms ... one can look at the latter to better understand the former. Before coming to life in music, the fugue or sonata already existed in myth." The principle of polyphony is therefore an echo in human expression of a world in which everything has intelligence, everything has personality, everything has voice. Polyphony assumes that these various beings are not just communicating individually and directly to human beings; rather, they are in networks of communication with each other, the human listener being simply a part of that network. Thus the discourse of the mythtellers is ultimately the discourses of nature overheard in something of their indigenous organization. That discourse has since narrowed itself to a condition that might best be called *homophony*. The term denotes the reduced sound of human language when it is used under the assumption that speech is something belonging only to human beings, and when "other-than-human persons, both animal and plant, have been disenfranchised – defined or spoken out of discourse into dumb brutes or unconscious vegetable matter, each depersonalized by man the cosmic orator, the name-caller."

Polyphonic form

I have been sketching the various horizons of being that sound in the voice of myth: the storyteller, the listeners, society in its past and present community, and finally, nature, felt to be the source of stories, an assumption that is still going strong in Homer's invocations to the Muses. Much of this context dwells as nuance in the voice of the teller. Other aspects are present in the language of the society in a way no translation can do justice to. Besides semantics, there are also syntax and prosody; these features of oral poetry can invoke a great deal of environmental polyphony, as I understand they do in classical Haida. And there is also the form of the story – or rather, the seams in the form, for the narratives of hunter-gatherer societies are full of seams, with stories bursting out of each seam, like the faces carved in the eyes of faces in the totem poles of the Pacific Northwest. Such narrative has the organization of a forest floor. It is wild, ecstatic and musical, expressing the shapes and flows of forest, sea and the sky.

This open organic form is as startling in its effects as nature. On the beach, just when the world seems hushed with the stillness of sea and rainforest, suddenly a raven starts speaking in proto-syllables. Polyphonic myth is like that. Without warning, a story will give talking space to some quite ordinary being or to an object one has forgotten has intelligence. In *Nangdldastlas*, the shaman steals into the village of the supernaturals beneath the sea. To make himself invisible, he is wearing two Chilkat blankets – ceremonial shoulder robes made of yellowcedar bark and mountain-goat wool with the faces of the mythcreatures woven into them. Edging into the house of the gods, he sees an unfinished blanket hanging on a weaving frame. It is like the ones he is wearing. Suddenly, the incomplete face of a creature on the blanket recognizes the mythcreatures on the shaman's blankets, and it speaks to them: "Tomorrow, one of my faces will still be unfinished, unfinished." The voice breaking into the storyline was probably startling even to the original hearers of this myth. Not only does the voice speak with the sudden surprise of the spiritual, but the whole dimension the voice comes from enters the story, making it tremble for an instant before another expanse of timelessness. This is a simple example of the way stories are encoiled spring-like within stories in mythtelling, in an oral poetry that embodies the shifting intelligent energies of the natural world.

Consistency

With so much polyphony, it is surprising that myths do not burst their seams altogether like milk-weed pods, giving rise to new stories everywhere. In fact, this dissemination happens all the time. Stories, or those bits of stories called motifs, are exchanged easily among people who recognize the behavior of the creatures in them. The peoples of the Pacific Northwest adopted each other's myths in spite of a linguistic diversity greater than that of the European language families. Adjacent tribes among the Australian Aborigines, some speaking different languages, shared sections of a major mythline. Of course, the exchange and recombination of motifs is relatively frequent with stories that are carried in memory, not in writing, by a semi-nomadic people. What holds the motifs together are the ecologies to which the myths are tied and, at the macroscopic level, the mythology in which the myths are nested. Landscape and social memory constrain the myth-teller. One cannot play fast and loose with the figure of the Raven without the audience saying, "No – Raven would *never* do *that*!" A violation in the presentation of a motif sends a ripple effect through the oral memory of a people so that the entire oral memory is violated.

One cannot overestimate the inertia of social habit. Myths are embodied in the customs of a people, and the customs replicate the essential patterns of a mythology with each of its aspects a sign pointing to another sign in an endless circularity. Pattern, as they say, is redundant. Over the house door, on totem poles, on dancing blankets, on bodies as tattoos – there are often the same motifs. The replication means that should any piece of the pattern be destroyed, the whole mythology closes up the wound by a self-healing consistency. Where social memory is embodied in every person, especially those marked by the kinship system, a mythology, so to speak, walks around and greets itself constantly between the individuals who carry it – or, I should say, who *are* it. In the northeastern Arnhem Land myth-songs, human beings, together with their totemic myth-beings, are divided into two separate moieties, called *dua* and *jiridja*. The myth-songs are associated with one moiety or the other: the Moon-Bone song is of the *jiridja* moiety, for example. The populations within a moiety then organize themselves according to a

number of particular dialect units (*mada*) and clans (*mala*), so
that everyone belongs to a specific dialect-and-clan pairing.
The Wonguri-speaking Sandfly clan is one such *mada-mala*
pairing. Any particular clan possesses sections, in both sacred
and non-sacred versions, of the main religious song cycles,
which trail across eastern Arnhem Land according to the wanderings of the mythical personages in these songs during the
Dreaming, and according to the moiety affiliation of the god
and of the clan who sings that god's song. Then each clan has
its own song cycles about the respective totemic creatures
who were created by the great personages of the Dreamtime.
The Moon-Bone song of the Sandfly clan is an example.
Taught by the song keepers to initiates, these songs root the
clan in its particular sacred gathering-place (such as the Clay-
pan of the Moon). The clan songs exist in sacred cycles for the
men, and non-sacred cycles for the women, and cycles shared
by members of both sexes. These cycles exfoliate into other
song cycles which may be known to a number of clans. All of
this mythsinging complexity gives context to the individual,
who is believed to contain the spiritual power of a particular
myth-person as well as being its living manifestation, an identity that comes to the individual through descent and *mada-
mala* membership. Like Aborigine society, traditional Haida
civilization preserved its coherence through exogamy, with
members of the Raven side marrying members of the Eagle
side, and *vice versa*. All the Eagles of the southern island of
Haida Gwaii came in succession from the womb of Jilaquns,
having been differentiated into several families in the process
of descent. The ancestor of the Raven side is a being called
Foam-Woman. The two moieties were comprised, in turn, of
matrilinear clans, each with its own storytelling sub-tradi-
tions. The clan, the basic unit of Haida society, is made up of
several households, the house being connected to the moiety
and the clan by its male owner whose honor comes to him

by inheritance through his mother. Kinship is therefore an elaborate system of interlocking mythological categories which all had to be learned. Learning the rules of kinship meant, in the case of Native Australian children, learning the hand gestures specific to the greeting of each family relative, as well as knowing how to identify the individual footprints of some two to three hundred clan members.

With all of these patterns of relationship made present daily to an oral people, one may say that the culture survives by being informational rather than materialistic in outlook. The Kula exchange between islands off the New Guinea coast is a vivid example of this orientation toward pattern. It involves tribes that differ in language, culture and race. The Kula is a custom of exchanging bracelets of white shell and necklaces of red shell, with the former always moving from left hand to right hand and from North and East to South and West, and the latter always moving in the opposite direction. The objects have no ornamental or commercial value – they are not hoarded, they are simply handed to the partner, red shell for white shell, white shell for red shell, marking by a gesture of reciprocation a continuing relationship between individuals and societies involved together in a great undulating web of pattern. A similar primacy given to symbolic exchange determines the non-materialistic quality of traditional Aborigine societies. It is evident to a lesser extent in traditional Haida society. There, the chief's prestige comes to him from the wealth he accrues, but since wealth consists largely of artistic objects valued because they speak pattern, and because wealth is even more prestigious if it can be given away ostentatiously (as it is in the potlatches), the exchange of symbols keeps the society consistent with itself. In this way, civilization is both the living expression of the mythology and an expression that reproduces the mythology. The society is written on itself; it is both itself and the memory of itself.

Improvisation

Less attention has been paid by scholars to the other face of
oral tradition – its improvisational side. This is partly because
twentieth-century students of mythology, led by Sir James
Frazer, were fascinated by agricultural fertility myths in which
a cycle of recurrence is pronounced. Hunter-gatherer societies are less concerned than agricultural societies are with the
predictable. Indeed, they are on intimate terms with the
unpredictable. Who knows what you will find on the beach
after a storm? When will an animal be found in the trap? The
improvisational quality of the life of the hunter and gatherer
is carried into their forms of mythological expression, which
for nomadic cultures are ideally weightless, like a story.

The improvisational element in storytelling is what caught
the scholar Milman Parry's attention when he went to find
clues to the structure of Homer's epics in the oral poetry still
sung by bards in the roadside cafés of Montenegro in the
1930s. Albert Bates Lord describes the milieu as exceptionally
noisy – pattern could get lost here: "The farmers of the nearby
villages drop in ... They come and go ... The shopkeepers and
caravan drivers have come with their merchandise. They are
critical, gossipy and restless." In such a noisy milieu, the story-
singers have to be masters of improvisation. Dan Yashinsky,
my storytelling colleague, puts it this way: "They have to be
able to stretch or condense, and bring on the battle scene
quickly when the inebriated shepherd in the corner calls for a
round of double rakis." The academic collectors of these
songs found the most variation, in different versions of the
same song sung by the same men, at the endings of these
songs. That is because half the time the storytellers never
got to finish them. As to the adaptability of oral tradition,
there is the story of how Milman Parry, sitting there with his
notebook and observing the bard performing in front of

197

him, found himself incorporated as a figure into that and subsequent retellings of the epic of Olaf. "That was not a grey falcon," Lord jokes, "but Professor Milman Parry the Glorious!"

This sort of spontaneous insertion or substitution in a narrative happens all the time in storytelling. It is a feature of performance, answering to the storyteller's freedom to adapt a story to a particular milieu. I have heard Alice Kane tell the Breton wonder tale of "Ivon Tortik" many different ways, dramatizing it for an audience of children, sentimentalizing it for an audience of young adults. She seems to make up the story as she goes along, all her changes being unconscious decisions. Yet it is always the same story of poor Ivon the hunchback who went to get a straight back from the fairies and returned with pockets full of gold to marry "Margaridde, the Pleumeur Miller's daughter." And there are always the same key phrases, like the one just quoted. Evidently, the essential pattern of the tale together with its key phrases are held intact in the storyteller's memory as a sort of musical score for improvisation. Milman Parry saw that the bards of Montenegro generated their versions from a memory hoard of couplets and epithets flexed and ready to fill the right rhythm. As I mentioned earlier, the storytelling act is dialogical rather than monological. There is a give-and-take with the listeners happening all the time during the telling of a story. That exchange can be quite explicit. It is common, I understand, in African oral traditions for someone in the audience to interrupt the story, in the right place, with a question. The question becomes occasion for the storyteller to use a feature of the story in order to teach. Dennis Tedlock describes how in Zuni mythtelling, in New Mexico, the narrator starts the story with a loud, decisive word: *so'nachi!* It is a framing device, having the effect, "Now we're taking it up." The listeners give the response, *e.so*, affirming that they are prepared to step into the space of the story. Even before this response has died, the teller delivers the next part of the opening formula: *sont'ino–te*: "Now it begins to be made long ago," to which the listeners respond again. *E.so!* Then, throughout the story, there are pauses, statements that call for an obligatory response from the audience, other breaks from the frame of the story, and, in one documented case, the substitution of the word *nocapi.we* (coffee) in the dinner supposed to be served by a god straight out of mythtime (this provoked laughter). What I am suggesting by this example is the dimension of self-conscious performance in storytelling. The particular Zuni story is a type of narrative of long ago called a *telapnanne* – long ago, but not so long ago as creation time – and therefore not a strictly sacred story. And the Zuni are known for their love of extravagant language. For these reasons, the give-and-take between teller and listeners is explicit. The dialogic act is incredibly subtle in sacred mythtelling when rendered by a master-storyteller like Skaai. Still, somewhere between the acknowledgment, through body language, of performance in the space and inspiration of the sacred and the more overt indicators of performance (in many cultures the storyteller enters the village on stilts!), there is a range of narrative improvisation that allows a story to be a response to its particular community. It is from other sources – the invisible editing out of audience "noise" by the untrained anthropologist, the static authority of a story transfixed as text, the deliberate spellbinding effect of western European storytelling traditions – that we get the notion of a telling as frozen in one direction, like a printout from a script.

Adaptation —

Oral tradition evolves, and evolution itself is a mental process intertwining consistency and improvisation, having the mental characteristics of memory, trial and error, comparison of alternatives and selection. The analogy with biological evolution, so considered as mental or at least informational, inches us closer to the mythtellers' sense of nature as a playground of minds. It may also explain how an oral tradition perseveres through change by making use of change, while remaining an effective mapping of those minds.

In regard to change and variation in an oral tradition, it is the storytelling act that is the seed-bed for new stories. Here is where rearranged motifs and sub-stories have the potential to issue as new narratives. A particular sub-story may pop loose from its main story to become a finished narrative in its own right, or a particular motif, learned from an adjacent tribe, may join with a cognate motif already in the oral tradition. Or an oral formula may suddenly sound in an unexpected place. In the Haida stories told by Skaai, the familiar phrase "Your father's father asks you in" anticipates the sudden presence in a myth of the Old Man White-as-a-Gull. There is a barrier on this process of improvisation, as we will see, but that barrier does not intrude on the freedom storytellers all enjoy to tell their stories differently in order to discover which effects work best for which milieus. If they improvise well on a particular story-pattern, they will repeat that improvisation until the story acquires the smoothness and lustre of a pebble found on the beach. But it is probable that most of the time, stories are *essentially* unchanged by the conditions of performance. Their underlying patterns of emotional expectation and release remain undisturbed. In fact, the repeated performance of a story often leaves that story more true to its inner score, enforcing, by the test of the pleasure of many kinds of listeners, its homology over time. My analogy here is with biological consistency, the way a child sometimes resembles an ancestor more than its immediate parents. The conditions of performance edit out variations in the story which do not, after repeated tellings, turn out to fit its deepest feeling patterns. The test of actual performance can also sponsor effects that give those patterns of feeling a better expression, as happens when a storyteller borrows narrative touches from a repertoire of similar stories. Alice Kane, who is not Slavic, seems to release in any Russian tale she tells the whole sound of the oral culture that lies behind that tale, simply because she has heard so many Russian tales and has an ear for their particular poetry. For these reasons of performance pleasure, an individual storyteller's repertoire will favor conformity and conservation. A principle of natural selection seems to be active here, ensuring that the most deeply expressive version of a story is the one that survives longer. There is a kind of boundary eliminating the grossly deviant variation.

That is just one boundary – the boundary between pattern and variation on that pattern, between score and improvisation, in the storyteller's performance memory. Of course, there is also the social memory, which is to say the narrative repertoire or mythology of the culture as a whole. There is another membrane here: it falls between the individual repertoire and the social repertoire. Beyond that boundary, change cannot directly go. I say *directly*, pursuing the analogy with evolutionary biology and having in mind the so-called Weissmannian barrier which prevents changes acquired by an individual over a lifetime from passing directly into the DNA. Somatic variation cannot be encoded directly into the genotype without upsetting the whole coding of the life-molecule. Social memory is like the life-molecule. It consists of polyphonically patterned scripts, sets of instructions for being a society. Acting conservatively on the individual storyteller's repertoire, it determines what is permissible in the recounting of a myth. "No – Raven would *never* do *that*!" The musical score from which performative variations are uttered is a set of instructions handed down to the mythteller by an elder, an ancestor or a god – the ones whose presence in the story, if not at the storytelling event itself, is felt in the formula "they say." A violation of the score is an infringement on the sacred, the sacred being the culture's patterns of memory and expectation, its mythology. Thus, a boundary protects the deepest sources of power in a myth just as a boundary protects a special source of power in nature. Greek oral tradition identifies Mnemosyne and the Muses, the Daughters of Memory, with the mountains, sacred locales beyond the reach of human beings. To think of the sanctity of pattern in a myth is to consider something that cannot be said to exist, except genotypically. Incapable of being talked about, it is felt in each cell of the story it informs.

The two barriers I have mentioned do not, however, render oral tradition static and repetitive. I have emphasized its improvisational quality, and there is much evidence of this in the Pacific Northwest cultures, with artists developing local and even individual styles. Ronald Berndt says that the great song men of eastern Arnhem Land add a touch of new mastery to the old rhythms, extending or abbreviating the original versions as the mood seizes them – and "there are outstanding song men who compose their own songs or receive inspiration from some spiritual source." In a society where everybody is unselfconsciously a narrative artist, or at least knows the art of listening, there is a mixed pool of possible story bits and motifs: some tried-and-true, some distorted and essentially untellable, some of them myths that exist more as narrative gestures or resonances than fully formed stories. Some of these can spring into voice, given the right circumstances. For example, among several of the indigenous Alaskan peoples, there is the memory of a terrifying volcanic eruption that wiped out a village. (Indeed, one such catastrophe was the reason for the migration of an entire Athapaskan people to New Mexico, where they became the Navajo.)

Listening

The motif of the volcano can be found imbedded in many different stories from this part of the world. The event intrudes on the silence of social memory in time, giving its impulse to a variety of stories. Each of them, in one way or another, naturalizes the catastrophe in terms of the particular tribe's mythology. In one case, the catastrophe is linked to a disgrace done to a clan totem – in another, to the wanton destruction of fish or animals, with a powerful deity seen to be taking revenge by means of the natural catastrophe. Improvisational linkages of this kind show that a mythteller has spliced two narratives together according to a common feeling pattern latent in both. In this way, a new story is released into the social repertoire, rather like a genetic reshuffling or mutation. But the release cannot be sudden.

It cannot be sudden because the release happens at the level of the individual storyteller's repertoire. The story has to be told and retold until it passes the test of narrative art, and then the further test of the society's repertoire of acceptable mythological experience. The story has to conform to the patterns of narrative pleasure and the patterns of being a society. Only then is the society ready to move mythically in the direction indicated by the story. Even then, the society shifts its overall mythological memory subtly, not in a way that disrupts its hierarchy of narrative experience. Consequently, change acts *indirectly* on the repertoire, and only becomes irreversible after a period of accommodation during which the new myth is being perfected and the motifs of the culture, including the insights, feelings and skills invested in those motifs, have, as it were, caught up with the event. At this point, what was once an unspeakable catastrophe, and later a descriptive account in the nature of anecdote, has been regularized in terms of the deeper structures of myth.

The volcano catastrophe stories are, for the most part, demonstrations of the conservative aspect of myth. Several of these stories affirm the continuity of tribal traditions, in the face of the catastrophe, by mentioning a survivor, a young woman of high family who is alone in the menstruation hut above the village when the town burnt up. It is she who searches among the ashes for the symbols of her people and is found singing a dirge when she is rescued. A type of story that shows the more innovative face of mythtelling is what is known as the contact story, the story about the first encounter between natives and whites. There are several of these narratives from the Northwest Coast, and they are of special interest because they account for an irreversible historical change that came with white civilization, rather than an event in nature that is more easily naturalized into a *status quo ante*.

There is a Tlingit story of the meeting with the French navigator LaPérouse in 1786. The story was collected, not verbatim, in 1886. It is still widely told, and verbatim versions have been recorded and published. The event happened in Lituya Bay, which the story says is a place of malevolent supernatural powers: four canoes of natives were drowned there just before the ship was sighted. Whether the drownings happened coincidentally with the arrival of the ship or sometime earlier, the feeling patterns that find expression in the setting of the encounter are ones of desolation and foreboding. Then the ship came – it seemed like *Yéil*, the Raven himself, surrounded by a flock of small crows (these were evidently the ship's rowboats). A war canoe was launched, but the people turned back to shore in the face of what appeared to be the gods. Then an old person, one whose "life was far behind him," and nearly blind, makes direct contact with the supernaturals by going aboard the ship. He thinks the men are Crow People in their human forms, and the rice they are offering him is worms. To this point, the historical event is still interpreted in terms of original mythological seeing. The place of contact is the beach-boundary where exchanges happen, where things, good things and bad things, are given by the sea to the land. But then comes the break with the past. The old man was persuaded to exchange gifts with the foreigners and he returned to the shore with some goods and food. He decided that these visitors were not supernatural beings after all: they were merely human, and it wouldn't be such a bad idea to trade with them.

Commentators on this, and other contact stories like it from the Pacific Northwest, emphasize the feeling patterns of the story, the relationships between states of feeling which are the essential meaning of the story apart from its variation in the telling. "The background for the event of contact is an unsettled period of loss and foreboding, constituting perhaps a type of prophecy." The mistaken apprehension of supernatural beings by a blind old man, then his correction of the misperception, "represents the initial clearing out of a cognitive and experiential space in which the two cultures come to establish structures of communication and exchange." By "clearing out of space," the commentator implies the suspension of a mythology that is not constructed to handle this sort of intrusion. For, next in the story, the atmosphere of miscomprehension is replaced by mutual understanding and advantage. "It has almost the quality of a parable: of blindness being replaced by sight, of scales falling from one's eyes. Told and retold over successive generations, the parable becomes a map of social relations in this new historical world, with all the necessary emotional warnings and encouragements built into it."

The two kinds of stories I have mentioned – the catastrophe story and the contact story – show how change is incorporated into an oral people's way of telling. In both kinds of stories there is a rupture in the narrative where the event has made its impact, leaving a zone of inexplicability which the mythtelling tradition does not immediately provide for. But

incorpora- tion of change

it provides later, probably after the consequences of the initial shock have settled into a pattern of social experience which the mythtellers draw from to interpret the event with, using the appropriate shadings of courage, in the one case, and opportunity, in the second. That is how an oral culture deals with new sources of meaning. And the informal world of personal narrative too! Everybody has an unformed story within them that turns on a historical event. Where was I when the Berlin Wall was torn down? Or, for members of another generation, when President Kennedy was shot? When the Second World War ended? Or, for a mother, before the Baby and after the Baby. The personal before-and-after myths are already there for the telling. They just need to be woven across a gap.

Nonetheless, in oral memory as in personal history, there may come a point where change imperils the whole system of its accommodation. The gap is too great, too abrupt. It cannot be woven, even as a painful memory, into an enduring narrative tradition. Padraic Colum writes of the Irish famines of 1846 and 1847 when, after a centuries-long struggle, the Irish language gave way to modern English among the people of Ireland. How that catastrophe affected everything that belonged to the imagination may be guessed at from a sentence written by George Petrie, who made the great collection of Irish music. In the preface to this collection, Petrie laments that he came into the field too late. "What impressed him most about the Ireland after the famine was, as he says, *the sudden silence of the fields*. Before, no one could have walked a roadway without hearing music and song; now there was cessation, and this meant a break in the whole tradition." Colum goes on to say that what was true for music was also true for the songs and sagas. "The song perished with the tune. The older generation who were the custodians of the national tradition were the first to go down to the famine graves. And in the years that followed, the people had little heart for the remembering of 'old, unhappy far-off things and battles long ago.'" Not long after the famines in Ireland, a similar colonialist holocaust swept through the Queen Charlotte Islands so that by the year 1900 a Haida civilization of six to seven thousand people was reduced by smallpox to some six or seven hundred individuals. Today, only a few native speakers know the old language; the classical Haida that Skaai used for his stories was archaic even when he told them at the beginning of the twentieth century. The Native Australians, in spite of contact with cultivators from New Guinea 7000 to 8000 years ago, did not adopt the habits of cultivating seeds, wearing clothes, building houses or using the bow and arrow. The power of the Dreaming was too great. Yet an elder of the present day said that as soon as the young people take up the customs of the whites they are in some inner way dispirited: "They no longer have the vision .... "

The subsequent history of a once oral people is a record of the recovery of a tradition in a different form, after an attack that has almost meant the death of the race. In the face of the storm of modern civilization, it is a testament to the power of an oral tradition that it survives at all. Yet it takes only one person to remember properly. And if that one person can remember as well the catastrophe that almost destroyed the ways of his people, and if he or she can build its account into the story, then the oral tradition, being inoculated against forgetfulness, is stronger. I believe the Pacific Northwest myths of the volcano reflect upon the continuity of oral tradition in this way. But the grandest example of a storyteller making the reclamation of an oral tradition the very subject of his story is found, strangely enough, among the ancient Greeks, the form-givers of European civilization.

Homer: storytelling at risk

The *Odyssey* tells of a world shattered in the aftermath of the Trojan War. It ought to have been a quick victory for the war-bands that set out from the little Akhaian kingdoms. Most wars begin with the heady promise of a quick ending. But the siege of Troy took nine years and devastated the Greek leadership. The survivors were scattered by storms all over the Mediterranean and many more died during the next ten years. In nineteen years, a community can forget its own stories. That, precisely, is the threat that hangs over Odysseus' island kingdom of Ithaka, where the forces of forgetfulness battle the forces of recollection. The son, Telémakhos, has no memory of the father. Is he dead? Is he alive? A hero must not die without a story because a death with no story is no death at all. A death that cannot be told is an unfinished life; a death without particulars is unremarkable. In an oral world where identity is upheld by memory, Telémakhos is in danger of becoming a non-person. He sets out beyond Ithaka to discover if there is in the oral tradition of the various scattered Akhaian kingdoms some resonance that speaks of his father. Meanwhile, Penelope loyally weaves and unweaves the threads of memory of her husband, and in a court filled with the agents of amnesia she cannot stray farther than the doorsill to search out news, depending on the eyes and ears of every traveller to be her own. But she is losing power – "Or did I dream him?" – and even her parents are encouraging her to embrace a future with no past in it. Into this vacuum in the communal memory of Odysseus pour the suitors, carrying on like an unending fraternity house party. They have lost track of the number of animals they have slaughtered – they have forgotten order.

This is the situation at the beginning of the *Odyssey*, which reconstructs the social memory of the Akhaian peoples in the aftermath of the Trojan War. The poem tells of the loss and recovery of tradition as a drama of forgetting and remembrance. All of the unworthy people in the story are poor listeners; all of the worthy people good listeners and therefore good storytellers. Of all of the storyteller listeners, no one listens more keenly than Odysseus. The master of stratagems needs to find out if after nineteen years he still exists in oral memory. If he does, he knows that his people are not extinct, and he knows that he can regain his place, carefully, in the reality that is made of stories. For this reason, it is one of the most poignant scenes in the story – I think of the *Odyssey* not as an epic but as a kind of polyphonic story-box – when the hero is brought face-to-face with the master-storyteller of the court of Alkínoös –

> *that man of song*
> *whom the Muse cherished; by her gift he knew*
> *the good life, and evil –*
> *for she who lent him sweetness made him blind.*

This Demódokos seems to know the myths of the Akhaian peoples: he sings of Arês lovemaking with Aphroditê, of Poseidon, Hermes and Apollo. Here in this out-of-the-way kingdom is a bard who knows the myths of Odysseus' own kin. Heartening as this is for Odysseus, it is even more heartening when Demódokos celebrates in song the events of the Trojan War, naming Akhilleus and Agamémnon and even Odysseus himself. At this, the great hero cries: after nineteen years the oral tradition of his race is intact. But what about his own reputation, which is the reputation of Ithaka? Has it survived war and shipwreck and the unravelling of time? Odysseus sends a piece of the choicest meat over to the blind harper saying, if you can sing "with such great style your songs of the Akhaians,"

Now shift your theme, and sing that wooden horse
Epeios built, inspired by Athena –
the ambuscade Odysseus filled with fighters
and sent to take the inner town of Troy.
Sing only this for me, sing me this well,
and I shall say at once before the world
the grace of heaven has given us a song.

And Demódokos sings it vividly as if he had been there, "or heard it all." Odysseus is left weeping again, in sorrow for the death of comrades, for sons without fathers and fathers without sons, wives without husbands, and for an oral tradition and the civilization that walked around within that oral tradition, that has been lost and found. Everything is at stake – every memory, every story, every lineage, every cultural value and inherited wisdom. Those left at Ithaka are being pressured to forget; others have been pushed to the margins where the work of remembering is still going on: an aging father tending his grove of trees, an aging swineherd keeping count of Odysseus' flocks, tending order – "I know: I could count it all up." But the old are about to cross over into death – death which silences remembering, death which makes remembering urgent human business. Odysseus weeps at all of this. But most of all he weeps because a renowned singer of tales has included him in his repertoire.

Odysseus then proceeds to tell his own story. It is a set of Sinbad the Sailor-like adventures all hanging on the theme of threat to cultural memory. There are accounts of the danger-ous world of direct experience, of experience unmediated by memory, where one is at the mercy of the sea-god who when he is moved to anger shakes the whole earth. There are stories of temptations to oblivion: the Lotus Eaters, the Oxen of the Sun, the Sirens, Circe who can make men forget who they are (even Odysseus has to have his memory jogged when he is with Circe). And there is the myth of Hades, where Odysseus goes for missing pieces of the story so that he can reconstruct by storytelling the oral history of his people. Conscious that he is preparing the oral fabric that he will take his place in when he returns to Ithaka, aware that he is weaving himself into existence, Odysseus the trickster is not above inserting some white lies into the oral network to see how it will respond. In this way he periodically tests the web of memory, and its bearers, for veracity. In an oral culture, there is no official version of anything. No single version of Odysseus legislates his reality. Consequently, he is different things to the different minds and ears of his listeners – hero, father, husband, king, master. Eurykleia, for example, hears in him the sharp-tongued child of privilege she once nursed. Altogether, these memories make up the oral tradition of Odysseus, but no single story, not even the one that Odysseus tells himself, is authoritative. Only by provoking from his particular listener of the moment an answering story can Odysseus determine his location on the map of cultural memory.

It is important to the suspense of this task of cultural reclamation which is the theme of Homer's *Odyssey* that we are never really sure whether it will succeed or not. We are not sure, that is, until we hear the story and realize that because we are hearing it the story *has* succeeded. There is a moment in Book Fourteen when Odysseus appears in disguise to his loyal swineherd Eumaios, when the account suddenly and deftly slips into a special quality of past tense: "Eumaios – O my swineherd! – answered him." At that moment, the story has the air of already being told; it has *succeeded* in being told. Do you remember long ago how you – O my swineherd! – showed hospitality to a stranger in a world where "All wanderers and beggars come from Zeus"? I deceived you, Eumaios – and the deception was necessary then

– but you were loyal! When Odysseus utters tenderly, "O my Eumaios," the story he is recounting in the immediate present to the swineherd is the property of some future telling, even as it is being told in the apparent past. And so an oral tradition has been restored. The oral tradition of the *Odyssey* keeps referring to itself in this and many other ways. In the *Odyssey*, storytelling reflects on itself. Heard by the sons and daughters of the original Akhaians, the story offers wise counsel about a time when an oral tradition almost vanished, and a people with it. This wise counsel is given by the storytellers who took name and inspiration from the blind bard Homer, himself immortalized in the story in the figure of Demódokos.

Mythtelling, the human dialogue with environment, survives because its patterns are weightless – they occupy no time or space. The patterns are metaphors for perceptive states of feeling and knowing. Accordingly, like the Kula custom, a myth is felt to exist invisibly in the spiritual realm, the actual told story, like the shells, being simply its outward and visible form. Of course, there are visual reiterations of the myth everywhere in an oral culture – on totem and mortuary poles, clan tattoos, and body-maps of the hunting grounds. But these material reproductions are essentially aids to memory, not to be cherished over and against the intelligence thought to dwell in their patterns. It is therefore the portability – in memory and communication – of a symbolic, or I should say spiritual, culture that allows it to exist for as long as it has (some 30 centuries in Haida Gwaii). The totem poles are erased quickly by wind and weather, but the intellectual and sensual patterns persist. Only when myths are monumentalized by being written down is there an inflexibility – and an amnesia – built into an oral tradition. Then voice is silenced and the principle of boundary essential to mythtelling suddenly becomes as impermeable as the substance the myths get written on.

Ἑρμῆν ὕμνει Μοῦσα Διὸς καὶ Μαιάδος υἱόν,
Κυλλήνης μεδέοντα καὶ Ἀρκαδίης πολυμήλου,
ἄγγελον ἀθανάτων ἐριούνιον, ὃν τέκε Μαῖα
νύμφη ἐϋπλόκαμος Διὸς ἐν φιλότητι μιγεῖσα
αἰδοίη· μακάρων δὲ θεῶν ἠλεύαθ' ὅμιλον
ἄντρον ἔσω ναίουσα παλίσκιον, ἔνθα Κρονίων
νύμφῃ ἐϋπλοκάμῳ μισγέσκετο νυκτὸς ἀμολγῷ,
ὄφρα κατὰ γλυκὺς ὕπνος ἔχοι λευκώλενον Ἥρην,
λήθων ἀθανάτους τε θεοὺς θνητούς τ' ἀνθρώπους.
ἀλλ' ὅτε δὴ μεγάλοιο Διὸς νόος ἐξετελεῖτο,
τῇ δ' ἤδη δέκατος μεὶς οὐρανῷ ἐστήρικτο,
εἴς τε φόως ἄγαγεν, ἀρίσημά τε ἔργα τέτυκτο·
καὶ τότ' ἐγείνατο παῖδα πολύτροπον, αἱμυλομήτην,
ληϊστῆρ', ἐλατῆρα βοῶν, ἡγήτορ' ὀνείρων,
νυκτὸς ὀπωπητῆρα, πυληδόκον, ὃς τάχ' ἔμελλεν
ἀμφανέειν κλυτὰ ἔργα μετ' ἀθανάτοισι θεοῖσιν.
ἠῷος γεγονὼς μέσῳ ἤματι ἐγκιθάριζεν,
ἑσπέριος βοῦς κλέψεν ἑκηβόλου Ἀπόλλωνος,
τετράδι τῇ προτέρῃ τῇ μιν τέκε πότνια Μαῖα.

TO HERMES

Sing in me, Muse, of Hermes, son of Zeus and Maia,
guardian of Kyllene and Arkadia with its sheep, the
messenger of the gods, the luck-bringer whom Maia
mothered.

Beautiful she was with her flowing hair – but she scorned
the company of the gods and lived instead in the shadows of
a cave on Mount Kyllene. That was where Zeus came to her
during the dark hours when no man or god could see, and
when Hera of the white arms was sleeping. But when the
mind of Zeus achieved its purpose, and her tenth moon was
stationed in the sky, and the son was born – then everything
was plain enough! For then there was brought to light this
wily, cunning, night-watching, dream-bringing,
cattle-driving bandit child to hang around the city gates with
thieves. He was destined to do great things among the
deathless gods. Born at dawn, he was playing the lyre that
afternoon, and by evening he had filched the cattle of
Apollo. All this on the fourth day of the month, on that day
the lady Maia bore him.

This is how it happened on that day. Some say his mother
laid him on swaddling clothes on a winnowing fan. But he
couldn't be contained in that sacred cradle: he soon slipped
out of the high-roofed cave. Outside he found a tortoise
waddling along, feeding on the rich grass at the cave-mouth.

"Ha!" said the infant. "There's some luck here! I will
address this creature courteously:

"Hail to thee, friend! Hail to thee, O nimble slender
dancer, companion at the feast. Tell me – where did you get
such a beautiful shell, living in the mountains? I'll carry you
inside – yes, you should be inside, away from danger,
especially with a glittering sparkling garment like that!
Come, I'll make you a musician."

Then he grabbed the tortoise and choked it. With a gouge of grey iron he scooped out its marrow. Then he bored holes in the shell and fixed stalks of measured reed to the holes he'd bored. He stretched ox-hide around the whole thing and attached the horns of a lyre. Then fitting the bridge to the horns, he strung seven chords of sheep-gut. That way he had a sounding-board made from the tortoise shell, the shell the mountain people use as a drum. It was a smooth invention.

He played the instrument awhile, then hid the treasure in his cradle. Other thoughts were coming to him, the sorts of thoughts that fill the hearts of rustlers when the night is dark as pitch.

The golden chariot of the sun had sunk into the sea when Hermes arrived at Pieria looking for adventure. Pieria is where Apollo's celestial cattle graze on the meadows that are never cut. Hermes stole fifty of them. He drove them all over the land here and there, reversing their tracks, confusing the hoof-marks on the sandy plain. And he drove them backwards all the way to Pylos with their heads toward him so that it looked as if they were coming from where they were going. He took myrtle twigs and tamarisk, fresh green wood, and tied them to his feet, leaves and all, to brush away his tracks.

An old man digging in a vineyard saw him.

"Old man – you are working very hard to plant a vineyard, especially at your ripe old age. You'll have wine soon enough, if you keep quiet about this."

Over the shadowy hills and through the night plains Hermes drove the broad-chested cattle of Apollo. Backwards they went, to the Alpheus river. There they munched on lotus flowers and marsh marigold wet with dew. At that place, some say, at Pylos at the ford of the Alpheus, Hermes, while he was tending them, made the first fire. This is what

he did. He took a shoot of the flowering shrub called daphne
and fitted it to his hand. And he put dry twigs and tinder in
the fire-trench, twirling the laurel stick upon them, the male
drill in the female stock, you see – like the phallic pillar in
the laurel grove of Cephalenitanum; there's a story about that
too! Then when the flame broke out he blew on it to keep it
going, and he took two bellowing cows, threw them on
their backs and cut their throats. He roasted them there. The
hides he stretched out on a broken rock, as even now is
done. Then he carved twelve perfect dinners. A longing for
the sweet scent of sacrifice came over him – he was a god,
you see, and that, some say, is the first sacrifice that was
made. Then he took the trophy of his thieving, burning the
heads and feet in the fire he had made, and scattering the
ashes all around so no one could see what he had done. Last,
he threw the sandals in the river.

He was back in his mother's cave by morning. They say
he slipped through the bolt-hole of the inner chamber door
like mist on the breath of autumn. And there he lay like an
ordinary innocent in his swaddling. But he kept one hand on
the lyre.

He could not escape the intuitions of a mother:

"Well, now – where have you come from in the night,
I wonder. Wearing shamelessness like a cloak too!
I'm thinking Apollo himself will be here soon, and you'll
be wearing his fetters on your sides instead. You're trouble
to gods and men, that's for certain."

And then she added:

"Probably your father meant it that way!"

The son had words of guile even for his mother:

"Why are you trying to scare me as if I were a helpless
child that trembles at the scoldings of his mother? You know
I have invention in my heart. But do you know I am using it
for us? For us, Mother – unless you want to keep house in a

dark cave forever and never enjoy gifts and prayers and be rich in wheat-fields like the other gods. As for shamelessness – well, I too will be honored even like Apollo. Indeed, if Leto's golden boy bothers me, I think I'll go and bother him too. I'll go to Pytho and break into his temple and take all his tripods and cauldrons. You can come and watch, if you want."

And so they confided things together, the son of Zeus, and Maia the mountain nymph of Kyllene.

Aurora's daughter, Morning, daughter of Dawn, was rising from the ocean. It was time for Apollo to tend the sacred cattle of the sun. The great black bull was there, but the cows had wandered off – what a marvel! While Apollo pondered this, he saw an old man beside a vineyard.

"Tell me, old one – did you see any man following my cattle up the road?"

"Well, a man – no. And *following* cows – I can't say that I did. But, you know, it's strange what an old man sees when he spends the day until sunset digging about in his vineyard. Many people go by here, some good, some not so good. Who can say what is in the hearts of each and every one of them ..."

"Just tell me what you saw," said Apollo.

"Well, I think I saw a child. And he was driving your herd backwards."

Then Apollo knew a thief had come. He hurried to Pylos where the tracks led backwards. Along the path a long-winged bird, a crane, stood watching. Then Apollo knew who the robber was, for the crane is Hermes' bird.

Apollo, son of Zeus, the God of the Silver Bow, appeared on the Kyllenian mountain, his broad shoulders clad in purple cloud. The sweet fragrance rose from the forest-covered hill and from the grass where sheep were grazing.

He strode over the stone threshold into the dusky cave, did Apollo the Far-Thrower.

When Hermes saw him there, he curled himself up small in his cradle, his tortoise-shell beneath his armpit. But Apollo discovered him soon enough.

"Child – tell me right now, as you lie in that cradle, where my cattle are. Or else I'll cast you all the way to Tantalus and you can go steal what you can from the dead down there!"

"Apollo," the baby lisped, "why do you speak like this to me? Here am I, sleeping and sucking my mother's milk and wearing swaddling cloths around my shoulders and having warm baths. Do I look like someone who would steal cows? I was born yesterday: my feet are tender; the ground is rough on them. It would be a wonder to the gods to think a new-born child could cross the threshold of this cave, let alone steal the sacred cattle. I didn't do it: I will swear a great oath on it."

Yes, he lisped as he said this: there was whistling in his breath, the story says. But his eyes twinkled and glanced every which way.

Then Apollo laughed. "Oh, you are a rogue, you are! I think the time will come when you'll be breaking into people's homes and leaving them bare, when shepherds wake up to find the hills empty of sheep. Come out of the gloom there, companion of the night. Yes, some day that's what you'll be known as – the Lord of Thieves." And Apollo lifted the brat out of his cradle.

But even then Hermes had his tricks. Caught in the hands of the god, he farted – he farted an omen, an evil belly-tenant he let loose, with rumblings of more to come. Then he sneezed prodigiously. Apollo dropped the child. He wanted to be out of that cave. But eager as he was to go, he had one last word to say:

"Think of this, Maia's child. These omens of your belly will guide me to the cattle – because you'll be leading the way." And Apollo grabbed the child by the neck.

"Where are you taking me?" cried Hermes. "Where are you taking me? Give me the right of justice! Let the matter be judged before High Zeus."

Quiet was snowy Olympus when those who know not death nor decay gathered in anticipation. Then stood Hermes and Apollo before the knees of Zeus the Thunderer.

"Apollo – where did you come by this prize, a new-born godling with all the makings of a herald, by the looks of him?"

"Father, I found the polished thief in the hills of Kyllene, and so perfect a rogue have I not seen among gods or men. He stole my cattle and drove them backwards down the coast to Pylos, wearing sandals made of shoots as if he walked on trees instead of feet. Then he denied it all, though a witness saw him."

Then Apollo took his seat and Hermes told another tale, this in the company of the immortals and before Great Zeus, the master of the gods. Listen to what he said:

"My father, Zeus – this is the truth of it, truly, since I am too young to know the ways of falsehood. Today at sunrise Apollo came looking for his shambling cows. He produced no witness from the gods. Instead, he forced me to declare a mischief under duress, threatening to throw me down to Tantalus – and I being born yesterday and he in his prime! Believe me – since you are my Father – that I could never have driven home these cattle, and, as I love you, you know I am innocent of this. I swear before these fair-made porches of the immortals that I am innocent. And one day I will take vengeance on this pitiless accuser, mighty as he is and I but now a child."

So spoke Hermes. But he winked as he said it, with his wrapping on his arm: he did not cast it down.

Zeus of the Aegis laughed long and loud at this; he laughed at this sly-witted child. Then he bade the brothers make peace between themselves and find the cattle, Hermes leading the way.

No one takes lightly the orders of Zeus, who gives his orders lightly. So they sped, the radiant sons of Zeus, to Pylos at the ford of the Alpheus. There Hermes drove the cattle out of a cave. But Apollo saw the flayed skins still stretched on the high rock.

"How would one who was born yesterday manage to skin two of my cows?"

And Apollo took the infant and tied bands of willow around his feet. But the bands started to intertwine; they sprouted with blossom; they wove around the feet of the cattle and, turning to full-grown willows, made a bower over all the field.

"I slaughtered only two," Hermes said, "and I made of them twelve perfect portions as sacrifice to the gods."

"Twelve gods," Apollo asked. "Who is the twelfth?"

"I am," said Hermes.

Then Hermes took his lyre and he sang songs of praise to each of the immortals. He sang of the deathless gods and how the dark earth was at first, and how things were made and appointed to each of the immortals to command. To Mnemosyne, first of the gods, he sang – the Mother of the Muses, for the Muse came down upon Maia's son that day. Then the rest of the gods by rank and birth he honored, standing there at the left side of his brother, playing and singing. And Apollo was charmed as the notes passed into his very soul.

"That is worth fifty cows," said Apollo, overcome. "Perhaps we will be of one mind yet, as we are of one heart with this music. Tell me – have these gifts been always yours or did someone teach them to you? For your song fills my ears beautifully, and no one – on Olympus or anywhere – has such a gift. No, not even the Muse herself who knows the dances and the lovesome sound of the flute. I promise you this: I myself will lead you to Olympus and install a place of fame for you there – you and your mother, Maia, too."

Then Hermes summoned all his cunning:

"I would feel fortunate if you took up my art. This day you have heard it, and to you I would be kind in everything. Let the joys of the lyre be your care. Take this gift from me and gain glory by it, and bear it at the festivals and the dances. And whoever touches it with a skilled hand, and with art and reverence, the voice of the lyre will teach him the rest: it is easily played by skilled practice. And it suits you, Apollo, for it is in your nature to know what things you wish. They say you know the art of prophecy. You can tell the futures – now that is a most useful art."

And he handed the instrument to Apollo, who touched each string in turn, astonished at the sound.

"Truly," he said, "there are three things in one to be had for the asking: gaiety, love, and sweet sleep. I will give you my whip, Hermes, and you will be the keeper of the heavenly cattle and god of all shepherds and herdsmen."

"Let us both watch over them as they graze," said Hermes. "The cows and bulls will bring forth calves, and the livestock will increase."

And while they watched the cattle grazing, the ever-agile Hermes cut some reeds, and he made them into the kind of pipe the shepherds play. And again Apollo was enchanted.

Back to snow-clad Olympus they came, two brothers, rejoicing in the lyre and the new art, the far-heard music of the reed pipes. And Zeus was glad of it.

And Hermes offered Apollo the shepherd's pipe. "The art of prophecy, Apollo — now that is a most useful art ... "

Apollo laughed and said to him, "I fear you will steal my house out from under me, if not the instrument you just gave me. For that, you have from Zeus to be the guardian of the ways of barter and exchange among the men and women of the earth, for you certainly lead the world in bargaining. And you will have my three-pointed golden wand to govern with. But as for the art of prophecy — no, that is not mine to give. It is in the mind of Zeus alone to know the fortunes of each being, and I have pledged that none of the other gods but me should know his secret counsels. But Hermes, son of Maia, I will tell you this. There are three sisters, the Thriae, the mountain-goddesses of Parnassus, who sprinkle their heads with the white barley flour — they were once my nurses. In their form as bees they eat the honey-combs of the mountain, and when they are full of honey they speak the truth which they discern in pebbles. I learned the art from them when I was just a boy. This knowledge of the sisters I will give to you, and you may tell the fortunes of any man or woman lucky enough to come to your oracle. But promise this, by the great oath of the gods, that in all the things you do you will never steal anything from me. You will not even come near my house. Do you promise?"

This Hermes agreed to, and none other of the gods were closer to each other than the two sons of Zeus from that day forward.

"These gifts are for you, then," said Apollo, "and the cattle of the field, and the mules that toil, and the lions with their burning eyes, and white-toothed swine, and dogs, and sheep, and everything the wide earth nourishes: over all these are you the lord. And also you will be the herald into Hades."

And so Hermes moves among the mortals and immortals. He holds the herald's staff with its white ribbons; his round hat he wears against the rain, and the winged golden sandals carry him like the wind. To some he brings luck; some he tricks: always through the dark night he beguiles the tribes of mortal men and women.

Farewell to you, Hermes, son of Zeus and Maia: of you shall I ever be watchful and remember you in other songs.

CONTEXT

Literature

Literature began as an aid to memory, and it continues to serve myth in that role, preserving a few strands of myth from extinction in the way endangered animal species are preserved by zoos and exotic plants by botanical gardens. Only through literature and other forms of documentation do most of us have any memory of myth at all. The "Hymn to Hermes" enters posterity by way of a collation of thirty-one manuscripts (only one of which, sad to say, is actually possessed by Greece: the so-called *Athous*, in the monastery of Vatopedi on Mount Athos). The intrusion of literacy at a crucial point in Greek history – and Hebrew history too – has allowed oral traditions to outlive their original community and have meaning in another context 3000 years later. One hopes for a similar posterity for the myths of Haida tradition, documented by John Swanton in notebooks that he chanced to the mail in the spring of 1901, addressed to Franz Boas. However we judge Christianity, its missionaries and scribes captured the fading sunset of mythtelling cultures in many places. That is why we have a beautiful story like "The Wooing of Étaín" – although it exists fully in only one manuscript, discovered outside Ireland in 1937, the lone survivor of the Viking raids. There is a basic irony, then, in this matter of the contact of literate with oral cultures. Oral transmission and pure mythtelling are uprooted by cultures that have literacy in their arsenal; yet it is also because of that contact that even a museum version of a myth survives. And these potted versions can be the seed-bed for re-germinating kinds of oral tradition.

For students of myth, it is more important to discern the particular synthetic habitats that literature provides for myth than to blame the former for the demise of the latter. Typically, this human power-field called literature exerts its effect invisibly, like magnetic lines of force polarizing whatever falls under their influence. With literature, oral tradition becomes a managed pseudo-tradition, a series of abrupt dislocations created by each new text, with fragments of myth laid head-to-tail in such a way as to evoke the seamless continuity of real spoken tradition. What follows is a very commonplace example of this reconstruction of myth by literature. It is taken from a modern edition of a myth for use in a high-school textbook.

A textbook case

Textbooks of mythology for use in schools nowadays come in all shapes and sizes, and mythologies one never knew existed are represented in them. Altogether, the texts provoke an embarrassment of indecision for a teacher, like ordering dinner in a Chinese restaurant. What text shall I adopt? What is the most authentic version of a myth to use in the classroom? The questions are practically impossible to answer. Lacking a knowledge of the cultures the myths come from, knowing nothing about the virtues of the translation, and probably having an untrained ear for the storytelling voice, even the most conscientious teacher is at a loss. For many, it is easiest just to decide on the basis of the graphics. For these books explode with graphics. They offer the visual impact and information density of the high-tech culture students are used to.

Graphics are only one form of mediation. There are others more subtle. One of these is thematic organization. In most of these anthologies, myths from different cultures are arranged under common themes, such as "Creation Myths," "Myths of Descent," "Tricksters," "The Hero." While these thematic frameworks hint at a common language of men and women that we hope to find beneath multicultural diversity, they flatten the particular oral cultures that give us, or give up, their myths. In addition to these explicit homogenizing frameworks, there is a great deal of invisible mediation going on in the rewriting of myth. Unseen hands have been at work altering the story in all sorts of ways. The result is usually that the given version of the myth bears no relation whatsoever to the values of the people who once told it. Indeed, the literary version may be exactly the opposite of what the original myth enacts.

My example is from a high-school anthology typical of the genre in its caption quotes and point-form boxes and all the visual layout of the age of the word-processor. That may bother you a bit, but there amidst the clutter of modernity stand some old familiar myths, like nineteenth-century houses among high-rise office towers. There's "Demeter and Persephone" – that great myth about the relations between natural fertility and human power. It appears in almost all the anthologies. But, reading it (and you find yourself reading it more than hearing it), the myth seems to be a rather simple, sentimental, factually written story of a mother losing her daughter, then recovering her again, but for only part of the year:

> [Zeus] spoke to both Demeter and Hades. "Because Persephone ate four seeds in the Underworld, she will spend four months of the year with Hades. But always she will return to her mother Demeter to bring flowers and brightness to the earth." And Demeter and Hades and Persephone knew that this was the way it would be.
>
> Demeter sorrowed that Persephone would be in a world so far from the light for so long each year. But now her sorrow did not overwhelm her. She looked at the dry, barren earth, and the golden light of love came

into her eyes once more. She began to walk the fields and groves again, and again they flourished.

Clearly, the myth has been retold so as to focus on a mother's love for her daughter. It could be any mother, any daughter – all the elements in the retelling bring out that pathos: "She had a daughter who was her heart's joy. As Demeter loved the fields of grain and the trees laden with fruit, so her daughter Persephone loved flowers and the spring time. Her step was light and her smile was like sunshine." Mother-daughter affection is a very fine thing – but if these essentialist sentimentalities about human nature were all that mythtelling were about, myths would deserve their bad name. Demeter's sorrow is part of the myth, but it is not the whole part. In fact, in a full rendition of the myth, the sorrow brings the grain goddess to the country of King Keleos, a country of simple agricultural people whom Demeter blesses. This sub-story ties Demeter to the sacred site of Eleusis where women practised the ancient mysteries of agriculture. The modern retelling is silent about this matriarchy, as it is silent about the goddess Hecate, a key personality in the myth because she is an aspect of the Triple Goddess made up of Persephone, Demeter and Hecate – the green corn, the ripe corn, and the harvested corn respectively. We are beginning to see in Demeter a very powerful fertility goddess (her grandmother was Gaia, the Earth herself). As a fertility goddess, she represents more than just the fertility of the fields. According to the sources of this myth (none of this in the high-school anthology), she also knows the secrets of the marriage-bed, and blesses couples on their wedding-night. At the wedding of Cadmus and Harmonia, she drank too much of the nectar that was flowing like water at the party. Slipping outdoors, she lay with Iasion the Titan on a thrice-plowed field under the night sky. Zeus saw the mud clinging to the body of his sister. With the fury of a lover and a brother, he struck Iasion down. This was Zeus who himself slept with his sister Demeter when she was younger. It is clear from all accounts that Demeter doesn't have a husband. Nor is she particularly interested in finding one. I suspect that in some versions of the myth the mud Zeus saw was clinging to his sister's hands and knees. Obviously, no high-school textbook would want to get into this kind of detail. Yet, there is room, even in the introduction to the myth, for Demeter's sexuality. Sexual rites in her honor were once celebrated at Eleusis, when ecstatic priestesses symbolically represented her love affairs by raising a phallic object and where generations of mothers told generations of daughters the secrets of human sexuality. All of these fertility associations are missing from the modern rewriting.

Gone too is the tension felt between these fertility associations, focussed on Demeter, and the warrior power of the new Olympians, Zeus and Hades. Yet there is political history remembered in this myth. It is the story of the uneasy relationship between the ancient Mediterranean goddess cults and the new warrior cult of the Hellenes. The latter tribes swept down into ancient Greece, where their initial contact with the customs indigenous in the peninsula probably resembled Zeus's sleeping with Demeter (in fact, a form of rape by the king of the gods). In an earlier instance of the invisible alterations of mythtelling, which is a large part of the history of this subject, the indigenous myths were recorded in such a way as to give an aboriginal goddess like Demeter a place in the new system of worship – a strictly limited place. Yet it is still clear that Demeter is very much a goddess of the country people, Zeus a deity of the city-dwellers.

Myth is about human nature. But it is also about politics. Hidden inside the myth of Demeter is a memory of the end of the sacred cults of mother-daughter sisterhood and their absorption into the new cult of the Bronze-age warrior.

These politics are missing from the modern retelling – there is a silence where these politics used to be. A new politics silences the old politics in the revision of myth.

It is a sign of this invisible and invisibling politics that the editors of the anthology, probably as baffled by the version as any student reader, have supplied a journalistic subtitle indicating to teachers and students alike how the myth ought to be interpreted. The subtitle says: "This is a myth about the balance between life and death, and how compromise keeps our earth in order." Compromise? *Our* earth? The daughter of the goddess of farmers has been snatched away through a conspiracy between the warlord Zeus and his brother, Hades. Zeus says he will look the other way when the abduction happens. He has already raped Demeter; now Hades is given a chance to rape the daughter. Then Persephone (her sorrow in captivity is not mentioned in the retelling) is to be returned to her mother on schedule in the manner of visitation rights in a modern joint custody arrangement, so that she spends part of the year as wife of one of the new Olympian deities and for the other part of the year is allowed to rejoin her sisterhood. It is hard to say that the story is about "compromise" in any sense. It is a branch of a larger story in which the Hellenic patriarchs – Zeus, Poseidon and Hades – each forcibly marries one of the pre-Hellenic triple goddesses – Hera, Demeter and Persephone. So much exploitative politics is often concealed by that reasonable-sounding word "compromise."

And so much wisdom of the earth too – for the myth of Demeter in its fullest rendition echoes with the knowledge of the agricultural and seasonal cycles of the Mediterranean. This is a knowledge based on agricultural practice in a low key in settled village cultures, which the Homeric bards transferred into the hands of the Hellenic kings.

The example of the textbook Demeter demonstrates a myth held in suspended animation in two invisible contexts: an ancient context involving a transfer of power from plants to kings, and a modern context involving a transfer of power from storyteller to author. These are just two of many contexts in which myth is mediated by efforts of human *techné*, or making. Our access to the wisdom of the mythtellers is normally through certain reconstructions of this kind, with some features of myth blurred so that others can be held in amber.

Contexts of human making

This is true not least of all of the myths reproduced in this book, which present a sort of spectrum of told and made coloration. In that coloration, we may see how the context in which a myth is presented actually reshapes the story, directing it to take on the meaning of its often invisible context. By a brief recapitulation of the myth exhibits I have given, I will try to disclose some of these contexts, simply in order to open up the question. They are: language, agriculture, literacy, the individual, the city.

Skaai's stories are the product of centuries-old coevolution with nature. Their English translation could not possibly capture the full poetry of the classical Haida idiom Skaai used, just as that idiom itself cannot possibly capture the full poetry of nature. This introduces us to a first context of human making, the context of language – for language is a *techné*. It is a human construct designed to organize something as inexpressible as terror and as intangible as joy into a system of sounds. Language is a form of domestication. But it is not an air-tight form – a poet can use it to take something from nature or use it to give something back to nature with a prayer.

In a more pronounced domestication of the earth's thinking, the myths that became the tales of Étaín and Branwen were recreated from druidical knowledge by people who understood something of the natural powers of trees and animals and weather and stars that these Celtic shamans spoke of. But the retellers also had their own story to tell – a story of humanity living in the uneasy mixture of satisfaction and doubt of managed agricultural wealth. The technologies of plow and plow-horse and other instruments of imposed form become the context for the telling of myth in a country where you can still find the bones of the last of the wild Irish elk.

In another displacement of myth there stands a monument like the *Odyssey*. Homeric epic was passed down orally for some eight centuries and the tales of Odysseus are rich in the language and customs of oral community. But during the 7th and the 6th centuries BC, the stories were recorded by the new technology brought to the Greek communities by Phoenician traders. The technology of the phonetic alphabet allowed the storytelling schools to produce organized texts for a warrior society centralizing itself in cities. Here, then, is a context of mythtelling involving the deliberate cultivation of texts for the sake of civilized progress. This activity comprises everything we mean by literacy, and it puts a particular spin on inherited stories. Yet these stories are still in the form of oral poetry.

Finally, we have a tale like "The Earth-Shapers" by Ella Young, where seeds of the myth of the goddess Brigit, culled from various manuscript sources, are nurtured in the hothouse of literary prose. The prose is composed by an individual – indeed, by all accounts something of an individualist – and it is composed for a purpose: to provide a heritage for a people on the verge of independence. Almost exclusively a shaped artifact in itself, "The Earth-Shapers" answers more exclusively than do the other examples of myth-in-context, not to an idea in the mind of nature, nor to an idea in the mind of a society, nor even in the mind of a class of society, but to an idea in the mind of an individual. And an individual speaks with a different kind of power from any of the other contexts in which myth is domesticated by humanity. One of the powers the individual may speak with is the power of the city and all that an urban environment involves: printed books, education, industry, the sense of a significant future, alienation.

I will elaborate on these contexts of mythtelling one by one, trusting the reader to accept the fact that I am being very arbitrary. Of course, no overall social setting for myth can be represented by a single factor. Nor do the factors necessarily follow the historical order that is given here, which is the sketch of an increasing anthropocentrism of myth. I do not wish to condemn this anthropocentrism too severely in any case. In whatever way a myth is told, it is true to the people who believe in it. The principle of contexts only insists that a myth cannot be, or should not be, true for all people in all time.

The domestication of energies

In one respect, even told myths are made things, and nobody knows this better than a master-storyteller like Skaai of the Qquuna Qiighawaai. A discretion about craft is apparent in the way he plays with language. Skaai, like most oral artists, does not tell a story so much as do a dance in words. That dance is meant to evoke in the bodies of his listeners the movements of certain intelligent patterns out there in the wilderness. For him, meaning is not in words, it is outside them, in the mountains and ocean and sky. He keeps pushing the meaning away from words, aware that no human story can be the last word on anything. Even the formulaic *wansuuga* at the end of a line of his poetry does not mean "they say" or "it is said." In literal translation the word means "far-away saying from-hearsay," the components being *wan* (far away) + *suu* (root tenseless form of the verb 'to say') + *ga* (without direct evidence). A paraphrase might be "it is being said (without knowing for sure)." In Skaai's hands, the formula becomes a theatrical device, pulling the listener into a state of absorption, then disowning that moment of possession by pushing the action out of reach with a wry chuckle. Language here is a membrane for a world of poetry that already fully exists, in the darting red streak of a sapsucker or in the rainclouds gathering ominously over Hecate Strait. In this sensitivity to what's-out-there, Skaai is in the company of the Inu shaman Igjugarjuk, who told the explorer Knud Rasmussen: "The only true wisdom lives far from mankind, out in the great loneliness, and it can be reached only through suffering."

In his stories, Skaai does not reach meaning through suffering – but the blend of intensity and discretion in his craft suggests he does experience a privation felt by the best poets. This is the privation of language, the incapacity of words to coincide with the real. Everywhere his language is spare and imagistic, practically lacking in adjectives. Even when he mimics natural ontophonies, he does so in a way that reminds his listeners that mythtelling is one thing and what myth is about is something extraordinarily other. The other-than-human beings have the right to live out their own narratives on the other side of the boundary. Aware that the art of human surface dwellers amounts to just another story in a world of stories, Skaai answers the poetry of the earth in his own stylized way.

The achievement of style is a quality one hears in the master-storytellers. The virtuoso is so much in control of the medium that he or she can enact a drama of engagement and detachment with it, making narrative reflect on its own processes. That is why storytelling makes itself its own subject in the *Odyssey*. In the hands of the Homeric singers, the medium is fluently carved yet friable. Its perishability owes everything to the recognition that meaning dwells in the mountains with the Muse, the daughter of Memory and the Weather God. "Sing in me, Muse, and through me tell the story." I hear the same effect of wonder standing off from words in the fairy tales of Alice Kane. She likes to tell Arthur Ransome's story of "The Silver Saucer and the Transparent Apple." Sometimes, at the end of that story she brings before the eyes a scene of the Tsar's children spinning the magic apple of vision. It spins and it spins "and it turns into a soft blue light, and there spread out before them is the whole land of Russia. The ships at sea, the great rivers, the farmers at work in their fields, the merchants in the cities. The children, the children almost asleep." She says this more and more softly and slowly – this account of a trance, which is at once the enchantment of vision and the enchantment of the wonder tale. A spell is at work. But there is too much power here; such power, in human hands, is dangerous. And so she ends the story abruptly with the words: "The children, the children almost asleep. And perhaps they say, *It's time we stopped this.*" Language can only go so far in domesticating a world that exists before human making.

The domestication of speech

Domesticated speech – speech with fences around it: this is a notion about mythic expression in an advanced agricultural culture that has learned to enclose a portion of wilderness and call it a garden or pasture. Evident in the uniform narrative field of late Homeric and late Celtic myth, and organized according to the uniformity of actual fields, narrative speech is no longer wild in the sense of resonating with the cries of forest animals. Instead it thumps decisively with the rhythms of human making. Speech is now something that can be tamed or, as the rhetoricians of the post-classical tradition say, "cultivated," like a garden. It can be forged into an instrument explicitly to reorganize and contain the real. If we take Skaai as the prototype of the non-agriculturalist mythteller, these changes in the way a myth is meant to sound are striking – though the form of agricultural existence I am typifying here is that of the complex civilization – the civilization of courts and cities, not of cottages and village life. To this extent, the generalization is useful. In the shift from hunter-forager to agricultural livelihood, myths become enclosed within a structure of predictability based on the urge after the Neolithic to control the environment. For example, one of the techniques for regular measure and control is versification. It cannot be found in Paleolithic narrative, which takes its form from the changing patterns of nature. Versification schemes arise with agricultural myth, and copy the forms of human culture. Regular meter is a case in point. It is probably the beating of the priestess's drum in early Greek religious ritual that gives us the dactylic hexameter of the Homeric hymns and the other regular Mediterranean meters. The double beat of the spondee at the end of the line marks the point where the dancers brought their feet together suddenly in a double stamp before beginning another circle or *strophe*. Bringhurst speaks of versification as a "phonetic exoskeleton" placed on narrative, its model the imposed order of the garden: "In cultures that have mastered metal, the gardeners and herdsmen and blacksmiths of language are also present." The experience of voice measured out in regular units confirms domestication: a stanza is a chamber you stand in (*stantia*, an abode). It completes the illusion that the "gift" of speech is an ordering device that only human beings possess.

It is hard to apply a generalization about prosody to ancient Celtic oral narrative, which ranges everywhere in style, and much of which in any case is reconstituted by scribes ignorant of the old druidical measures. At one level of consideration we have the shamanistic chants written at different times by bardic writers and all attributed to the legendary *pennbardd* or "chief of bards" named Taliesin, who has been described as "druidism made man":

> *I have been a sow, I have been a he-goat,*
> *I have been a sage plant, I have been a boar,*
> *I have been a horn, I have been a wild sow,*
> *I have been a shout in battle,*
> *I have been a stream on a slope,*
> *I have been a wave on a stretch of shore,*
> *I have been a damp gleam of a downpour,*
> *I have been a tabby-headed cat on three trees,*
> *I have been a ball, I have been a head,*
> *I have been a she-goat on an elder tree,*
> *I have been a well-fed crane, a sight to see ...*

At another level we have prose romances almost ready to emerge as Arthurian narrative. Mostly, as in "The Wooing of Étaín," we have a mixture of styles. Yet in all this heterogeneity one can hear the vowel music, the wavering unemphatic rhythms, and the half-said things of the world of oral poetry. These are the speech habits of a culture still close to the gods, though typically in Irish and Welsh narrative the gods are transformed into the personages of saga and romance, to seem partly members of a historical world and partly outsiders moving in a prehistory of their own which is felt in the stories as a nostalgia. There are mountain and water gods, as in Haida tradition; but there are also concretely realized human personages obedient to their own complex psychology, as in the Greek. And these later, more humanized gods and goddesses, while ascribed to certain features of the environment like the fairy mounds, have very little to do with them. Aengus, the love god, may enter a story carrying a silver branch of apples – his is the gift of fertility to poet and lover alike. But there is no wider sense in which he is, let alone stands for, a specific indigenous natural process or an animal. In Irish myth – less so in the stories of the Welsh *Mabinogi* – the gods have lost their habitats and are beginning to behave like heroes and kings in the courts that resound with their praises.

The gods have not been silenced; in fact, they have been driven underground. There are no creation myths extant in Irish tradition; in their place are invasion myths, consistent with the expanding populations of Bronze-age agriculturalism. The myths speak of a truce between a new race of human settlers and the indigenous deities. The latter are left alone to rule the inaccessible and subterranean realms of the earth, reachable through the elfmounds. They are still there, these Children of Dana. And beneath or around them are the personages of an earlier stratum of gods themselves displaced by the gods of the Bronze-age invaders. These are the shadowy *Fomhóire*, the deities, probably, of a village agricultural people. In a legendary victory of the kinspeople of Dana over the Formorians, the life of Breas of the Fomóire is spared by the sun-god Lugh on condition that Breas teach the invaders the secrets of agriculture. A similar uneasy alliance obtains between the gods of power and sovereignty in Norse myth and the seldom seen gods of fertility, called the *vanir*, who move like light-beams in the uppermost branches of the world-tree. It often seems the case that a conquering people has a poor mythology of its own for dealing with the indigenous lore of the environments it invades. It has to speak through the myths it expropriates, bending them to its own images of supremacy. A consequence is that Irish myth as we have it remembers very little about the Formorians, except to associate them too easily with darkness and sterility just as the clans of the goddess Dana are associated with light and fertility. Apparently it is not only the knowledge of agriculture that is stolen from one people by another in this instance; the myths are stolen as well – to be retold as the invaders' own in the sharp oppositions of heroic vision. Many parts of the Judaic Bible from Genesis on show this pattern. Yet even while it is being swallowed, the indigenous mythology gives its shape to the conquering mythology like moss clinging around a rotted-out tree stump: the original tree has gone, yet it leaves its form on the moss.

All of these signs of imposition – of one mythology imposed upon another, of fences on wilderness, of versification schemes on polyphonic poetry – are signs of myth in a developed agricultural context. According to the terms of this imposition, a single boundary between the world of the human and the worlds of the other-than-human begins to harden in the recounting of myth, replacing all the nameless and familiar sanctuaries and power-sites of archaic mythtelling. The gods are driven underground as they are in Irish tradition, or they are chased into the fens and woods and driven up above the air, buried in the black sky. When civilization gains a greater hardness of purpose, with laws replacing tribal custom, the world of human effort is imagined to be pitted against a world of shadowy forces "out there" in the greater nature which threatens, eludes, and even goes so far as to mock the self-sufficiency of human culture. There is a paradox building up here. It involves an uncontrollable otherness that needs to be continually invoked as the necessary opposite to human order. In such a contest between the human will and abstract nature, the stage is set for the Greek tragedies to picture what happens when you push too far, when you "tempt fate," when you act blindly and exceed a certain limit. Then the fury of that abstract world rains down on you. Even more starkly in Virgil, we witness an arena in which human character as *virtus* (force, energy, personality) is matched symmetrically against *fortuna* (fate, necessity, the gods). The Old Testament, while more complex than this, often shows a similar oppositional outline, with the individual alternately placating or shaking his fist at a sky god who heaps fortune or misfortune on his chosen people almost as if by whim. The agricultural condition can offer relief and release only through transcendence – in this case, the worship of one new God to the exclusion of all others. That is the only way the "prison of this life" can be escaped. Judaism, Buddhism, Christianity, Islam, point to the transcendence of a limiting physical existence in which the self is felt to be imprisoned by its very efforts. These religions are agriculturalist: they sprouted and branched out with the agricultural conditions they offer release from. When the membrane boundaries of hunter-gatherer myth are replaced by the fence of the horticulturalist, the setting is complete for a myth of transcendence – but when a myth of transcendence arises, myth itself is transcended.

The domestication of the gods

Nature is a trickster like Shiva, giving with one of her many hands while taking away with another. Her unpredictability is so commonplace that it might be foolish to project on her the values and expectations of a structured moral framework. As the Voice in the whirlwind tells Job, such frameworks are an extension of human self-satisfaction. In dealing with nature or any of her people, the one thing you can be really sure of is that beings are intelligent and therefore easily insulted, and that acts have consequences. For life in a playground of intelligent roving energies, that is perhaps the best advice. What goes around comes around.

To the peoples of the Pacific Northwest, the capriciousness of nature was concentrated in the figure of the Raven.

He is what the psychologists call a trickster. The psychologists are speaking of some primal mischievous impulse in human personality related to the Freudian Id. Since tricksters can be found in every mythology, an argument is made for trickster-ism as a universal human trait, a so-called "archetype." Consequently, a god like the Raven is not really a god – he is simply another expression of the universal human Id. That is how anthropocentrism makes its claim, and has done so from the time of Herodotus (c. 484-425 BC), who represented the gods as aspects of human behavior, to the present time when readers of Freud and Jung speak of "the Trickster within." It seems remarkably species chauvinistic of psychologists to reserve for the human psyche qualities that are found everywhere outside it. Human beings are not the only tricksters in the universe: birds are tricksters too; so are Killer Whales; so is every creature that hunts or is hunted and every plant that finds a clever way of propagating. If you are a human hunter or forager you live cheek-to-cheek with natural ingenuity. If you shut that power out, it may come in the form of Hermes and steal your cattle. If you are too solemn about it, it may come in the form of the Raven and sleep with your wife.

That is what happens in one Haida story. Ranked among the young man's stories in the traditional narrative hierarchy, it is still a popular story among today's Haida storytellers. The Raven dupes Xhausghaana, the lonely and unchanging Fishing God. He makes Redshafted Flickers out of his own blood so the halibut fisherman can take some of their prized feathers back to his wife. While the Fishing God is busy gathering the feathers, the Raven is busy sleeping with the wife. Pounded to a pulp by Xhausghaana, dumped down the latrine hole, then defecated on by the wife, the pieces of the Raven are still capable of shouting insults up through the hole. The Raven's pieces next find themselves floating dreamily on the sea when a party of Haida paddle by in a canoe. "Why does the chief float about on the water?" one of the party asks indifferently. His options exhausted, the Raven wishes to be eaten by a black whale. After he has eaten up the whale's insides, he wills the whale to strand itself in front of a town. The Raven emerges from the whale's side, flies straight up, then at the edge of town takes the skin of an old man and lives there in the old man's form. Eventually the people ask the old man about what it was that flew out of the whale's belly. The Raven in the old man advises: "When something like this happened a long time ago, everybody fled from each other in fear." The people pour out of their village in panic and the Raven helps himself to their provisions.

In the story of the Raven and Xhausghaana the dance of transformations of the physical world determines the form of an apparently random narrative. The story is arbitrary and topsy-turvy, like the Raven himself, and the only thing you can be sure of is that is is not a good idea to be indifferent to the Raven, especially when he is in one of his plights. What goes around comes around. The bird is already in a terrible mood. He will get even with the villagers who ignored him.

This is the form of the so-called trickster in mythtelling before a myth of human power carves things up. Hermes, the lord of robbers to the Homeric singers, was probably like that. He seems to have been associated with a tradition of cattle-raiding as well as with the gentler pastimes of culture, such as music, that we think of in relation to the Greeks. As the god who conducts the souls of the dead to the Otherworld, and later as official messenger of the gods, he crosses boundaries effortlessly, like the Raven. He passes like a breeze through the keyhole, says the Homeric hymn. He is also inquisitive, like the Raven, and the inventor of many things, including fire, which he induced through the sexual twirling of the male drill in the female stock. He is the bestower of any lucky profit – the regular word for a windfall was also *hermaion*; but like the Raven who makes a whale wash up on the shore for the villagers, he can just as easily take everything away.

These were some of the customs of the Creto-Helladic civilization of southern Greece, whose god Hermes was, before the Hellenic invaders brought their new sun-god Apollo. It becomes a matter of expropriating the cult of Hermes which the invaders found there. The line of power is drawn between Hermes and Apollo. The gifts of civilization belonging to Hermes now pass to Apollo, most notably the gift of the lyre, the instrument, probably, of local popular traditions of singing and dancing that the Hellenic invaders found in Greece. The Hymn to Hermes says that Apollo was enchanted by this music. In return, Hermes asks for some of the power of the new conquering gods. "'Apollo, it is in your nature to know what things you wish. They say you know the arts of prophecy.'"

> Apollo laughed and said to him, "I fear you will steal my house out from under me, if not the instrument you just gave me. For that, you have from Zeus to be the guardian of the ways of barter and exchange among the men and women of the earth, for you certainly lead the world in bargaining. And you have my three-pointed golden wand to govern with. But as for the art of prophecy – no, that is not mine to give. It is in the mind of Zeus alone to know the fortunes of each being, and I have pledged that none of the other gods but me should know his secret counsels."

In fact, Apollo goes on to grant Hermes a limited power of prophecy. It is a safe power, the power to serve as the mouthpiece of Apollo, to be a mediator between two worlds. But it is nothing beside the power Hermes must have had when he was the god of the country-people – when travellers added a new stone for luck to the phallic pillars of stones, called *hermaion*, that grew by the wayside at the markets and town gates. Hermes is accommodated to the new Olympic pantheon now, given just enough of his former traits to make him interesting but not enough to make him dangerous. He has been humanized and housebroken. The storyteller has made him a son of Zeus, born to Maia, the spirit of a mountain, so the relationship with Apollo, now smoothed over, is that of two brothers. "This Hermes agreed to, and none other of the gods were closer to each other than the two sons of Zeus from that day forward."

We could call this outcome a "compromise." That would be Apollo's word for it. If Hermes could speak in his old voice, he might call it something different. He might call it a "sell-out." In fact, this condition of divine servitude is more than a sell-out because it is an attempt to separate human beings from a world of unpredictability, passion, sexuality, spontaneity and improvisation. Here in this hymn the conflict between wild order and cultivated order is referred to a power apparently above the level of the dispute, promising a resolution of the conflict. That authority dwells outside the story altogether, while drawing all the elements of the story to itself, like the vanishing point in perspectival art. The mediator of a structure of opposition, it keeps itself hidden from questioning, being little more than the idea that a certain kind of order, the order conveyed in the story, will prevail. That vanishing point exists in the Hellenic telling of the Hermes myths in the figure of Zeus – a sun to whom all the other gods, like flowers, turn their hot faces. He is the fulcrum of a set of balances that swings between two symmetrical contestants, Hermes and Apollo. Controlling the whole symmetry of the diagram as an abstract principle of order brooding above it, he is the god who announces in Book Eight of the *Iliad* that he can at any time draw all the other gods into himself on a great chain.

To say that such a transformation of mythtelling as this comes about as a result of literacy is to attribute too much to a technology. There are other larger factors involving the emergence of a class structure with a king at the top and the increasing sense that the planets and stars, not the animals and rivers and trees, tell the more certain story. Yet the enclosing of a story in a text is a drastic form of domestication. Literature is the mirror in which humanity regards itself. At the center of that pride is a notion of fixed recurrence. If you look at yourself in the bathroom mirror, you want to imagine yourself as the same (or better than) the day before. Literature generates and sustains that notion of fixity by monumentalizing a story in a way no mythtelling act can do. With the invention of writing, an act of mythtelling can become perfectly predictable. It cannot vary from the authorized version written down on papyrus or carved in stone. Moreover, writing, unlike mythtelling, assumes that a single mind is in control, and reinforces that illusion by habits of phrasing that suggest a consistency of consciousness. Fixing objects and values in the abstract mental space called literature, writing also fixes the habit of purposeful consciousness which accompanies the objects and events it abstracts. That is why literacy reinforces itself so quickly in the reading and writing skills of children. Literacy is not a skill – it is a mentality. It has been the major means of empowering the individual since Greek times, but the price of that empowerment is the muting and dispersal of other ways of knowing before the elucidation of conscious purpose. Among the first qualities of life to be muted by the specialized human power field of literature is the polyphony of oral myth. Body language, musical accompaniment, the breathing of listeners, the sense of event, the background noises of nature – all these go silent when language becomes a set of visual marks marching across a page. These symbols invoke their own kind of consciousness and authority, subtly pressing the newly created reader to choose which of two worlds is closer to the truth – the world of oral polyphony or the world of silent thought.

The domestication of consciousness

Faced with this fork in the road, the obvious choice for the comfortably literate person is to define language as a thinking instrument apart from sound. This is the choice Plato makes when he orients speech in relation to *logos*, or reasoning thought, and away from *epos*, or human speech as song. The changed orientation supports the ideal of an act of purer knowing in which not just speech but also the thinking processes can become a *techné* by which the reasoner can elucidate a single explanatory principle. The intimation of that whole truth impels the reasoner to expose as half-truths the opinions that stand for truth in the caves we inhabit. To that end, language is secondary to a true knowledge that resides, as Plato says, "in our minds, not in words or bodily shapes" and is a "conversation (*logos*) which the soul holds with herself ... I mean, to oneself and in silence, not aloud to one another." In these conditions of silent thought, the written page or, properly speaking, the self-reflective consciousness it induces, inserts itself like a crystal wedge between thought and feeling, between mind and body.

One may also say between one discourse and another – for the written page allows speech and consciousness to be enclosed by itself and then viewed as an object, and as one's own. In these arbitrary conditions, speech becomes a property of the individual, that newly created entity who perceives himself to be bounded by his own skin. Consciousness is henceforward to be restricted by the illusion of individuality.

The reasoner who wishes to appear to be speaking the truth must now organize a discourse so as to provide the illusion of purposeful consciousness – poetry and especially oral poetry being dangerously hit-and-miss at best. Consciousness, divided against itself by the membrane of the written page, is not merely an exclusively human property, it is an exclusively individual one. These are the psychological conditions for the emergence of the author as a context for myth.

There are good authors and there are bad ones – the good authors, as I say, give something back to nature with a prayer. Ella Young is a good author. Yet like any author she is at one or two removes from what she writes about, and so the silence of her page fills up with descriptive adjectives missing for the most part from the vocabulary of the mythteller. Those adjectives compensate for the loss of oral polyphony. And she gives myth a decidedly literary embellishment. In her style, and to a certain extent in Alice Kane's retelling, is the fayness of that period known as the Celtic Twilight; also the imagery and chamber music of the nineteenth-century symbolist poem. It helps to know this.

Also it helps to know that in spite of her country excursions Ella Young was, like most authors, a city-dweller. This is no small fact. The period of agricultural existence represents one of the great transformations of human life on the planet. The period of global urbanization is another. It has changed our attitudes about things. Our modern scepticism about myth goes back to the Athenian philosophers who renounced orally-told myth in favor of the individual's ability to objectify it in mental frames, and these were people who made a life for themselves in cities. One can see in the dialogues Socrates' nervousness outside the security of the city, pictured in the *Republic* as the ideal of social organization. His colleague Phaedrus remarks: "What an incomprehensible being you are, Socrates: when you are in the country, as you say, you really are like some stranger who is led about by a guide. Do you ever cross the border? I rather think that you never venture even outside the gates." And Socrates replies: "Very true, my good friend; and I hope that you will excuse me when you hear the reason, which is, that I am a lover of knowledge, and the men who dwell in the city are my teachers, and not the trees or the country." Of course, there is much in Plato that would have taken us in more fruitful directions: his *Seventh Letter* and the *Symposium* describe a mysticism that breaks over and takes hold of one, a mysticism beyond the limits of the written, which the Neoplatonists picked up on. There is much that would have taken us beyond the city walls, were it not for Aristotle. He holds himself apart from the early countryside sages, whom we have come to know as the Presocratic philosophers. He said they were too closely tied to the "continuous transformation" of the physical world and so had decided that nothing could be said for certain about a world that was "always and everywhere changing" (*Metaphysics* 1010a). *Wansuuga* – it is being said (without knowing for sure). Those oral sages chose to write in fragments of perception. Some chose not to write at all. Cratylus chose not even to *speak* about a world where nothing stayed in the same place for very long. Their thinking ran with the mythtellers and the people of the country, worshippers of the old gods, henceforth to be condemned by the enlightened city-dweller as "pagan" (*paysan*: of the country) and "heathen" (people of the heath).

These, then, are some of the contexts of myth: language, agriculture, literacy, the individual, the city. There are others. But one can see that this succession of man-made habitats begins to tell its own story. It is the account of an increasing privatisation of the narratives of Earth. One needs to be aware of these specialized environments. The contexts through which myth is remembered are also the contexts in which myth is reinvented by each succession of peoples.

EPILOGUE

"These things never happened, yet they always are."

SALOUSTIOS, *Of Gods and of the World*

EPILOGUE

The image on the cover of this book shows the eye of Tsaghanxuuwaji, the Sea Bear, on a replica of the pole that stood in the ancient Haida village of Tanu. That original pole is now in decaying pieces in the Royal British Columbia Museum in Victoria – but right outside the doors of the museum stands the replica, which was carved by Henry and Tony Hunt in 1966. Tsaghanxuuwaji is kneeling at the base of the pole, which is proper because he is holding up a mythology, a set of stories carved in images. As well, he is holding up the world of time and space, for the Sea Grizzly is one of the forms of Ttsaamus, the great pole standing on the ocean floor, grandfather of the Raven and nephew of the One in the Sea. Though sustaining a world, the god is not so much a structure as one of the processes of that world, and so he is linked with other life. The cropped photograph does not show it, but protruding from the mouth of the mythcreature is the pectoral fin of a sea mammal – a porpoise or sealion or small killer whale – being swallowed head-first. A full view of Tsaghanxuuwaji would disclose, at the lower left, his right arm in a conventional posture (forearm up, thumb up, fingers folded down over his palm) and, at the upper right, the small inverted head of a human being between the Sea Bear's eyebrows, where it doubles as his blowhole and connects him at the same time to his other body, that of Sghaana, the Killer Whale. One can see just a bit of that human head in the photograph as it is. Even so, the god in this image must be feeling very pinched. To add to his discomfort there is a black box carrying the name of an author and the title of a book – in fact, the identical title of many identical books. A god has been put to new uses.

This is the condition of myth in our time – the fleeting image of a god snatched away from his landscape and put up on display. Does his power still ripple out from under the printed letters? Does his eye judge us severely or does it hold in its gaze the innocence and candor of the universe?

That god-force may continue to exist in the world of human making, and even in the most banal of human constructions. The Aboriginal teacher Bobby McLeod said to Robert Lawlor, while walking through downtown Sydney, "With your mentality, these tall buildings are the result of the dreams and plans of architects, engineers, and builders. But the Aborigine also sees that the stones and bricks themselves have an inner potential – a dreaming to become a structure." If that is so, then even through their most fragmented images the gods still practise their power. In the Pacific Northwest, it was enough just to paint the eyes of a god on the prow of a canoe for the spirit of that image to help the fisherman see the fish that were hidden from him. In downtown Sydney, the essences of those bricks and stones have dreamed themselves through the minds and muscles of the builders into a building. It is probably not a very fine dream as Dreams go – likely it is a nightmare; nonetheless Bobby McLeod would say that the power of the Dreaming persists in the modern world. It persists even in the very forms that try to deny that power.

For people defined by Modernity, there is a problem with this claim – and I will get to that problem shortly. But first, it would be fair to the mythtellers to give that claim its fullest expression. In its fullest expression, the claim for myth is universal: myth has a life of its own, and with its own spiritual resources keeps finding clever ways of re-seeding itself, using every kind of human making to spread its potency.

That potency is strong throughout the history of the very culture – western European culture – that denies it the most. Forbidden literary status by the austerity of medieval Christianity, myth finds its voice in the narrative interlace of Arthurian romance, with many of the Celtic symbols kept virtually intact. Later, myth retells itself in the paintings of Botticelli and Titian and in the polyphonic narration of Spenser's *Faerie Queene*. Negated by enlightenment rationalism, it seeks a stage for itself in an opera like *The Magic Flute* by Mozart and in chamber-music concerts by earlier revivers of polyphony, like Bach. Denied authority by the utilitarianism and industrialism of the nineteenth century, myth keeps its voice in the fairy tales told by the peasantry, from which by way of nannies hired for the middle-class nurseries it succeeds in re-articulating itself in the literary wonder tales, like those by Ella Young. In the face of early twentieth-century democratic individualism, myth invents for itself the concept of the collective unconscious, which W.B. Yeats and D.H. Lawrence draw on. At the end of a century of scientific technology, myth exfoliates in New Age writing and in various market categories of popular writing and fantasy. Doubtless, myth will seek interesting ways to speak in future centuries as the languages of intelligent life on this and other planets are translated. The gods continue to speak to ears that are organs of the heart.

All this is the promise that myth sponsors – that if people could put aside, for a moment or for a lifetime, the language of the ego by which they administer creation, they would discover in themselves what Hindu scripture calls "the unborn world." The potency of that spiritual world lurks in even the tiniest overlooked particular.

Whatever we think of the claim myth makes on us, there is no denying that the potential of myth is always close at hand. The talking animals, the transformation at the boundary, the crossing into a surreal dream realm of power, the lifetime in an Otherworld that is only a second out of this one – these narrative elements are the stock in trade of modern fantasy and fairy tale. In a popular children's story like "Jack and the Beanstalk" there is a shamanistic journey through the boundary of the clouds, to steal from superhuman sky people the talismans of fertility – a hen that lays golden eggs and a harp with a human face that sings the music of the gods. In whatever trace or fragment myth speaks, it broadcasts the dream that if all of the seeds of myth with which the world is pregnant could only come together, the world would be re-born again in mythtime. If the pieces of myth could at least cohere in the unconscious of the individual, that person would be reborn in a spiritual empowerment.

Any reader of myth feels the sly tug of this claim – it pulls a person out of a dry rationalism back into some version of the Earth's poetry. However, this universal claim for myth holds certain dangers for the modern individual, and it is time, at the close of this book, to sound a warning. The warning is about the promise of redemption that mythology inevitably falls into in our time. For those of us lost in a modern oblivion, there is especially this dangerous allure of redemptive promise. I hope I may be forgiven for speaking personally of it, since I am always in danger of being one of its victims.

For me, it is a promise harbored in nostalgia for certain childhood moments when I felt the earth under my feet. Pine needles under bare feet. The mysterious life of the forest. The whisper of the wind through all the stillness of Pre-Cambria. The storyteller was nowhere – and everywhere. There was no mythtelling elder to guide me into the meanings of those sounds of the primeval. I was left, as I am left today, with an undefined yearning at the center of a solitude.

Into that solitude steps the mythteller – Skaai of the Qquuna Qiighawaai, or Homer, or the unknown song man of the Moon-Bone myth. He brings the prospect of a way of being on the earth that is different from what I have known. He brings a philosophy – an intellectual and emotional phi-losophy told in images, those images distilled from centuries of human beings treading warily upon the earth, rather than undertaking to rearrange its basic furniture. I am unaccustomed to his power. I stare at the words he has left on the page. I try to translate them, and I depend on the experience of scholars to reproduce in a modern tongue the language of the mythteller – but what of that numinous vocabulary? The power of the mythteller exists beyond normal interpretation, making the mythteller a dangerous figure. That figure is especially dangerous when taken out of context. Vulnerable to the lure of ancient meaning, we are ill-equipped to enter it as individuals. In such a state of distance and desire as this, we can see too quickly in myth a release from our alienation. And then there is the question that this redemptive promise is offered, not by an ancient humanity living within the earth's allowances, but by a more recent agricultural humanity, continuous with our own, which has reinterpreted all other forms of mythic experience in the context of its own redemptive vision. That singlemindedness transcends the wisdom of myth altogether. It catches us in a bubble world of our own longing that is manipulated by others. We forget that all the work that various peoples have done – all the work that peoples must do – to live with the Earth on the Earth's terms is pre-empted by the dream of transcendence.

What the mythtellers and the oral poets know is that truth cannot be captured in a solitary idea. It is alive and uncatchable. It tumbles about in the polyphonic stories told by the animals and birds and mountains and rivers and trees – not in some taxonomy of their separate identities but in the play of exchanges among them, which is the only way we really know nature.

Those stories are still there in the Earth, to be overheard by anyone who has the patience to listen. This act of listening is not enough in itself to reach wisdom – but it is a start. It is the opening of an aperture to what lies beyond our species chauvinism and the version of human history on this planet which that chauvinism has constructed for itself. Yet history is real too, and there are new patterns that are part of the long uneven narrative of human habitation on the Earth. The stories, old and new, will be told in new mixtures, with new tones, through new selves. Individuated consciousness is our destiny, and we embrace its power with the ironic playfulness it speaks, and also with an increasing humility for what it cannot speak. Only by hearing the many voices that are silenced will we recover a sense of a wider world than the one we make through our particular histories.

Then, when it becomes time to return to the languages of the Earth for meaning, we may discover what the mythtellers knew – that the wisdom of the Earth has ways of re-seeding itself. The wonder of it is that the process has not yet halted. I am glad that the re-seeding has fertilized the mind of my generation, and though I am not yet sure of its outcome, I dwell in hope that in whatever myths it speaks the process will continue in the generation to which my son belongs, and in his children, and his children's children.

10 *THE SONG OF THE MOON-BONE.* The whole song cycle was published as "The Wonguri-Mandjigai Song Cycle of
the Moon-Bone" in *Oceania*, 19:1 (1948): 16-50, with excerpted songs in general translation touched up in the chapter
on "Singing and Poetic Expression," in Ronald M. Berndt
and Catherine H. Berndt, *The World of the First Australians*
(1964; Chicago, 1968): 306-320.

Comprising 13 songs, this is one of the shortest song cycles
which the Berndts transcribed during their field-work. I reproduce the last two songs only, with ellipses, as in Berndt's
translation, to show repetitive singing. The Berndts explain
that some song cycles contain 200 to 300 songs, with each
song a separate piece in itself. The Moon-Bone cycle is a non-
sacred song of the Sandfly clan, and tells of their gathering before the first rains of the wet season at a particular large clay-
pan in Arnhem Bay which, after the rains, becomes a
billibong, or lagoon. This is where the Moon God lived in
ancestral time with his sister the Dugong (also called the sea
cow – a cetaceous animal who digs up the lily and lotus roots
in the lagoon with her tail). The song tells of the Sandfly
clanspeople digging all day for these plants just as their totemic ancestors did, meeting in the water the same creatures
they met, then, at the end of day, gathering to sing as they see
the New Moon rising with the Evening Star beside it.

The last two songs refer to the myth itself, using sacred-
secret words. In the myth, the supernatural being who became the Moon made this very clay-pan, then left his spiritual reflection in it as his Dreaming-center. His sister found
the place too dangerous because of the leeches, so she went
out to sea to become a Dugong. The brother changed himself into the Moon and made it so that after his death his

bones go into the sea and become a nautilus shell. Reborn from these bones, after three days he climbs back into the sky. The third significant being in the song is the Evening Star, a form of the Lotus Bloom, whose long stalk is a string held by the Spirits of the West. The spirits send out the Lotus Bloom to attract the Moon, and give him food so that he will grow and cast his bones away. Dozens of stars are sent out on strings by the spirit beings, each one for a significant place in the region.

15 *primitivism.* See Arthur O. Lovejoy and George Boas, *Primitivism and Related Ideas in Antiquity* (1935; New York, 1965).

15 *culture.* Brace C. Loring, *The Stages of Human Evolution* (Englewood Cliffs, NJ, 1979), 78

17 *Skaai of the Qquuna Qiighawaai.* He will be identified later with his stories.

18 *the Neolithic Revolution.* Gordon V. Childe, *Man Makes Himself* (London, 1956). See also Mark Nathan Cohen, *The Food Crisis in Prehistory: Overpopulation and the Origins of Agriculture* (New Haven, 1977).

19 *weeds and rodents and pests.* Alfred W. Crosby, *Ecological Imperialism: The Biological Expansion of Europe, 900-1900* (Cambridge and New York, 1986), 28-34

20 *Gunwinggu people.* Ronald M. Berndt and Catherine H. Berndt, *Man, Land and Myth in North Australia: The Gunwinggu People* (East Lansing, Michigan, 1970). *The tongues of the Lightning Snakes* is a section of a love song of the Ridargu-speaking clans of northeastern Arnhem Land, translated by Ronald and Catherine Berndt, *The World of the First Austra-*

lians, 315. For the Gunwinggu association of the Rainbow Snake with catastrophic floods, see *Man, Land and Myth in North Australia*, 49-50.

21   *Calvin Luther Martin*. See *In the Spirit of the Earth: Rethinking History and Time* (Baltimore and London, 1992), 22-76.

22   *three classes of deities*. Georges Dumézil, *Jupiter Mars Quirinus* (Paris, 1941)

22   *Uncle Bul*. Conversations in 1988 with Uncle Bul and the Aboriginal healer and activist Bobby McLeod, in Robert Lawlor, *Voices of the First Day: Awakening in the Aboriginal Dreamtime* (Rochester, Vermont, 1991), 373

23   *late Stone Age Europe*. See Marija Gimbutas, *The Goddesses and Gods of Old Europe, 7000-3500 BC: Myths and Cult Images* (London and New York, 1982) and her *The Language of the Goddess: Unearthing the Hidden Symbols of Western Civilization* (New York, 1989).

23   *The early Irish poets*. Nora K. Chadwick, *Poetry and Prophecy* (Cambridge, 1942), 58

24   *Alice Kane*. See her *Songs and Sayings of an Ulster Childhood*, ed. Edith Fowke (Toronto, 1983), and *The Dreamer Awakes* (Peterborough, Ontario, and Calgary, 1995), a collection of wonder tales.

24   *"at the thought's edge ... The gods come, unseen, to drink."* Robert Bringhurst, "Third Movement," lines 15-16, of *New World Suite: four movements for three voices*. First performed in Vancouver, October 1990. Bringhurst's major books of poetry are: *The Beauty of the Weapons: Selected Poems 1972-82* (Toronto, 1982, and Port Townsend, Washington, 1985);

Pieces of Map, Pieces of Music (Toronto, 1986, and Port Townsend, Washington, 1987), and *The Calling: Selected Poems 1970-1995* (Toronto, 1995). His translations of the extant works of the great Haida oral poets will be identified when they are cited hereafter.

28 [*STTLUUJAGADANG*] / *SAPSUCKER*. The title appears in parentheses because when Skaai told the poem he did not identify it. Yet the poem was evidently meant to stand on its own as a myth. Skaai of the Qquuna Qiighawaai ("Those Born at Qquuna") came from an Eagle clan that identified itself with this now abandoned settlement. Probably born in the 1830s, John Sky (to give him his Christianized name) was an old man when he was introduced as a master-storyteller to John Swanton, the young field anthropologist commissioned by Franz Boas. "Sapsucker" is therefore a gift from a white elder to a young person without his feathers. The Haida text is edited by Robert Bringhurst from Swanton's transcription, MS Boas Coll. N I.5, American Philosophical Society, Philadelphia. For an account of Skaai, see Bringhurst, "'That Also Is You': Some Classics of Native Canadian Literature," *Canadian Literature*, 124-5 (1990): 32-47. Reprinted in W. H. New, ed. *Native Writers and Canadian Writing* (Vancouver, 1990). Skaai was described in the Ashley Lectures given at Trent University by Bringhurst, March 1, 3 and 10, 1994. For Skaai's stories in the 1900-1905 translation, see Swanton, *Haida Texts and Myths: Skidegate Dialect* (Washington, DC, 1905).

34 *sghaana*. The root meaning of the word is something like "supernatural power," and is applied to the Killer Whale, the "animal of power" (*sghaana ttigha*) whose form the supernatural mythcreatures take. *Sghaa* is a shaman. For the translation difficulty posed by *sghaana*, see Robert Bringhurst and

Ulli Steltzer, *The Black Canoe. Bill Reid and the Spirit of Haida Gwaii* (Vancouver and Seattle, 1991), 163. For *dal* and *maia*, see Ronald M. Berndt, *Australian Aboriginal Religion* (Leiden, 1974), 15-16.

37 *Coneflower*. K. Kindscher, "Ethnobotany of the purple coneflower (*Echinacea angustifolia*, Asteraceae)," *Economic Botany*, 43: 4 (1989): 498-507

37 *Dawatt Lupung*. John Goddard, "Paradise Logged," *Saturday Night*, 109: 1 (February, 1994): 48-52. For the information from the *Gunwinngu people*, see *Man, Land and Myth in North Australia*, 32.

42 *the Kaminuriak herd*. Roderick R. Riewe, "The Inuit and Wildlife Management Today," in Milton M.R. Freeman and Ludwig N. Carbyn, ed. *Traditional Knowledge and Renewable Resource Management in Northern Regions* (Edmonton, 1988), 31-7

47 *Job Moody of the Sttaawas Xaaidaghaai*. In John Swanton, *Contributions to the Ethnology of the Haida* (Leiden, 1905), 94-96. Swanton does not identify Job Moody as the mythteller here. The identification is made in the Haida text of the story, found in Swanton's papers by Bringhurst. In Moody's account the boys are fishing for trout. Several other stories of this type can be found in Marius Barbeau, *Haida Myths, illustrated in argillite carvings* (Ottawa, 1953), 16-33, 69-77, though the stories are likely to be Nishga or Tsimshian. Barbeau's notes are also untrustworthy. The frogs are, in fact, northern toads, misidentified by the first Europeans.

51 *Hlqinnuhl*. Or Cumshewa, on the east coast of Moresby Island. See Bringhurst and Steltzer, 53.

54 *XHUUYA QAGAANGAS / RAVEN TRAVELLING.*
"Raven Travelling: Page One: A Lost Haida Text by Skaai of
the Qquuna Qiighawaai, Transcribed at Skidegate in October
1900 by John Swanton, Edited and Translated by Robert
Bringhurst," *Canadian Literature*, forthcoming. The whole
myth bearing this title is eight times as long as the opening
scene translated here. The section appearing in square brack-
ets is a related piece that Swanton heard separately from Job
Moody and inserted into Skaai's text.

62 *Peterborough Petroglyphs.* See Joan M. Vastokas and Romas K.
Vastokas, *Sacred Art of the Algonkians: A Study of the Peterborough Petroglyphs* (Peterborough, Ontario, 1973).

63 *rock paintings.* Peter Murray and George Chaloupka, "The
Dreamtime animals: extinct megafauna in Arnhem Land rock
art," *Oceania*, 19 (1984): 105-116

64 *parts of that story have become blurred.* The cave-gallery paintings
of the Unggumi clans of the Kimberleys serve as an increase
center, primarily for rain. The Unggumi spokesperson told
the anthropologist A. Capell in 1938 that rainfall is diminish-
ing because the headman whose duty it is to "touch up" the
paintings has not been doing so. "Conversely," Capell writes,
"when in 1938 rain fell in June at Walcott Inlet while members of the Frobenius Institute Expedition were copying cave
paintings in the vicinity, the moral was soon pointed!" See A.
Capell, *Cave Painting Myths: Northern Kimberley*, Oceania and
Linguistic Monographs, Number 18 (Sidney, 1972), 2.

64 *the Songlines.* Bruce Chatwin, *The Songlines* (1987; Harmondsworth, Middlesex, 1988). Strehlow's famous study is
Aranda Traditions (Melbourne, 1947). For *outside* and *inside*

versions, see Ronald M. Berndt and Catherine H. Berndt, *The World of the First Australians*, 327.

65 *"put themselves in spirit."* See *Man, Land, and Myth*, 19. In *Australian Aboriginal Religion*, 8, R.M. Berndt points out that the Dreaming does not refer to a period when the world, as Aborigines know it, was created. The landscape is already assumed to be there. Rather, the Dreaming refers to the process of preparing that world for humans.

65 *mythline of the honey-ant ancestors.* T.G.H. Strehlow, "Culture, Social Structures, and Environment in Aboriginal Central Australia," in Ronald M. Berndt and Catherine H. Berndt, ed. *Aboriginal Man in Australia: Essays in Honour of A.P. Elkin* (Sydney and London, 1965): 121-145, at 129

66 *A.E. Newsome.* "The Eco-Mythology of the Red Kangaroo in Central Australia," *Mankind*, 12:4 (December, 1980): 327-333

68 *the first rock.* Swanton, *Haida Texts and Myths: Skidegate Dialect,* 110

70 *"it fits together snugly."* The Black Canoe, 67

70 *Demeter.* Robert Graves, *The Greek Myths*, 2 volumes (Harmondsworth, Middlesex, 1955), I, 92-6, for these identifications

72 *Ayer's Rock.* Bill Harney, *To Ayer's Rock and Beyond* (Victoria, Australia, 1988), 104

73 *Táin Bó Cuailnge* ("The Cattle Raid of Cooley"). *The Táin, Translated from the Irish Epic Táin Bó Cuailnge* by Thomas Kin-

sella, with brush drawings by Louis le Brocquy (1969; London and New York, 1970), 63-4. The second quotation is at 252.

76   *Brennus.* Junianus Justinus, *Historiarum Philippicarum,* xxiv. 6.

76   *Joseph Campbell.* See the *Historical Atlas of World Mythology* (New York, 1988), volume I, part 2. The quotation that ends, "These people thanked the animal" is from *The Power of Myth* (New York, 1988), 74. See Paul Shepard and Barry Sanders, *The Sacred Paw: The Bear in Nature, Myth, and Literature* (New York, 1985). For *seals as human-looking fairies,* David Thomson, *The People of the Sea: A Journey in Search of the Seal Legends* (1954; London, 1980). Among the many Scots and Irish clans and families who claim a seal as an ancestor is my family.

77   *Agnes Haldane.* The story is found, among several variants, in Barbeau's misnamed *Haida Myths,* 117-129. In quotation from this myth, Nishga misspellings have been corrected and translations have been provided by Bringhurst. In the story, Laxangida means "Fishrake Place," a place where eulachon were fished with rakes, now simply called Angida, a village site about 30 km upriver from Kincolith, opposite the present village of Greenville. The Naga'on household owned a village site right next to Laxangida.

86   *TOCHMARC ETAINE / THE WOOING OF ÉTAÍN.* With its pronounced matriarchal focus, Celtic myth returns again and again to the situation of a goddess who is loved at once by her divine husband and by a mortal king, on whose realm she bestows the gifts of poetry and fertility. The Irish storytellers, like the Haida, grouped their tales in suites, and *Tochmarc Etaine* is actually the title of three related myths, the second of which is reproduced here. Mentioned in the ancient lists as Prime Stories, these short narratives were evi-

dently foretales (*remscéla*) to the saga of Conaire Mor, the Great King of Tara, regarded by several clans as their ancestor. The foretales depict Conaire's descendance from Étaín, the goddess of astonishing beauty who was a poet and Otherworld helper to kings.

The Étaín tales were recorded in the ninth century in a manuscript lost to the Viking raids. An incomplete retelling was made by monks during the second half of the 11th century in a manuscript called *The Book of the Dun Cow* (*Lebor na huidre*), so named after a famous cow belonging to Saint Cíaran of the cathedral of Clonmacnois where the story was rewritten. In 1937, the first complete version of the three linked tales was discovered in a 14th-century manuscript, the *Yellow Book of Lecan*, now in the National Library of Ireland. Among several references to the Étaín myth is a 16th-century embellishment found in the Egerton (1782) collection in the British Museum. The text reproduced here is that found in the *Yellow Book of Lecan*, published by Osborn Bergin and R.I. Best in *Eriu*, 12 (1937): 137-193. The translation is based on this text and on texts from *The Book of the Dun Cow*, reproduced by A.H. Leahy, *Heroic Romances of Ireland*, 2 volumes (London, 1905-6), II, 145-161. The section describing Eochaid's vision of Étaín ("There is a poem that tells of how he first saw the goddess ...") is inserted from the Egerton manuscript, adapted from Leahy, *Heroic Romances*, I, 12.

The piece of regular verse standing as overture to the tale is transposed from a later position in the story where Midir reveals himself to Étaín on the rise at Tara. Leahy notes that composition in regular verse is commonly done for descriptive moments in the sagas. This poem has fewer internal rhymes than is usual in regular Irish verse. The first appearance of the god Midir to the mortal Eochaid shows a second kind of descriptive style, which is achieved in a prose succession of images, sometimes with no verb or with the same verb repeated so as to give a brilliant word-picture. The style seems to be reserved for descriptions of the supernatural and may be a scribal memory of the ancient druidic forms. I have tried to recreate it in the account of Eochaid's vision of Étaín bathing, a scene probably influenced by epiphanies of a goddess in the Greek and Latin classics.

The first three paragraphs of the translation are a condensed paraphrase of the first foretale, which tells of the birth of Aengus and how he obtains Étaín for Midir by clearing twelve plains and creating twelve rivers (only nine are named in the story) for the King of Ulster and by giving the king his daughter's weight in silver and gold. The phrase *elfmound of the Boyne* refers to the Newgrange tumulus in County Meath.

101 *Síd Ban Find.* On Slievenamon in County Tipperary. The third mythological foretale goes on to tell how Eochaid and his men proceed to dig up the elfmounds until Midir offers to return Étaín. Instead he produces fifty women who resemble the goddess perfectly. Eochaid, hoping to identify his queen as the one who is the best at pouring drink in Ireland, makes his choice and is satisfied. But he chooses wrong. Eventually Midir comes to tell him that the woman Eochaid has chosen and has now slept with is in fact the daughter of Étaín, pregnant when she left the king. The child born of Eochaid's incest is driven out, but she is brought up by herdspeople until she is noticed by King Etarscél, who takes her as his wife, to become the mother of the Great King Conaire.

104 *cyfarwyddyd.* Alwyn Rees and Brinley Rees, *Celtic Heritage: Ancient Tradition in Ireland and Wales* (London, 1961), 212. *Druid* (Welsh, *derwydd*) is derived from the root *drui* meaning "wisdom."

105 *xhaaidhla.* Bringhurst and Steltzer, 16

107 *widdershins.* In Irish custom until fairly recently, the sun- wise or right-hand-wise turn was considered lucky; the widdershins turn unlucky. Except for turning a plow-team at the end of a furrow, it was proper to perform all actions right-hand-wise. Séan O Súilleabháin, *A Handbook of Irish Folklore* (Dublin, 1942), 373

108 *a Haida myth.* "John Sky's 'One They Gave Away' translated from the Haida by Robert Bringhurst," in Brian Swann, ed. *Coming to Light: Contemporary Translations of the Native Literatures of North America* (New York, 1994), lines 428 and 436

108 *Mabinogi.* See the endnote for the myth of "Branwen" placed at the beginning of chapter 5.

109 *Gráinne.* Padraic Colum, *The King of Ireland's Son* (1920; New York and London, 1926), 126, 301, 302

111 *"moment that can not be seen."* Marjorie Halpin, *The Graphic Art of Robert Davidson, Haida* (Vancouver, 1979), 11

112 *Sir James Frazer.* See *The Golden Bough: A Study in Magic and Religion* (London, 1922): 525-547.

113 *boundary between ... what it is functionally useful to know.* This argument is made by Gregory Bateson and Mary Catherine Bateson, *Angels Fear: Towards an Epistemology of the Sacred* (New York, 1987), 69-81.

114 *A Buryat story.* Translated from Russian by the storyteller Kira Van Deusen as "The Hunter with the Tiresome Wife" (unpublished). There are many stories with a similar plot and

meaning, including a Balinese one involving the folk hero Adji Darma, which Gregory Bateson retells, *Angels Fear*, 78-9.

116 *Uncle Bul.* Conversations in 1988 with Uncle Bul and Bobby McLeod, in Lawlor, *Voices of the First Day*, 373. The phrase *other elders* refers to members of the Walbiri, a Western Desert people, quoted in Nancy D. Munn, "The Transformation of Subjects into Objects in Walbiri and Pitjantjarjara Myths," in M. Charlesworth, H. Morphy, D. Bell and K. Maddock, ed. *Religion in Aboriginal Australia: An Anthology* (St. Lucia, Queensland, 1984), cited in Lawlor, 36.

117 *"dialogues with the spirits."* See *Dialogues avec les esprits*, on CD *Gabon musique des pygmées Bibayak: chantres de l'épopée*, by Pierre Sallée, Musée des arts et des traditions de Libreville (Ocora: Radio France, 1989). The recording referred to was made at the Elone Encampment, Minvoul, Gaboun, March, 1973. For *the tabla*, I thank Brian Sanderson, a student of the *tabla* traditions in Luknow, India, for this information.

119 *myths arranged in suites for performance.* For example, the story of "The Woman who Married a Bear" is linked in Tsimshian performance tradition with the tale of *Gunaxhneisemgad* (Haida: *Nanasimget*), who went to the world beneath the sea. Skaai's *Nangdldastlas* is the first movement of a three-part suite mapping the world of human beings in relation to the sea, then the forest, then the sky.

119 *"common surface people."* The Haida is *xhaaidhla xhaaidaghaai*. Another epithet is "ordinary surface birds" (*xhaaidla xitiit ghidaai*). The idea is common in the original metaphysics of America. "The Islands at the Boundary of the World" is a translation of *Xaaidlagha Gwaayaai*. See Bringhurst's notes to John Sky's "One They Gave Away."

120 *Walter of the Qaayahllaanas.* The myth is *Ghungghang lanaagha gha nang xhitiit ttsinhlgwangxidaghan* ("In his Father's Village, Someone Was Just About to Go Out Hunting Birds") by Walter of the Sealion People (Walter McGregor). Transcribed by John Swanton in *Haida Texts and Myths*, 264-268, edited and translated by Robert Bringhurst (unpublished).

125 *THE EARTH-SHAPERS.* A literary composition with no known source in manuscript tradition, this story is the preface to the myths of the goddesses and gods of Ireland recreated by Ella Young in *Celtic Wonder Tales*, illustrated by Maud Gonne (1910; Edinburgh, 1985), 3-11.

The Celtic tribes that reached Ireland from the 6th century BC on brought with them a mythology in which Brigit, "the exalted one," was prominent. Her traditions transcended those of local deities in western Europe, providing a focus of worship and unity among diverse tribes such as the Brigantes, who took their name from the goddess whom Julius Caesar called "the Gaelic Minerva." In Ireland, she was one of the spiritual elite of wizards, druids, artisan-gods and chieftain gods and goddesses called the *Tuatha Dé Danann*, or the children or the clanspeople of the goddess Dana. Dana (or Danu) is the ancestral goddess and Earth Mother. Her kin are Aengus, the youthful and impetuous god found in many love stories; Ogma, the god of writing and eloquence and the guide of souls; Nuada, the king of the Dé Dananns who led them into Ireland; Midir, associated by his name with judgeship; the Dagda, who with his Cauldron of Rebirth represents the processes of fertility; and Manannán, a sea god later assimilated to the divine clan by mythtellers in the 11th century.

Much of Irish mythology was recorded from folk echoes of oral tradition by Christian scribes anxious to preserve a heritage and merge it with the new belief. For that reason, one needs to be careful about matters of provenance. For example, the arts of oral poetry, healing and midwifery are sacred to Brigit, who is also said to be the patroness of domestic animals. *Imbolg*, the name of her feast day of February 1st, means parturition and refers to the birth of animals in the spring. But these attributes are more firmly invested in the 5th-century saint of the same name who is said to have founded the major religious center on the plain of Kildare at a sanctuary long sacred to the Druids (*Cill Dara* – "Church of the Oak"), and so it is possible that the magic cloak and some other attributes passed through literature from the saint to the goddess, rather than the other way round.

With their talismans – the spear of Victory, the Sword of Nuada from which no opponent escaped, the Cauldron of the Dagda, and the Stone of Destiny, which cries out when touched by the rightful king – the gods move through a number of worlds: Tir-na-moe, "the Land of Heart's Delight"; Tir-nan-Oge, "the Land of the Ever Young"; and Moy Mell, "the Delightful Plain."

134 *Ella Young's version.* "The Golden Fly," *Celtic Wonder Tales*, 129-141, at 141, as told by Alice Kane, *The Dreamer Awakes*

134 *sghaalang.* Bringhurst and Steltzer, 163

136 *"Everything is different, the balance is gone."* Marie-Louise von Franz, *Number and Time* (Evanston, Illinois, 1974), cited in Lawlor, *Voices of the First Day*, 252

137 *the unborn, to the living, to the dead.* See *Voices of the First Day*, 35-43.

138 *the Aranda verb.* T.G.H. Strehlow, *Aranda Traditions*, xx-xxi. For *Inu words for snow*, Margaret Visser, "It' snowing what to say," *Saturday Night*, 109:1 (February, 1994): 30

138 *the Cetacea.* Stirling Brunnell, "The Evolution of Cetacean Intelligence," in Joan McIntyre, ed. for Project Jonah, *Mind in the Waters* (Toronto, 1974), 52-59

139 *perception is a kind of breathing.* Richard Broxton Onians, *The Origins of European Thought: about the Body, the Mind, the Soul, the World, Time and Fate,* 2nd ed. (1951; Cambridge, 1954), 75 and 82-3. For an account of thought categories as derived from bodily functions or states, see George Lakoff, *Women, Fire, and Dangerous Things: What Categories Reveal about the Mind* (Chicago and London, 1987).

140 *one of Plato's dialogues.* See *Phaedrus,* 275a.

142 *"Excess of sorrow laughs. Excess of joy weeps."* William Blake, *The Marriage of Heaven and Hell* (1793), plate 8, line 26, in David V. Erdman, ed. *The Poetry and Prose of William Blake* (Garden City, New York, 1965), 36

145 *A Tlingit elder.* Elizabeth Nyman, with Jeff Leer. *Gágiwdul.àt: Brought Forth to Reconfirm. The Legacy of a Taku River Tlingit Clan* (Whitehorse, Yukon, and Fairbanks, Alaska, 1993): "The History of the Taku Yanyèdí," lines 284 and 257 (p 24-5, 22-3)

145 *Exodus 3:14.* "I will be what I will be" – an interpretation of the Authorized Version's "I am that I am" or "I am what I am." See Northrop Frye's comment in *The Great Code: The Bible and Literature* (New York and Toronto, 1982), 17. For the epithet of the Raven, see Bringhurst and Steltzer, 49.

146 *Jaime de Angulo.* See *Indian Tales* (New York, 1953), 240.

150 *BRANWEN VERCH LLYR / BRANWEN, DAUGHTER OF LLŶR.* The standard Welsh text is Ifor Williams, ed. *Pedeir Keinc y Mabinogi* (1930; Cardiff, 1964), but for tradition's sake the extract reproduced here is from the first edition of the Welsh stories, which has given its title to subsequent editions and translations: Lady Charlotte Guest, *The Mabinogion. From the Llyfr Coch o Hergest and other Welsh manuscripts, with an English Translation and Notes.* 3 volumes (London, 1838-49), III, 81-140. Lady Guest's edition is based on one of two Welsh collections in which the story survives: *Llyfr Coch Hergest (The Red Book of Hergest)*, written between 1375 and 1425, now in the Library of Jesus College, Oxford. The other manuscript is *Llyfr Gwyn Rhydderch (The White Book of Rhydderch)*, of the period 1300 to 1325, National Library of Wales, Aberystwyth. Welsh manuscript history suggests some of the *Mabinogion* material had been written down earlier in the form in which we have it, and there is more than sentimental reason to suppose that the myths were given shape by Rhygyfarch ap Sulien (died, 1099), a learned scholar-storyteller who wrote this lament: "Nothing is of any use to me now, but the power of giving: neither the law, nor learning, nor great fame, nor the deep-resounding glory of nobility, nor honor formerly held, not riches, not wise teaching, not deeds nor arts, not reverence of God, not old age; none of these things retains its station, nor any power" (MS Cotton Faustina C1, Part II, fols 66-93).

152 *Matholwch.* The text identifies him as the king of Ireland, and the action of the story next moves to that island to the west which the goddesses favored. In these mentions, and at the end of the tale, I have omitted the historical naming that grew on top of a myth of a raid upon the Otherworld. "The Island of the Mighty" is the name that the original text gives to Wales.

167 *"Night, thou foule Mother of annoyance sad ..."* Edmund Spenser, *The Faerie Queene* (1590), III. iv. 55. I am quoting the J.C. Smith, ed. *The Poetical Works of Edmund Spenser*, 3 volumes (1909; Oxford, 1961). Spenser follows sources in Hesiod (*Theogony*, 116-125, 211-225), Virgil (*Aeneid*, V.721-39, VIII. 369) and Cicero (*On the Nature of the Gods*, iii.17).

167 *Gallic War. De Bello Gallico*, vi. 18. They defined "the division of every season, not by the number of days, but of nights; their birthdays and the beginnings of months and years they observe in such order that day follows night." For night as belonging to the spirits, see T. Gwynn Jones, *Welsh Folklore and Folk-Custom* (London, 1930), 196.

168 *Hajime Nakamura*. See *Ways of Thinking of Eastern Peoples: India, China, Tibet, Japan*, translated and ed. Philip P. Wiener (1964; Honolulu, 1981), 350.

168 *The Voyage of Bran*. Edited and translated by Kuno Meyer (London, 1895). The phrase is still heard in connection with storytelling in Ireland.

170 *"Something encircled his hat ..."* "John Sky's 'One They Gave Away,'" lines 46-54. The quotation that begins, "unwilling to eat in this way," is at lines 326-30.

172 *mab*. Or, "the material pertaining to the god Maponos." See Eric P. Hamp, "Mabinogi," *Transactions of the Honourable Society of Cymmrodorion* (1972-3): 95-103.

173 *"Summer Song."* Caitlín Matthews' translation. *Mabon and the Mysteries of Britain: An Exploration of "The Mabinogion"* (London and New York, 1987), 24. Hafgan could also mean "Summer-White" and, as such, is pitted against Arawn in his grey-brown hunting outfit, suggesting winter. See R.S.

Loomis, *Wales and the Arthurian Legend* (1956; London, 1977), 81.

174 *"and of all he had ever seen to converse with …"* As translated by Gwyn Jones and Thomas Jones, *The Mabinogion* (1948; revised edition, London, 1989), 5-6

175 *"Radiance, Son of Light."* Caitlín Matthews' translation, 27

175 *compert.* W.J. Gruffydd first hypothetized an original unity to "The Four Branches" involving the destiny of the hero, Pryderi. See *Math vab Mathonwy* (London, 1928) and discussion in Jones and Jones, xii-xvii.

178 *Birth, adventures, disappearance, death.* For archetypal narratives of spring, summer, autumn, winter, see Northrop Frye, *Anatomy of Criticism* (Princeton, NJ, 1957), 163-223.

180 *reciprocity between subjective and objective knowledge.* The spirits who dictated to the poet W.B. Yeats the metaphors that became *A Vision* (1925; London, 1937) were evidently deeply versed in the structure of Celtic mythology.

183 *THE ODYSSEY, BOOK EIGHT.* In his postscript to the translation, Fitzgerald points out that "Three or more Greek dialects and perhaps half a millennium of Greek hexameter poetry contributed to Homer's language" (1962, p 506). For Homer, living not much before 850 BC, the events at Troy some five centuries earlier were a rich tradition of war-songs and mythology that had grown around a historical nucleus – like the account of the war-bands from Wales who were demolished in the attempt to bring back from a distant place their own tribal woman of beauty. And like the tellers of

"Branwen," the teller of the *Odyssey* describes the events in images from his own world.

It is a world in which there was no conception of law (Homer describes instead councils of elders interpreting tribal custom), no uniform religion (the Apollo of the *Iliad* is spoken of as a local Asiatic deity), no statuary, and, in spite of one reference to it in the *Iliad*, no writing beyond the keeping of accounts and lists. Nor was there what the later classical age called "rhapsodists" – the reciters of epic whom Pindar called "singers of stitched verse," explaining that they held a wand during their performance as a symbol of their right to be heard. Instead the singers (this is Homer's word: his musical Greek probably had a tonic accent) accompanied themselves on a lyre as Demódokos does.

Demódokos is more than a court poet of the time; he is the memory of the blind bard from which a tradition of epic singing, extending as long as English literature, took name and inspiration. He is put into the story, more out of devotion than for the sake of advertisement, perhaps originally by a family whose hereditary occupation it was to sing the epics, or by later rhapsodists and *Homeridae*, the "spiritual kin" of Homer, who were his interpreters and teachers.

The *editio princeps* of Homer was published at Florence in 1488 by Demetrios Chalcondyles. Reproduced here are lines from the scholarly edition by Thomas W. Allen, *Homeri Opera*, volume 3 (1908, 2nd ed., Oxford, 1917).

188 *Alice Kane.* From a retelling of a story in *The King of Ireland's Son* by Padraic Colum (1881-1972). See Alice Kane, *The Dreamer Awakes*. Fairy tale readers will be familiar with the starker versions of this story found in Grimm ("The Six Swans") and Asbjornsen and Moe ("The Twelve Wild Ducks").

189 *"moving in tune to the words of the speaker."* William Condon and Louis Sarle, "Synchrony Demonstrated between Movements of the Neonate and Adult Speech," *Child Development*, 45 (1974): 456. The second quotation (*"a sort of mating dance"*) is from T. Berry Brazelton's article in Marshall H. Klaus and John H. Kennell, *Maternal-Infant Interaction* (St. Louis, Missouri 1976), 74.

191 *"Mythic structures prefigured later musical forms."* Claude Lévi-Strauss and Didier Eribon, *Conversations with Claude Lévi-Strauss*, translated by Paula Wissing (Chicago, 1971), 177

192 *"other-than-human persons ... have been disenfranchised."* Calvin Luther Martin, *In the Spirit of the Earth: Rethinking Time and History*, 29

193 *Nangdldastlas.* Translated by Bringhurst as "One They Gave Away," lines 234-5

194 *shared sections of a major mythline.* R.M. Berndt, *Australian Aboriginal Religion*, 8; T.G.H. Strehlow, "Culture, Social Structure, and Environment in Aboriginal Central Australia," 128-9

194 *northeastern Arnhem Land myth-songs.* Berndt, "The Wonguri-Mandjigai Song Cycle of the Moon-Bone," 17-18

195 *traditional Haida civilization.* See Swanton, *Contributions to the Ethnology of the Haida*, 92; J.H. Van Den Brink, *The Haida Indians: Cultural Change mainly between 1876-1970* (Leiden, 1974); Marianne Boelscher, *The Curtain Within: Haida Social and Mythical Discourse* (Vancouver, 1989), 140

196 *The Kula.* Bronislaw Malinowski, *Argonauts of the Western Pacific* (1922; London and New York, 1961)

197 *Albert Bates Lord.* See *The Singer of Tales* (1960; New York, 1976), 13-29. Yashinsky's quotation is in "Thunder: A Story-teller Visits the Library," *Wilson Library Bulletin*, 65:5 (January, 1991), 53.

198 *"Ivon Tortik."* Alice Kane, *The Dreamer Awakes*

198 *Dennis Tedlock.* "Ethnography as Interaction: the Storyteller, the Audience, the Fieldworker, and the Machine," in Regina Darnell and Michael K. Foster, ed. *Conference on Native North American Interaction Patterns* (Ottawa, 1982), 80-94

202 *Ronald Berndt.* "The Wonguri-Mandjigai Song Cycle of the Moon-Bone," 18, 17

203 *The motif of the volcano.* Stories of this type may be found in Marius Barbeau, *Haida Myths*, 17-33, 68-76. But beware of the editor's attempt to pursue a thesis about a recent migration of Mongolian peoples who told these stories.

204 *a Tlingit story.* Michael Harkin, "History, Narrative, Temporality: Examples from the Northwest Coast," *Ethnohistory*, 35:2 (Spring, 1988): 99-125. Quotations which follow are Harkin's. See recent versions of these stories in Nora Marks Dauenhauer and Richard Dauenhauer, ed. *Haa Shuká, Our Ancestors. Tlingit Oral Narratives* (Juneau, Alaska, and Seattle, 1987): stories by Yaaneekee (Charlie White), 293-297; Jeenik (Jennie White), 299-301; Asx̱'aak (George R. Betts), 303-309.

206 *"the sudden silence of the fields."* Padraic Colum, Introduction to *An Anthology of Irish Verse. The Poetry of Ireland from Mythological Times to the Present* (1922; New York, 1948), 10

207 *"They no longer have the vision ... "* Uncle Bul to Robert Lawlor, 1988, in *Voices of the First Day,* 373

215 *TO HERMES.* Greek manuscript tradition mentions the names of hymnists who may have been singing the stories of the gods long before Homer, and so even more with the 33 extant hymns than the two epics the title "Homeric" refers to the tradition rather than the master. The hymns to Hermes and the other goddesses and gods were sung as preludes (*prooimia*) to recitations of stories from the epics, and they were sung at festivals associated with contests like the games that followed the snake priestess's festival at Delphi and the games at Olympia and Nemea in honor of the mountain god. Since that time of the games in the 5th century BC, until the edition of Demetrios Chalcondyles (Florence, 1488), the hymns received little attention from literature, which favored instead what it regarded as the definitive and monumental expression of Homer. Only 31 manuscripts, scattered throughout the libraries of Europe, form the basis of the authoritative text by T.W. Allen, *Homeri Opera*, volume 5 (Oxford, 1912), from which the hymn is translated here, with its invocation reproduced in the original Greek.

227 *"Demeter and Persephone."* In Celia Barker Lottridge and Alison Dickie, ed. *Mythic Voices* (Scarborough, Ontario, 1991), 213-219, at 215. The second quotation is at 213.

232 *something of an individualist.* Raised on the Presbyterian Shorter Catechism in County Antrim, northern Ireland, where she was born in 1867, Ella Young plunged into the Irish literary renaissance happening in Dublin around writers like Standish O'Grady and George Russell. She moved to the United States where she held a lectureship for many years in Celtic myth and Gaelic literature at Berkeley, spending her

free time in New Mexico with the Zuni peoples, close to Frieda and D.H. Lawrence. She died in 1956. See her autobiography *Flowering Dusk* (New York, 1945).

233 *wansuuga.* Robert Bringhurst, "Oral Tradition and the Individual Talent," second of the Ashley Lectures given at Trent University, March 3, 1994

234 *Igjugarjuk.* Hother Ostermann, *The Alaskan Eskimos, as described in the posthumous notes of Dr. Knud Rasmussen. Report of the Fifth Thule Expedition 1921-24* (Copenhagen, 1952), x, 97-99

235 *"The Silver Saucer and the Transparent Apple."* Alice Kane, *The Dreamer Awakes*; Arthur Ransome, *Old Peter's Russian Tales* (1916; London, 1971), 6-21

236 *"phonetic exoskeleton."* "Earth, Technology, Polyphony and Ancestors." Lecture given at the University of Salamanca, May, 1990. Privately circulated. The comment is elaborated in Bringhurst, "Everywhere Being Is Dancing, Knowing Is Known," *Chicago Review*, 39: 3-4 (1993): 138-147.

237 *Taliesin.* Translated from the *Book of Taliesin* by Jean Markdale, *The Celts: Uncovering the Mythic and Historic Origins of Western Culture* (Rochester, Vermont, 1993), 235. Originally published as *Les Celts et la civilisation celtique* (Paris, 1976). Legend makes Taliesin a 6th-century bard. See Markdale's chapter on "Taliesin and Druidism," 223-251, where "druidism made man" is quoted (from Henri Martin, *Histoire de France*, I, 55).

238 *invasion myths.* R.A. Stewart Macalister, ed. *Lebor Gabála Érenn* ("The Book of the Taking of Ireland"), 1-5 (Dublin:

Early Irish Texts Society, 1938-41): volumes 34, 35, 39, 41
and 44

240 *virtus vs. fortuna*. Sean Kane, *Spenser's Moral Allegory* (Toronto
and London, 1989), 9-11

241 *The Raven and Xhausghaana*. By Xhiiw of the Qquuna Qiighawaai, in Swanton, *Haida Texts and Myths: Skidegate Dialect*,
130-131

245 *planets and stars*. See Giorgio de Santillana and Hertha von
Dechend, *Hamlet's Mill: an Essay on Myth and the Frame of
Time* (1969; Boston, 1977).

246 *"in our minds, not in words or bodily shapes."* Seventh Epistle
342c. *Plato's Epistles*, translated by Glenn R. Morrow (New
York, 1962). The second quotation is from the *Theaetetus*
189e-190a. *The Dialogues of Plato*, translated by Benjamin
Jowett (Oxford, 1953).

247 *"what an incomprehensible being you are, Socrates."* Phaedrus
230d-e

248 *the Presocratic philosophers*. Bringhurst, *The Beauty of the Weapons: Selected Poems, 1972-1982* (Toronto, 1982), 48

250 *"These things never happened, yet they always are."* The phrase is
from the preface to the compendium of Greek mythology
written for the emperor Julian (361-363) in his effort to restore pagan and especially Hellenic worships into the Christianized empire of his predecessor Constantine the Great.

252 *Bobby McLeod*. Lawlor, *Voices of the First Day*, 49

ACKNOWLEDGEMENTS

A book is really the product of a community, and in the case of this book the community is a close-knit one. Besides Robert Bringhurst and Alice Kane, it involves Dennis Lee, the leading exponent in Canada of a polyphonic poetry in which several voices are scored across a poem in the improvisational manner of the mythtellers. Lee saw what the manuscript of this book might become, and moved it closer to its best self. Robert Carter gave the book insights from his study of Oriental value. Johanna Hiemstra, storyteller, suggested how the book could be shaped around its stories. Anna Gartshore proposed the form of the Epilogue. Robert Lawlor has been a source of meaning for me. He has ventured as far as anyone I have studied into the grandest context for any recreation of a metaphysics of the Earth. When that metaphysics is practised, it will owe much to the writing of Calvin Martin, prehistorian and philosopher of the Palaeolithic. He has been a first friend of this book. So has Gordon Teskey, whose work on allegory is crucial to the task of shaking myth free from the eidetic metaphysics which has captured it since the time of the Greeks.

I acknowledge the colleagues and students who brought perceptions to the book: Nicole Bauberger, Stacey Brown, Andrea Lawson, Margaret Poynton, and Brian Sanderson.

Kelly Liberty helped the book in many ways, and was the guardian of its solitude.

I am deeply grateful to all these individuals.

ABOUT THE AUTHOR

Following education at Upper Canada College and Carleton University, Sean Kane began a scholarly career at the University of Toronto and the Warburg Institute, London, specializing in Medieval and Renaissance Studies under William Blissett and Northrop Frye. His *Spenser's Moral Allegory* (University of Toronto Press, 1989) is a study of the conflict between neoclassical theories of power and the neoplatonic philosophy of nature in the work of the Elizabethan poet-thinker.

After teaching at University of Toronto, he joined Trent University, outside Toronto, an experimental institution specializing in collegial undergraduate instruction. At Trent, Kane teaches courses in oral literature in the English Department and in Cultural Studies, an interdisciplinary program in the theory of culture and modernity, which he chaired when the program was founded in 1978. He is the editor of *The Dreamer Awakes*, a collection of wondertales told by Alice Kane, with an introduction by Robert Bringhurst (Broadview Press, 1995).

Sean Kane lives on the Otonabee River, in Peterborough, with Kelly Liberty and their son Owen.

Publisher: Don LePan
Cover photograph: Lilita Rodman
Research: Susan Stott
Copyeditor: Karen Denis

The text of this book is set in
the digital form of Monotype Bembo.
The Greek passages were set by hand in Monotype Porson
by Aaron Benson at Dreadnaught Design.

This book was designed by George Kirkpatrick and printed
on 70 lb Zephyr Antique Laid paper.

greg FRancis

Physics 205-206